Conversations with Leslie Marmon Silko

Literary Conversations Series

Peggy Whitman Prenshaw
General Editor

Photo credit: Nancy Crampton

Conversations
with Leslie Marmon Silko

Edited by
Ellen L. Arnold

University Press of Mississippi
Jackson

Books by Leslie Marmon Silko

Laguna Woman: Poems by Leslie Silko. Greenfield Center, New York: Greenfield Review Press, 1974. Tucson, Arizona: Flood Plain Press, 1994.

Ceremony. New York: Viking, 1977.

Storyteller. New York: Viking, 1981.

The Delicacy and Strength of Lace: Letters Between Leslie Marmon Silko and James Wright, ed. Ann Wright. St. Paul, Minnesota: Graywolf Press, 1986.

Almanac of the Dead. New York: Simon & Schuster, 1991.

Sacred Water: Narratives and Pictures. Tucson, Arizona: Flood Plain Press, 1993.

Yellow Woman and a Beauty of the Spirit: Essays on Native American Life Today. New York: Simon & Schuster, 1996.

Rain. With Lee Marmon. New York: Whitney Museum, 1996.

Gardens in the Dunes. New York: Simon & Schuster, 1999.

www.upress.state.ms.us

Copyright © 2000 by University Press of Mississippi
All rights reserved
Manufactured in the United States of America

08   07   06   05   04   03   02   01   00   4   3   2   1
∞
Library of Congress Cataloging-in-Publication Data

Silko, Leslie, 1948–
    Conversations with Leslie Marmon Silko / edited by Ellen L. Arnold.
        p.   cm. — (Literary conversations series)
    Includes index.
    ISBN 1-57806-300-0 (alk. paper) — ISBN 1-57806-301-9 (pbk. : alk. paper)
        1. Silko, Leslie, 1948—Interviews.   2. Authors, American—20th century—
    Interviews.   3. Women and literature—West (U.S.)—History—20th century.
    4. Indians in literature.   5. West (U.S.)—In literature.   I. Arnold, Ellen L.
    II. Title.   III. Series.

PS3569.I44 Z888   2000
813'.54—dc21   00-036338

British Library Cataloging-in-Publication Data available

Contents

Introduction

Leslie Marmon Silko appeared on the American literary scene in 1977 with the publication of her brilliant first novel, *Ceremony.* Having already published numerous short stories (many of them anthologized in the 1974 collection, *The Man to Send Rain Clouds: Contemporary Stories by American Indians*) and a book of poems, *Laguna Woman* (also in 1974), Silko was a rising star of what has been called the Native American literary renaissance, ushered in by N. Scott Momaday's 1968 Pulitzer Prize-winning novel *House Made of Dawn.* *Ceremony* has since grown steadily in popularity and critical acclaim to achieve a secure place in the new American canon. Silko's subsequent work includes her autobiographical mixed-genre collection, *Storyteller* (1981); the apocalyptic epic, *Almanac of the Dead* (1991), described by many critics as one of the most important novels of the twentieth century; *Sacred Water* (1993), a volume of prose poems and photographs that Silko originally made by hand and later published through her own Flood Plain Press; her collected essays, *Yellow Woman and a Beauty of the Spirit*, (1996); and most recently, the lyrical historical novel, *Gardens in the Dunes* (1999). The variety and scope of her writing have established her as one of the most creative and versatile of living American authors. Silko is also widely known and respected in Europe, where, as she and Rolando Hinojosa discuss in a 1987 conversation, ethnic American authors have been accepted as mainstream American writers, in contrast to their marginalization as minority authors at home. The sixteen interviews collected here suggest some of the profound ways Silko's work has helped to reshape contemporary American literature.

When I interviewed Leslie Marmon Silko in August of 1998, she had just finished her third novel, *Gardens in the Dunes.* Eager to continue the birthing process of her newest creation, Silko talked enthusiastically for many hours about the novel, its connections to her life and other work, her writing process, and the important role of her readers in completing her texts. Silko grants interviews very sparingly, yet she is a remarkably generous and outspoken interviewee, shifting readily from playful humor to thoughtful analysis, personal reflection to impassioned anger over social and political issues. Presented with a prepared series of questions, she works hard to provide full and honest answers. Provided an open structure and plenty of time, her responses range widely, yet always circle back in an amazing coherence, reflecting the storytelling tradition in which she grew up at Laguna and the oral forms—the repetitions and cyclically recurring thematic patterns—that are so character-istic of her work.

Silko states in a 1977 interview with Dexter Fisher that the single most important influence on her as a writer was growing up in Laguna Pueblo and "listening to the people and to the way the stories just keep coming" there. To Donna Perry, in a lengthy 1992 interview not included in this volume, she describes her family as "book people"; even her great-grandmother and old Aunt Susie, who passed on to her orally so many of the old stories that found their way into her books, were educated at Carlisle Indian school and consid-ered book learning an important strategy for survival against the destructive pressures of the dominant culture (317).[1] Again and again in her interviews, Silko tells the story of a life-changing moment that came to her in the fifth grade at Manzano Day School, a private school in Albuquerque where her parents took her rather than send her away to Indian boarding school. Ill-prepared by her BIA schooling, lonely and unhappy, Silko discovered in a class assignment to weave spelling words into a story, as she puts it to Ste-phen Pett in 1992, a sense of "incredible pleasure and satisfaction and secur-ity and even power" that never left her. As a student at the University of New Mexico, writing came easy to Silko, and she was pleased when her short stories won prizes and were solicited for publication. Motivated by her father's success as a tribal leader in the 1950s in helping Laguna Pueblo win back a portion of the land taken by the federal government, Silko had long intended to study law. It was not until she withdrew in frustration halfway through the University of New Mexico's Indian Law Program that she began to think of herself as a professional writer. Convinced that the legal system would never achieve justice for Native Americans, she decided writing would be a better tool. "The most effective political statement I could make is in my art work," she tells Laura Coltelli in 1985. "The most radical kind of politics," she reiterates to Hinojosa in 1987, is "language as plain truth." Silko's commitment to truth and justice has only intensified over time, driv-ing the evolution of her work and thought.

Silko's responses to interviewers' queries have remained remarkably con-sistent over the almost twenty-five years this collection covers. At the same time, they reflect an unfolding of ideas and methods from a clear center in elaborating patterns like the spider's web that is the hallmark image of her writing. This development is never a progression, for nothing is ever left behind. Laguna, its stories and events, relationships and traditions, provide the subject matter and themes of her early work—the short stories and poems, *Ceremony* and *Storyteller*. Yet Laguna and the inclusive, communal world-view that characterizes it remain at the heart of her later work as well, as the settings and thematic scope of her writing expand to encompass the Americas and Africa in *Almanac of the Dead*, and Europe in *Gardens in the Dunes*.

It is Leslie Silko's heritage as a Native American and the influence of the oral tradition on her work that have most fascinated her interviewers. The earliest interviews in this collection—those conducted by Norwegian scholar Per Seyersted and American scholars Larry Evers and Dennis Carr before the publication of *Ceremony*—establish the themes that will structure her inter-views as well as critical attention to her work for the next quarter-century. In almost every interview Silko reminds us that the source of her inspiration is the living oral tradition—the stories she heard growing up at Laguna from family and community—and the land and spirits those stories evoke. When interviewed by Seyersted in 1976, Silko had recently returned from two dif-ficult years in Alaska, which had emphasized for her the centrality of Laguna to her identity and sense of well-being. Far from home in an oppressively rainy climate and experiencing a great deal of emotional distress, Silko wrote to reconstruct the desert landscape that offered her "a sense of familiarity almost like certain places being a parent or relative." As a person of mixed ancestry and heritage—Laguna, Mexican, and White—Silko grew up with a sense of "strangeness" to both the Laguna community and the outside world. The security that grew from her relationship to the physical landscape was reinforced by a sense of time tied closely to both place and narrative, so that, she tells Seyersted, in Laguna there is the sense that people and events do not "pass away"; rather "they are still there, they are still a presence" in the places that held them. For Silko, the most important thing for a writer is to remember "where he or she has come from" and that "the words that you use . . . are coming from your origin, they are coming from your ancestors."

Though she describes storytelling to Dexter Fisher as a "natural resource" for Indian people, Silko does not think of herself as a storyteller in the tradi-tional sense, but specifically as a writer. For her, the oral tradition is not just a body of old stories or the performance of communal acts of telling, but a way of life. As she expresses it to Kim Barnes in 1986, it is "a whole way of seeing yourself, the people around you, your life, the place of your life in the bigger context." In an oral tradition, Silko points out to Perry, all "information is stored in narrative" and "every interaction reinforces a narrative vision of oneself and one's belonging" (323). Silko does not draw on the oral tradition as a source nor does she attempt to "preserve" the old stories, which, she explains to Kim Barnes, is not really possible anyway, because the "stories have a life of their own" and die out when they are no longer needed. Rather Silko is participating in a living oral tradition that is now evolving on the page as well as in spoken language. In her interview with Barnes, Silko discusses ways that she attempts to communicate the "feeling or flavor or sense" of live storytelling by manipulating space on the page in *Ceremony*. In later interviews, she discusses her ongoing experimentation with style, form, and genre toward this end, for example her bonding of the visual with the written word in the interplay of text and photograph in *Storyteller* and *Sacred Water*, and of text and image in *Almanac of the Dead*.

Her interviews reveal that Silko has been deeply influenced by her reading in Euro-American narrative traditions as well. Shakespeare, William Blake, Edgar Allan Poe, Jorge Luis Borges, D. H. Lawrence, Henry James, Gertrude Stein, Isak Dinesen, Flannery O'Connor, William Faulkner, Maxine Hong Kingston, Toni Morrison, and Dorothy Allison are among the many writers she mentions whose work she admires. Silko also voraciously consumes nonfiction, and both *Almanac of the Dead* and *Gardens in the Dunes* involved extensive research in history, theology, economics, physics, botany, and psychology, including a break in the writing of *Almanac* to read the complete works of Sigmund Freud. The interviews that focus on *Almanac of the Dead*, especially those conducted by Laura Coltelli in 1985 and 1993, Ray Gonzalez, Donna Perry, and Linda Niemann in 1991 and 1992, and Thomas Irmer and Matthias Schmidt 1995 demonstrate a complex narrative theory taking shape for Silko in the interfaces of Native American and Western worldviews. The relatively simple ideas of space-time inherence she describes to Seyersted are layered with concepts from particle physics, chaos theory, and philosophy to explore time *as* narrative in *Almanac of the Dead*, and the interrelationships of narrative and perception in *Gardens in the Dunes*. Always concerned to bring to light hidden and silenced histories of brutality and oppression in the Americas, Silko enfolds linear accounts of historical events within more indigenous conceptualizations of time as cyclically recurring narrative patterns that hold out possibilities for human survival and healing.

Interviewers have sometimes attempted to focus on Silko and her work as exclusively Native American and to dichotomize Native and Western beliefs and practices in their questioning (a pattern that is repeated in a great deal of the criticism). Silko gently but insistently refocuses her interviews to high-light interconnections with Western and other traditions and literatures. In her 1992 interview with Linda Niemann, Silko complains that many reviewers and critics of *Almanac* saw only anger and vengeance in the novel, ignoring its humor and its optimistic prophecy of global spiritual reawakening. Though she is resolute in her exposure of the destructive systems of thought and practices that drive the consumption of the natural world and indigenous peoples by Western colonialism and capitalism, Silko has always maintained, as she tells Seyersted in 1978, that "the destructive impulse [does not] reside with a single race or a single group." The survival of the human race and the healing of the world, she continues, are dependent not on "particular tribes, not particular races or cultures" but on being part of "something larger," on a restored relationship of the individual to humanity and world. Silko reiter-ates this idea most eloquently to Coltelli in 1985: "I like to think of myself in a more old-fashioned sense, the way the old folks felt, which was, first of all you're a human; secondly you originate from somewhere, and from a family, and a culture. But first of all, human beings." Differences are impor-tant to understand, she says, but she writes "to realize the wonder and power of what we share." More than a decade later, Silko makes this a primary theme of her third novel, *Gardens in the Dunes*. In the interview that I con-ducted with her in 1998, she describes *Gardens* as the most conventionally structured and "literary" of her novels, and yet potentially the most subver-sive, because of the way it explores connections between Native American and Euro-American traditions and beliefs. "Our human nature, our human spirit wants no boundaries," she declares.

The interviews collected here reveal Silko as a writer who understands her work to be positioned in the complex intersection of multiple fields of influ-ence—historical and cultural, social, psychological, and spiritual—that both shape and are given expression in her texts. To Coltelli in 1985, she observes that the writing process is for her "mostly subconscious." She writes without an outline, to "discover what I don't know." The power of this "process of enlightenment" (Boos) is evident in a number of mysterious connections she describes to several interviewers. For example, to Seyersted, in 1976, she tells the story of learning after writing "Tony's Story," a short story based on the actual killing of a New Mexico trooper, that the witchcraft element of her story, which she thought she had imagined, had actually been part of the legal defense of the Indian man tried for the murder. To Robin Cohen, in a

1998 interview not included in this collection, Silko recounts a similar discovery that an old Yaqui testimonial, written in Spanish and Latin, has recently come to light that had been smuggled north to Tucson in the clothing of Yaquis escaping from revolution in Mexico, much like her invented almanac in *Almanac of the Dead* (61).[2] The most dramatic example of the prophetic power of Silko's work is *Almanac*'s prediction of the Native uprising in Chiapas, which occurred two years after the publication of the novel. Silko understands these connections as the unconscious accumulation of detail, as an elision of memory and imagination. Yet, her sense of her writing as an expression of spiritual forces outside herself is evident in her vivid account to me of her European promotional tour for *Almanac*, when she was welcomed to Germany by the ancestor spirits residing there, an experience that figured profoundly in the creation of her next novel. At the same time, Silko freely acknowledges that the spirits are not always kind, and her writing makes heavy demands on her personal relationships and emotional life. In her introductory note to Coltelli's 1985 interview, she comments that a novel can be "a voracious feeder upon the psyche." In every discussion of *Almanac*, she describes her withdrawal from friends and family as she was "ridden" by spirit entities who had designs for the novel that were beyond her control, and which were reflected in larger events surrounding the publication of the novel.

In a portion of our 1998 conversation not included in this volume, Silko also talks at length about her discomfort with the way the publishing industry is shaping contemporary American literature by focusing on marketability. She is frustrated by the push to "produce" on a schedule that prevents her from exercising the careful attention to every word and the extensive rewriting she was able to lavish on *Ceremony*. Yet, she describes an excellent working relationship with Michael Korda, her editor at Simon & Schuster, and feels she has successfully resisted "outside sensibilities" and "the demands of the market" in the editing of her subsequent novels. Silko decries what she terms the "cult of the author," which glorifies the physical bodies and personalities of writers at the expense of their work. She resents attempts to read her novels too biographically or to make assumptions about her personal life based on her fiction. In our published interview, she was anxious to lay to rest long-lived rumors that she had offended people at Laguna by publishing secret clan stories. On the contrary, she feels she was given a responsibility to keep the stories "active in my life," and expresses confidence that "I've never divulged anything that was kept secret."

Silko's interviews also reflect tensions around the necessity to sell herself and her work, and the toll that public appearances and interviews take on her as a writer, both in terms of time and energy, and in terms of the "competing texts" such conversations create. Yet she values very highly the direct exchange with readers that public appearances and interviews allow. She believes that the most important meanings of her work emerge in the interfaces of her subconscious mind with the larger world, and in the responses and interpretations of her readers. In this sense, Silko reflects intersections of the oral tradition with postmodern and reader-response theories: the written text, like the old stories, "has a life of its own," and its meaning continually evolves in exchange with its context. Nowhere is this clearer than in her discussion with me of the history of *Ceremony*'s acceptance. As Silko observes, "When *Ceremony* first came out, it was considered to be really challenging, for the most sophisticated reader. And then gradually, graduate students could read it, then juniors and seniors in college. . . . Now, precocious juniors in high school suddenly can read *Ceremony*." The culture has changed around the novel, but the novel has also shaped the reading milieu by teaching people how to read and think differently. Thus Silko's work participates in the evolution of American and world culture, helping to bring about the "new consciousness in the hearts of all human beings, the idea that the earth is shared and finite, and that we are naturally connected to the earth and with one another," as she puts it to Irmer and Schmidt, that her novels depict.

Because of the complexity and cultural specificity of Leslie Marmon Silko's work, her interviews, while rare, have been vital to critical interpretation of her poetry and fiction. This volume includes a large percentage of her substantive interviews, selected for the depth of their contributions to the understanding and appreciation of her achievements. I am especially pleased to be able to include Laura Coltelli's 1993 interview, which was published in Italy and has been difficult to obtain in this country, and the online interview with Thomas Irmer and Matthias Schmidt, which has not previously appeared in print. The interviews are reprinted as they originally appeared, with only minor corrections of typographical or obvious factual errors. They are arranged chronologically according to the dates they were conducted.

I would like to thank Emory University's Institute of the Liberal Arts for summer research and travel funding, and Appalachian State University and East Carolina University for institutional and staff support. Special thanks go to Glenn Ellen Starr-Stilling of Appalachian State's Belk Library for her skill and persistence in locating many of these interviews. I am grateful to Gregory Salyer, who published the first full-length study of Silko's work in 1997 for the Twayne US Authors Series and provided the core of the Chronology in this volume. I would like to thank my husband Chip Arnold for his unflagging encouragement and sound advice, Janet McAdams for her ongoing friendship and collegial support, Seetha Srinivasan and Anne Stascavage of the University Press of Mississippi for their patience and help, and most importantly, Leslie Marmon Silko, for the wonderful talent and the generous gift of time and energy that made this project possible.

ELA

Notes

1. Donna Perry, "Leslie Marmon Silko." *Backtalk: Women Writers Speak Out* (New Brunswick, New Jersey: Rutgers UP, 1993) 313–340.
2. Robin Cohen, "Of Apricots, Orchids, and Wovoka: An Interview with Leslie Marmon Silko," *Southwestern American Literature* 14.2 (1999): 55–69.

Chronology

1948   Leslie Marmon born 5 March to Leland (Lee) Howard Marmon and Mary Virginia Lee Leslie in Albuquerque, New Mexico, the oldest of three sisters. Grows up in Laguna Pueblo, New Mexico, about 50 miles west of Albuquerque. Attends Laguna Day School, the local Indian school run by the Bureau of Indian Affairs, through the fourth grade.

1958   Enters Manzano Day School, a Catholic school in Albuquerque. Here, in the fifth grade, Silko has an important first experience with writing, creating a story out of assigned spelling words, an event that marks for her a turning point in her life.

1964   Enters the University of New Mexico.

1965   Marries Richard C. Chapman. Robert William Chapman born.

1969   Graduates Phi Beta Kappa with a BA in English from the University of New Mexico. Begins law school at the University of New Mexico in the American Indian Law School Fellowship Program. Separates from and eventually divorces Richard Chapman. Publishes her first short story, "The Man to Send Rain Clouds," in *New Mexico Quarterly*.

1970   Leaves law school after three semesters; returns to the University of New Mexico to take graduate courses in English. Leaves the university to teach at Navajo Community College at Tsaile, Arizona. Awarded a National Endowment for the Humanities Discovery Grant. Marries John Silko.

1972   Cazimir Silko born.

1973   Moves to Ketchikan, Alaska, and begins writing *Ceremony*.

1974   Publishes seven short stories, including the title story, in *The Man to Send Rain Clouds*. Publishes *Laguna Woman: Poems*. Receives 1974 Award for Poetry from *The Chicago Review*.

1975   "Lullaby" selected as one of the twenty best short stories of 1975.

1976 Returns to Laguna. Her one-act play of "Lullaby," adapted with Frank Chin, is first performed.

1977 Wins Pushcart Prize for Poetry. *Ceremony* published.

1978 Moves to Tucson, Arizona, begins teaching at the University of Arizona. Begins correspondence with James Wright that becomes *The Delicacy and Strength of Lace*.

1980 James Wright dies of cancer. Silko's film, *Estoyehmuut and the Gunnadeyah* [Arrow Boy and the Witches] is completed.

1981 *Storyteller* published. Begins notes for *Almanac of the Dead*.

1982 Completes videotape, *Running on the Edge of the Rainbow: Laguna Stories and Poems*.

1986 *The Delicacy and Strength of Lace*, edited by Anne Wright, published.

1988 Wins University of New Mexico's Distinguished Alumnus Award.

1991 *Almanac of the Dead* published.

1993 *Sacred Water: Narratives and Pictures* published by Silko's own press, Flood Plain Press.

1996 *Yellow Woman and a Beauty of the Spirit: Essays on Native American Life Today* published.

1999 *Gardens in the Dunes* published.

Conversations with Leslie Marmon Silko

Interview with Leslie Marmon Silko

Per Seyersted / 1976

From *American Studies in Scandinavia* 13 (1981): 17–25. Reprinted by permission.

Laguna, New Mexico, January 7, 1976

Per Seyersted: You went to school in Albuquerque, didn't you?

Leslie Marmon Silko: Right. Four years I went here to the day school, just across the road here, and then I finished up school in Albuquerque.

PS: Did you feel it was difficult to be outside the Laguna environment?

LMS: Well, I've never encountered any kinds of vicious racial confrontations. I suppose it was more a feeling very strange, everything about Albuquerque and the kids I was going to school with, and that whole setting was very strange, kind of alien, and I moved through it as best I could, which I think most of the people from the Pueblos and from the reservations do even now. We move through the city, we talk with the people, but there's an extreme amount of tension that one feels and it can only be described as strangeness. We were fortunate that our parents sent us to small schools, not to public schools, and at the Catholic schools, of course, they were very strict about any sort of teasing and things like that, so we were pretty secure there. But I can remember one fall after hunting season we'd all done well, and we got deer and my dad's aunt over at Paguate dried the meat and made jerky out of it. I can remember in the eighth grade taking my lunch to school. I hated to get up in the morning to make my lunch, and I would take a large handful of dry meat and stuff it into my paper lunchbag and then maybe put in a candy bar and an orange and that was my lunch. This was a girls' school; my classmates on either side of me kind of jumped up and kind of scooted back, and they said, "What's *that*? It looks terrible," and I said, "Will you want to taste some of it?" and they said, "No!" Fortunately I was old enough, or maybe secure enough, not to feel . . . or at least I wasn't conscious of feeling ashamed of having brought that. It also had to do with my attitude which was I was always . . . I made the most of being different, and so I can remember laughing at them and telling them, you know, actually taking a piece of meat—and these are eighth grade, ninth grade girls—and either sort of shoving a piece of meat, of this dry meat toward them and watching them jump as if it were a snake or something. I mean, I took that attitude that *they* were the ones that were silly and not myself that thus . . . So it was that I was aware of encountering, but it was that kind of conflict more than it was any kind of brutal or vicious kind of . . . it was more subtle.

PS: Compared to many other people who are not "in the mainstream of the American life," wouldn't you say that you have had a great security, a great strength in the fact that you are solidly based in your own culture, and that as you said, you feel the *others* were strangers?

LMS: Yeah, just maybe I think of it more in terms of even just the place. A lot of these hills and mesas I showed you this morning: there's a sense of familiarity almost like certain places being a parent or relative, in other words, being related to the land in a familiar way, and there's a kind of security there which I always feel. You know, when I was going to the university, during the school term I lived in Albuquerque, but as soon as we would leave Albuquerque and gradually drive back into this area, a feeling comes just of being in a place. Not to mention that I have always felt . . . when the people here like the sacristan that we met up at the church . . . you know, I remember Joe from the time I was so little that I wasn't in school, and he remembers me, and there's also, of course, then, that kind of security. There again I . . . when that security is tied in with people . . . of course, people pass away, eventually . . . that's the beauty of the land, you know, that these things . . . and this is why it is important to me: my father tells me stories that his father told him about certain places, and it is as if when one goes back to these places that all of those past things that happened in that place, in a sense, their presence is still there, and so you don't lose it, even though human beings may pass away and old age comes and so forth. And there's a sense of having even with one's relatives back through the years . . . that somehow they are still there, they are still a presence. So, yes, then you have this, and it never fails. I was afraid when I came back from Alaska that maybe somehow it wouldn't feel that way anymore. Two years in Alaska was the longest I have ever been away from this part of the country. It was magical. I came back and maybe I felt it more strongly than I ever had.

PS: You have chosen to write about a number of male characters, haven't you?

LMS: Yeah. I guess it goes back to the fact that when I was growing up I never thought of myself as having any sort of gender one way or the other. I

mean, certainly I was aware that I was a girl, but if you've noticed my grandmother, she is in and out and she is seventy-four—when she was growing up
she was a Model A mechanic, and even now, my uncle has a coin-operated
laundry here and she fixes those machines and she carries heavy things. So
she was there when I was growing up, and my father had three daughters, I
was the oldest, and my father made no connections between the fact that we
were daughters and not sons. He took me deer-hunting when I was seven
years old, and then when I was a little girl I can remember when the crews
would come to plaster the house, that they were women. The people who
plaster the houses here traditionally have always been women, men do not
plaster houses. So in all my surroundings I never . . . I mean, I realized I was
a girl, but I never saw that one's experiences or one's activities had to—either
in my own family or just around me—I never made the connection that because of one's sex one would be limited to certain kinds of experiences. I
had a horse when I was eight years old, and as I got older I would go up
north to the ranch—this is an area I write about a lot—and I would help them
gather cattle and drive cattle.

PS: So because of your own experience and because of the manners and
customs of the Laguna pueblos . . .
LMS: Right—

PS: It simply was natural to you to have seen many aspects of what otherwise mostly men do . . .
LMS: Right. And not to think that, not to feel that, in terms of the consciousness that I . . . that there was something that one must exclusively be
forced to stay within one consciousness.

PS: How do you look upon black aesthetics, the fact that some blacks feel
that only blacks should write for blacks, only blacks can judge anything
written about the blacks. Is there any such feeling among Native American
writers, and do you share it?
LMS: I think it depends on whether the . . . if the non-Indian writer wants
to attempt to create a consciousness and pass off this consciousness as an
Indian consciousness. I think there is an area where I would tend to say that
that's on very uncertain, unsteady ground, that sooner or later in one's imagery and one's handling of that consciousness this non-Indian writer is going
to get herself or himself into trouble. I think that the most important thing
that any writer, any writer should remember in writing about any other person

or group or culture is for the writer to remember where he or she has come from, and to always remember one's own experiences, and to be true . . . or at least not to forget that the eyes that you've seen these people and these things with and the words that you use and the feelings you are putting into the work are *yours,* and they are coming from your origin, they are coming from your ancestors, and so that to always remember, then, always keep that one thing straight, a perspective, *then* if one is honest one does not pretend to be the expert upon blacks, or the resident expert on upper-middle class college professors or whatever, we keep this perspective. I think that's most important. Oliver LaFarge was a pioneer; he was the first, perhaps, to discover the difficulties when one attempts to take on the consciousness of a person worlds away from one's own culture. He would have done much better to have done a novel about the Eastern person, the white person who cared very much for the Native American people, but who was Harvard educated, an ethnologist. Then he could have given us the different kinds of emotional things of the conflicts which he must have gone through, because I know that at that time, that the Navajos didn't always embrace him with open arms. But we don't get this, and as a writer I feel that that's the important thing. I think that's where the center lies.

PS: Yes. Unless you are a commercial writer.

LMS: Right. I guess, when I talk about writing I am always thinking about writing from the heart. And one must write from one's heart. And that seems to me so much more valuable for everybody, and as a Native American people we could learn so much from an honest account from a person like La-Farge which we do not have; we could learn a lot about how *he* felt. We know how *we* feel, or the people they knew how they felt to have him around.

PS: You mentioned your father and your grandfather and all they have told you. Don't you feel that you have quite a store of material at the back of your head that you can call back at your leisure and in time bring to something, that you have a great *donnée* of material that you can use when it suits you?

LS: Oh, right, precisely. I think of even my technical skill as a storyteller as a birthright. I recently went up to Laguna-Acoma high school and spent all day with English classes. I said to them: "You know, they talk about different geographical areas and different groups of people having a resource, like they have uranium, they have gold, they have timber as a resource. This area is very interesting," I said. "Doesn't it seem interesting to you that Simon Ortiz would come from Acomita, and I would be at Laguna, and then there's this one other guy, Robert Fernando, who one day just out of the blue sat down and wrote a fine short story?" I said, "Don't you think there's something suspicious about this?" I said, "Because I do. Certain areas and certain people have another kind of 'resource'," and I said, "I think we all have it, we are very fortunate, we are lucky. Our greatest natural resource is stories and storytelling. We have an endless, continuing, ongoing supply of stories." And I said to them, "All of you have this and you should not forget it, and you shouldn't look upon Simon and myself as some kind of accident." I think it is something that many people here already possess, it is a part of the way of life, storytelling is. When you meet somebody around Laguna, you take a lot of time; you say, "Hello, how are you? Say, did you hear about what happened the other night?" And then you take the time to start at the very beginning of what happened the other night. "My goodness, it started at noon the day before," and then you go into this very detailed telling, including the dialogue, of what so and so said to so and so. Well, this is something that the people have always done; this is something you hear from the time you are a little child. It's you talk about having a sense of the story and of recounting the story, just what elements need to be there and which don't. The people, all the people that I've ever known and continue to know, have given this to me.

PS: Yes. But still, you wouldn't say that just anyone here could write a story like "The Man to Send Rain Clouds"—you have gained something from what you have read, too, haven't you?

LS: Oh, right, I've . . .

PS: . . . some sense of technique, at least?

LS: Yeah. I did a lot of reading when I was a child. There, again, I think, indirectly having developed this great appreciation for stories, I loved to read; and I loved the fact that you could go to books and inside of books were more stories, and stories from other places, and people around here have a tremendous appetite for stories and they don't even care where they came from. And so, yes, I did a lot of reading.

PS: What did you mostly read?

LMS: When I was thirteen or fourteen, I was very much interested in American authors, John Steinbeck and William Faulkner, and oh, Edgar Allan Poe. Possibly again, what one reads is determined by the kinds of books that one finds. I can remember encountering Shakespeare in high

school and not liking Shakespeare very much, and then falling in love with
him in college. Well, the first kinds of things I've read I can remember is
Faulkner and Steinbeck and Poe. I don't know how much this most recent
story I've written [Silko was here referring to "Escape Story"], the structure
and all sorts of things turning in upon themselves, whether Borges, the Ar-
gentine, I'd love to read him, I became fascinated with him, maybe some of
my most recent experiments and things were indirectly from him. Also Flannery O'Connor—I use her all the time in my classes, and I tell my students,
"Look, look what she's done." The students'd say, "Oh, she just writes about
the same old area and countryside." "Well," I said, "yes, that's true. I understand as a person, especially as she was ill in her later years, she really didn't
move around very much," and I said, "and that in a sense is one of her
greatest achievements, just to take these same sorts of things again and again
and again to make these magnificent stories, you know."

PS: Yes. Do you use much invention or do you have so much inherited
that you do not need to go much beyond that?

LMS: Well, you know, I never know how much I imagine and how much
is actually what I have heard and have forgotten and it comes back. Sometimes it can be rather frightening. Some other things I can't account for: One
of the stories I wrote, the Tony story, the killing of the State policeman. OK,
my father talked about it, and I heard other people talk about this incident
that took place. I sat down and wrote this story, and in the story I took it
from a very specific point of view, Tony's point of view, and I thought at the
time that I was inventing this whole thing with the witch. Well, Larry Evers
at the University of Arizona got very intrigued with the fact that Simon had
written about the State police killing and *I* had, and so Larry started to do
research into the old trial records and so forth, and he found that the man,
the accused not only told the psychiatrist he thought the state policeman was
a witch—it was also used as a defense in court in the trial. Now, I tell you,
when it was happening I was four years old, I couldn't have read it in the
paper. I didn't know very much about it. Anyway, Larry sent me the letter
and I kind of got almost physically ill to read that what I thought had been
my imagination turned out to be true. But I started to go back over the details
of the killing, and I can remember my dad—you know how my dad talks,
you've been talking to him—he told me about the killing of the policeman
and he said, "They put the cop's body in the car and they set that car on fire,
and later on when the people went and found the remains (and then this is

my dad, the way he likes to talk) all that was left of that cop would fit into a shoebox," you know. I go back now, and what I must have known, and what must have clued me in a kind of subconscious way was that you burn witches' remains, and see, that was one part of the story that I had heard and it had been impressed upon me by Dad—they had burned the state policeman's body. That was the clue, the key. But I never know, I never know until much later, and then people will come to me and say, "How did you know this?" or "Where did you hear that?" And then they will tell me something, you know, and they'll say, "This actually happened." And all I can think is that maybe as a little child I listened awfully closely or something, maybe I was always listening, I don't know.

PS: How far back do you remember?

LMS: I sometimes remember things when I was two or three, but the trouble is, living with people like my people here are, just the way my dad is always telling things, you lose sense of whether you really are remembering it or whether you just heard it. One's own history and experiences are being recounted constantly . . . you hear it so much, you don't know whether you are really remembering it at that moment when you were two years old, or whether you just remember them telling you about it.

PS: How do you feel about the American Indian Movement?

LMS: I feel that they're on one road that runs parallel to the road that I travel. I've seen the kinds of things that they talk about, I've been up in South Dakota and North Dakota; I've friends up there. In other words, I can sympathize and understand what they are saying. But there's no subtlety to their view. They oversimplify the world. They oversimplify things, and I'm bored with the oversimplification. They'll say, "This person here, so and so, he is in jail now, the reason he is in jail is because he did something while he was drinking, and the evil system has him in jail, the corrupt white system has him in jail and he is going to rot there." OK, I know a lot about the American justice system and that part is true. Once you've thrown in jail, unless you have lots of money for a fancy attorney, that's where you're going to stay. OK, that part is true. But what they miss is all of the personal subtleties and the unique experiences and aspects of this individual's life which have brought this person to this place in time. It is much more important to explore all of the possible depths and all of the possible details of a person's life and to range through time—back to a time before this person was born. This is how you begin to understand why these things happen. I feel it is more effective to write a story like "Lullaby" than to rant and rave. I think it is more effective in reaching people. A.I.M. is simply another political group, and I find them too similar to other American political groups.

PS: How do you feel about the Bicentennial—do you have feelings about it?

LS: Oh, I do, definitely, I have all kinds of things to say—I think it's one reason I'm very anxious to try to get the novel out during 1976. I just want to make sure that during this year when all of this sort of celebrating is going on, that Americans can be reminded that there are different ways to look at the past 200 years. I just want to make sure that beside all of the rhapsodizing about Paul Revere and George Washington and Benjamin Franklin that Americans are reminded that this great land, this powerful nation they are celebrating was established on stolen land. It was the resources, the metals, the minerals, it was the water, it was the coal, that enabled those people who came to America to build this nation. In this Bicentennial year we should remember, we should remember that it was on this stolen land that this country was settled and begun. In Anglo-Saxon law, in common law, when something is stolen, no matter how many times the stolen property changes hands, in common law, that piece of property still belongs to the original owner. It doesn't matter whether the people take the stolen article in good faith. The property remains stolen. As long as this fact is acknowledged, then I'll be satisfied, and they can celebrate all they have done with this stolen land and the stolen resources and they can pat themselves on the back for the achievement.

PS: What Native American writers do you like?

LMS: It's probably better to tell you what I *don't* like rather than what I do like as I like most of all the . . . Also, there are so few of them. What I don't like: Well, again, I hesitate to go on about what I don't like. Let me just say that I see things, then, in poetry sometimes that seem to me a bit precious, or somehow it seems that the writers are bowing to expectations—that is, they feel that they are expected, because they are Native Americans, to write in a special way.

PS: In subject matter and attitudes more than in technique?

LMS: Well, even now in technique. I think it is probably the white writers more than any who have actually dictated what they think "Indian writing" should be. People like Rothenberg and, of course, Gary Snyder perfected the "white shamanism" movement. The attitude of the white shaman is that he knows more about Indians than the Indians know. It has happened with Indian graphic art and painting. The people who buy the paintings tell the Indian artist, "Don't do that, that's abstract—Indians ought to only do realistic sorts of paintings," and, "Oh, don't paint that, that's a picture of a drunken man passed out on the street of Gallup. That won't sell in our gallery, you know." In other words, white patrons have very much controlled and molded it. I can see it happening with the writing—publishers using Jerome Rothenberg's chants as a standard for judging poetry that Native Americans may write because Rothenberg appeals to the romanticized notion of what Native American literature is.

PS: Do Native American writers as of today feel any pressure from publishers as to what to write, how to write?

LMS: I don't think we are aware of any pressure yet. If there is going to be any pressure in the future, probably not a pressure to be angry as with the blacks, but perhaps more of this pressure to fall into some of these preconceived . . . having people like, not Rothenberg specifically or someone like that, saying, "Why are you writing about 1952 GMC pick up trucks and Ripple wine?" You know, "Why aren't you writing about . . . ?" In other words, if there is any pressure it might be a Carlos Castaneda-Don Juan backlash, where Indian writers might be expected to always write about ethereal, mystical sorts of things when in fact those may not be the feelings they experienced at all.

A Conversation with
Leslie Marmon Silko

Larry Evers and Denny Carr / 1976

From *Sun Tracks* 3.1 (1976): 28–33. Reprinted by permission.

Q: How long has your family, the Marmon family, been in this house?

S: Well, this house we're in now is the old Santa Fe depot. I guess Grandpa Marmon bought it off the Santa Fe railroad when they changed the tracks. The railroad used to come right by here, and it went all the way around the village. In fact, there's a funny story that Harvey Paymella was spreading around the University of New Mexico. I wrote a poem about it. It's not a very good poem, I think, but it explains Harvey's Hopi theory on Laguna population. Harvey was saying that this is what the Hopis say. The fact that the Santa Fe railroad used to come so close to the village, right around it, the fact that there was a train that came by every morning about four a.m. and blew its whistle and woke everybody up, well, that explains why there are so many Lagunas around today. Disregarding Harvey and his scandalous Hopi population theory, the fact that the railroad came through here was very important. It had a great impact on the pueblo.

Q: The coyote poem we were talking about (*"Toe'osh*: A Laguna Coyote Story," *Carriers of the Dream Wheel,* Harper & Row, 1975), does the Marmon family come into that poem?

S: "Some white men came to Acoma and Laguna and they fought over Acoma land and Laguna women, and even now some of their descendents are howling in the hills." Well, I don't know how the rest of the Marmons feel about that line. Also, it isn't just the Marmons. I would have to include the Gunns, Paula's family, and the Pratts. John Gunn and Walter Marmon, my great-grandfather's brother, came to Laguna after the Civil War. In fact, I have seen John Gunn's blue uniform, Civil War uniform. I tried the coat on; I wore it. They came to this part of the country as government surveyors. My great-grandfather came out a little while later after Walter was established. He began to write a memoir of his years here. I think it would have been very interesting, but he never finished it. He came out here in the late 1870s and died about 1935. As far as I know he was just to the part about coming as far

as Albuquerque when he died. He got there by train, and then rode on horse-
back to Laguna. When he got here his legs and his behind were so blistered
that he walked the last twenty miles because he couldn't bear to be on the
horse. That's as far as he got. So what I know of him comes from what my
grandmother mentions or my dad.

They had a contract with the government, and they were the ones who laid
out the bench markers which are all around here to this day. Climbing around
in the hills you'll find a really old corner, brass bench marker, and that's one
of the ones that either Walter or Robert put in. My great-grandfather married
a woman from Paguate. They had two children, and then she died. Then he
married my great-grandmother, her younger sister. They had nine or ten kids,
one of which was my grandpa. I guess he taught school over at Acoma for a
while.

One anthropologist has written about the Marmons and the impact they
had at Acoma pueblo. His account emphasizes the fact that they were Presbyterians. I think maybe he gets the Marmons confused with old man Gorman
who cleared out right around the time the Marmons came in. They bought
the Gorman mission. It's true they were Presbyterians. My great-grandmother
had been sent to school at Carlisle, Pennsylvania, and she was a very strong
Presbyterian. Anyway, it's funny that the anthropologist thought it was so
disruptive, when you look around here now and see how many people show
up at the Presbyterian church. My grandfather and his brothers and sister
never practiced that religion at all. I think maybe the ethnologist was only
dreaming or wishing. Maybe he was a latent Presbyterian himself. Anyhow
that's some of the background. My great-grandfather was a governor here at
Laguna one year. I imagine that caused quite a stir.

Q: The river seems to be important to you in your writing. Is it important
here at Laguna?

S: Well, look where all the Marmon houses are here by the river, down in
below the village. They put us in this place. I always thought there was
something symbolic about that, sort of putting us on the fringe of things. The
river's really close by. It's just a short walk from here, and I was always
attracted to it as a kid. I loved the river very much, but I knew it was a small
river, and I didn't make any great demands on it. It's just a great place to go
and play in the mud and splash around. There are willows and tamarack, and
there are always stories. You just hear them. The river's the one place where
things can happen that can't in the middle of the village, obviously. I guess

from the very beginning there was always the idea that the river was kind of a special place where all sorts of things could go on. I got stuck in the sand down there once, and my grandma pulled me out and switched me. But I kept going back, even when I was twelve, thirteen, fourteen, except by then my idea of the possibilities for the river had grown. They included not only catching minnows and little frogs, but I began to realize the possibilities which the people have forever realized. The river was a place to meet boy-friends and lovers and so forth. I used to wander around down there and try to imagine walking around the bend and just happening to stumble upon some beautiful man. Later on I realized that these kinds of things that I was doing when I was fifteen are exactly the kinds of things out of which stories like the Yellow Woman story, I finally put the two together: the adolescent longings and the old stories, that plus the stories around Laguna at the time about people who did, in fact, just in recent times, use the river as a meeting place. The river was a sort of focal point bringing all those together. The stories about places give one the ideas or materials, at least, for fantasies and dreams or expectations. All of your expectations and your feelings about the place are developed by what people say about it. And you are better prepared in turn for the stories that people tell and have always told about the place.

It goes back to the function of the stories, these gossip stories. No, I don't look upon them as gossip. The connotation is all wrong. These stories about goings-on, about what people are up to, give identity to a place. There are things about the river you can see with your own eyes, of course, but the whole feeling of the place, the whole identity of it, was established for me by the stories I'd heard, all the stories: the early stories, the goings-on, and the warning stories about the old man who lost a team of horses in the quick-sand at a certain point on the river. That's how you know, that's how you belong, that's how you know you belong, if the stories incorporate you into them. There have to be stories. It's stories that make this a community. People tell those stories about you and your family or about others and they begin to create your identity. In a sense, you are told who you are, or you know who you are by the stories that are told about you. I see now that the ideas and dreams and fears and wonderful and terrible things that I expected might happen around the river were just part of an identity that the stories had made for it. By going to the river, I was stepping into that identity. And I think it happens for other individuals, families, and clans. That's why stories are told by clans.

Stories were important in this way for us Marmons because we are a mixed breed family. People in the main part of the village were our clanspeople because the clan system was still maintained although not in the same form it would have been if we were full blood. The process went on, but it changed slightly for us. The way it changed was that there began to be stories about my great-grandfather, positive stories about what he did with the Laguna scouts for the Apaches. But then after World War I it changed. Soon after that there came to be stories about these mixed-blood people, half-breeds. Not only Marmons but Gunns and Pratts too. An identity was being made or evolved in the stories the Lagunas told about these people who had gone outside Laguna, but at the same time, of the outsiders who had come in. Part of it was that the stories were always about the wild, rougish, crazy sorts of things they did. Maybe greedy and bad, there were both positive and negative things. But the identity was made for our families, and we're a big bunch of people now. So that happened.

In a sense it made it easier for me than for somebody like Simon Ortiz who doesn't have that kind of separate identity. A very different set of possibilities are open to him because he is a full blood Acoma man whose father is very involved in the religious things. There's a whole different set of stories and expectations for him that sometimes can constrict him. I don't say that negatively, of course, it's just different. I have great latitude by contrast.

Q: Many contemporary poets are remaking or "rescuing" songs and stories from old BAE reports, and their efforts are often thought of as the Native American oral tradition. You seem to be working from a more vital source, from what you hear now, rumor, gossip, and the like.

S: Yes, that's probably the basis for my acquaintance with language. For a long time I was sort of self-conscious about not knowing the Laguna language better than I do. I had that in that one poem about my grandfather. I always had the feeling that he died too soon. And I was given to feel—by some of those poets—that to be a worthy human being if you were coming from a pueblo, you should know the stories just the way the anthropologists reported them. Yet I was never tempted to go to those things and do what they did. There were some things that I heard and some things that I knew, and I thought, well, you know, you've just got to stick with it, with what you've heard, with what you have. I figured that anybody could go to the anthropologists' reports and look at them. I have looked at them myself, but I've never sat down with them and said I'm going to make a poem or a story out of this. The more I think about it, I realize I don't have to because from the time I was little I heard quite a bit. I heard it in what would be passed off now as rumor or gossip. I could hear through all that. I could hear something else, that there was a kind of continuum that was really there despite Elsie Clews Parsons. In 1930, you know, she wrote off Laguna as a lost cause. She said it had no kiva, that it was dead. I think she wrote that somewhere. And the same went for the "oral tradition."

I guess somewhere along the line I must have been hearing, and you still can. It's like last year at Laguna Feast they had a trash fight. There were some Navajos down at the trash pile, and they had a fight. It's called a trash pile fight. Every year at Laguna Feast there are these incidents. I always loved stories about them so much that the things in the anthropological reports looked dead and alien. I couldn't do anything with them anyway, even though theoretically they came from here. So I leave those things to those people that are so impoverished that they have to go resurrect them.

I also know the attitudes of people around here to those reports. You don't know how accurate they are. I started writing a story about ethnologists just continually milking their informants, kind of reversing that. When I started to write, I started to laugh. I never did get past the first meeting. This Charlie Coyote type starting to size up the anthropologist; he's talking about someone else who's been in the kitchen all this time pretending not to understand what was going on. After he leaves they start discussing, "What'd you tell him that for? Those are outrageous lies." I've always been real leery of the kinds of things that the ethnologists picked up, another reason not to fool around with it.

Q: The kinds of things you do pick up, how do you give them form? How does a Leslie Silko poem develop?

S: I just go at it. Somehow it just starts to come together. With the coyote story [*"Toe'osh:* A Laguna Coyote Story"], I wrote it after I came back from a writers conference in Wisconsin. At first, it started out to be something just about Simon Ortiz and about the conference back there. And then . . . then, somewhere I started to think about the coyote thing because Simon had read one of his coyote poems. He'd been talking about *Toe'osh.* Then all of a sudden I did this big switch. I started thinking that all these years there have been all these things. One was this Navajo story that the students told me about when I was teaching at Navajo Community College. I started remembering all these other things. It was like suddenly seeing that there are other kinds of coyote stories than just the ones in the BAE. Then I knew exactly how these things had to be said. I figured out what kind of coyote stories they were going to be. They were going to be like that one about the Lagunas, the politicians, and the turkeys. Once you see those connections, then it's easy. It's getting around to where you can see that's the hard part.

Q: Earlier you mentioned a talk you had with one of your neighbors this morning about that poem. Would you talk about her reaction again?

S: Well Nora was talking about the part about the coyote chain, that old story. I guess she was excited to recognize it. It's very, very sketchy the way I've got it, as little as I could say and still get across what happens.

Q: Would you read that part?
S: O.K. This is part seven of the poem.

> They were after the picnic food
> that the special dancers left
> down below the cliff.
> And *Toe'osh* and his cousins hung themselves
> down over the cliff
> holding each other's tail in their mouth
>   making a coyote chain
> until someone in the middle farted
> and the guy behind him opened his
> mouth to say "What Stinks?" and they
> all went tumbling down, like that.

So this morning I guess Nora's grandchildren ran across that story in *Carriers of the Dream Wheel.* She said that she had her grandchildren read the poem to her, those things, and then that got her started. It brought up that story. Then my fantasy of what was probably said was, "Well, the way the story really goes is like this. . . ." Then I think she went ahead and told them that and said how, when she was young, how many of those stories she'd heard. She was talking about an old man and her dad and how they would sit around the stove. Then, jokingly, before they began, say, "The storyteller cannot begin. The storyteller cannot tell stories unless there's some parched corn or pinons at the least." So someone would have to jump up and get this for the storyteller before he would begin. Otherwise he wouldn't. So she was recalling that this morning. She said that there were one or two stories that would take almost the whole evening just to complete and by that I would imagine from like five or six all the way to I don't know what time. People around here aren't too strict about when you go to bed. You just sort of go when you want to, so it could have been like eleven at night.

So the younger kids came across this poem and in reaction she said let me tell you the whole story. One of my frustrations in writing, you know, is that unless you're involved in this, in these stories, in this place, you as a reader may not get it. I have to constantly fight against putting in detail and things that would be too tedious for the "outsider." At the same time I have to have some sort of internal integrity there in the piece. But I'm satisfied with that. What I was doing in that coyote piece wasn't to retell it just the way it would be told by someone like Nora here. I hope the young kids have or develop a taste for the longer versions too. This one's really a funny one. Coyote comes over to the edge of this mesa and peeks over and he sees these dancers. The way my aunt describes it, the dancers are from a dance society that no longer exists, it's completely died out, so they were very special. And they had laid out all the food that they were going to eat after they got done dancing or practicing dancing, or whatever. Whatever they were doing down there was kind of mysterious. So the story is kind of cinemagraphic, the opening scene is like the opening scene of a movie. Coyote is peeking over the edge, and there are all these nice things down there, and the dancers are laying them out not knowing that Coyote is peeking over. You get the sense that Coyote's all alone. Then he kind of goes "Mmmm, wow. It looks good, but it's way down there." I guess it's on a mesa where it's miles to go around and get down. So finally he has an idea. He runs back from the edge, and he starts calling, "Ooooh, ooooh," you know, calling all his cousins. And they gather, and he says, "I've got this idea. Look. Look down there." And they all look, and they're excited, but they say, "Well, how are we gonna get it?" And he says, "Ah, that's why I've called you. I have this brilliant idea, and this is how it's going to work." Some of them are kind of doubtful, and they say, "Wow, this is really high, and if anything were to happen. . . ." "No, no, don't worry." And then, you get the coyote chain, so that in the longer version it's really funny because when it finally happens, when one farts and they all fall down, it's even better because Coyote's been reassuring all the others, telling them there's not a thing to worry about, that everything's gonna go fine. I've thought about this a lot. The one thing he hadn't taken into consideration happens. So the longer version is really a lot of fun. It's a good story.

Q: Working from these longer versions, then, does condensing become a problem for you in your work?

S: I guess the problem with condensing comes from the fact that the people around here have a lot of time, or they make time, to talk. So the people really appreciate hearing a good story, and a good story was a story that would last long enough at least. It was one that has all kinds of details and gestures. When you tell certain things, you might be expected to act out these facial expressions and gestures and so forth. So the Laguna stories, whether they're the very old time ones like coyote stories or whether they're something that happened at the last Laguna fiesta, there has always been a problem condensing them for the outsider, for the non-Laguna. One of the things I recall reading in one of the anthropologist's books was the Lagunas had a seemingly inexhaustible capacity for cataloguing and listing and also hearing the reciting ceremonial detail. There's the same sort of inexhaustible capacity for describing places and directions. In describing places and directions, there are stories that identify the place. These kinds of things make condensing a problem. It all depends on how much you want to make your stories acceptable to communities outside this one. I condense, but I try to be very careful to preserve the essential quality that stories have that makes them stories. If that is cut, then you've ruined the whole thing.

Q: What about witch stories, you use some in your novel and other places, where do they fit into contemporary Laguna oral tradition?

S: It wasn't until I went out to Chinle that I ever heard witch stories, because people here don't consider it to be a polite subject for conversation. I agree with Simon, although I always have to qualify with the fact that I was growing up down here at the foot of the village and up at the mill, that there's just not a whole lot of that that goes on anyway. Simon has said, too, that when a community is, in the catch phrase, together, where things are fairly orderly, where the livestock and the food supply is good, where some widespread series of deaths of religious leaders hasn't hit, where everything is in good shape within the pueblo view, then there's not going to be any witchcraft. It goes against the definition of witchcraft. Witchcraft is happening when the livestock are skinny. Simon has said, and my sense is pretty much the same, that there's not much of that that happens around here. It can almost be said with pride. The occurences are rare, and when they do occur they were handled by everybody. It wasn't like just one person dealing with it.

The whole Navajo thing seems different to me. First of all, witchcraft activity is incessant. It seems to touch almost everybody, and the means by which the Navajo seem to be attempting to deal with it were a little bit more like on an individual family basis. Tremendously expensive ceremonies and payments of money to medicine men seem to be necessary, whereas when the pueblo people worked these things out, you would have some kind of community thing not so much focused on the sick one. Navajos get so specific. This kind of sandpainting for this particular patient. Navajo perception of witchery seems much more widespread and involved. What I'm getting around to saying is I never heard many of those stories here, except for the classic. I heard that one and that says just about everything you need to know about witches. I heard that one, but that's the only one. I *never, never,* while I was growing up, ever heard anybody say so and so's sick or so and so died because of witchcraft. But the whole time I was in Chinle and Lukachuchai, it was so and so's got a rash on his hands because he did this, and so and so wrecked her car, and that was obviously because so and so caused it. The stories are all over there, you can't avoid them. If I hadn't gone up there, I probably never would have gotten into witchcraft in my writing.

Once I got into it, I began to try to understand how witchcraft fits into the whole scheme of things. That's when I got more interested in witchcraft as it *might* have occurred around here. I develop some of that in the novel.

Q: Does the Black Corn story appear in the novel?

S: The Black Corn story is there. I have the whole story at the beginning now, but we're going to cut it. But it comes into the novel at various points, I will still have some fairly direct references to it. It's there in so far as everything Arrow Boy sees in the Black Corn story, the main character in my novel sees, but in a different form. Arrow Boy in the story sees them in their cave. And part of the curse and prophecy thing is there, the jumping through the hoop three times. Towards the end, everything Tayo sees is what Arrow Boy saw, but in a different century and a different form. It's there, it almost has to be. There's just no way around it. The reason I first put the Arrow Boy story in the beginning was to clue people in who might not know. It was an afterthought, so I'm putting it out again. I think it works without that whole thing in there, that's the way I wrote it in the first place.

In the novel, I've tried to go beyond any specific kind of Laguna witchery or Navajo witchery which is why that one story is so important, that sort of curse-prophecy thing. I try to begin to see witchery as a sort of metaphor for the destroyers or the counter force, that force which counters vitality and birth. The counter force is destruction and death. It's one of the things that Ben Barney and I have worked out. We have tried to get away from talking about good and evil. Part of it is a kind of affectation. We're trying to affect the old, old, old way of looking at the world, but I think a lot of it is still implied. It's just that in recent years we've gotten into the habit of talking about black and white and good and bad. But back when, it was force or counter force. It may seem corny, but it is the idea of balance, an idea that the world was created this way. In the novel it's the struggle between the force and the counter-force. I try to take it beyond any particular culture or continent because that's such a bullshit thing. It's all Whitey's fault, that's too simplistic, mind-less. In fact Tayo is warned in the novel that *they* try to encourage people to blame just certain groups, to focus in on just certain people and blame them for everything. Then you can't see what the counter people or the counter forces are really doing. I think that's important, and I wanted to get that in. So, what I'm trying to say is that ultimately I go way beyond any kind of local experience I might have had.

Q: There's a passage in the novel, isn't there, that begins something like, "white people created witches," but then somebody says, "that's too simple, white people are only tools which the witchery manipulates. They invented white people."

S: It's sort of outrageous. Another name for the counter forces are the manipulators. That comes out in the old story, which I'm sure is in Parsons, about one of the many times when our mother got pissed off at the people. It was the magician who came down from the north. I have that story in the novel. The magician was showing the people all kinds of tricks, how to do this and that and the other. He'd make water come out of the north wall, he'd touch a log and it would jump up and become a mountain lion, and the people's eyes were getting real big. And the twin brothers who were caretakers of the corn mother altar got excited. Everyone was standing around watching this guy. He was going through a whole routine, and everybody got all excited and involved in this magic, and they forgot to take care of the altar. At one point the magician says, "You guys want some of this magic?" And the twins say, "Yeah, yeah, boy we could really use that for the fields. We could do anything. We wouldn't have to work anymore. This is fantastic. We'll take some." And they got all involved, and in the meantime the corn mother gets very angry, and she says, "Well, if they're so happy with that, then I'll just leave them with it. Go ahead and see how far it takes you." The whole point being that they've become manipulators. They create nothing. They merely take what is around, whatever it is, whether it's a simple sleight of hand or some of the magician's tricks or whether we're talking about using races of people or philosophies or technologies. What should emerge is that the manipulators, the white people, according to this awful story I made up, will be manipulated. The whole point of the novel is that they're trying to manipulate everybody. One of the big battles Tayo begins to have to deal with is to keep the end of the story right. They're trying to manipulate him into doing something that would change the way the story has to go. It goes back into the ceremony thing that started long ago, and, of course, it goes on and on. So they're manipulators. They cannot originate things. That's why they jump into animal skins, and that's why I had that note that live animals were horrified of them.

Q: How is it that the Japanese come into your novel?

S: Well that's a long story and it's very interesting. I got mixed up with some Asian-Americans, writers, but long before that there was this woman who was our clan mother. She's the one who had to come and give pudding to my father at Easter or he would turn into a frog, that sort of lady. Her son went over to Japan after the Korean War, and he married a Japanese woman, and he lives there. But he would come back and tell us that the Japanese have lots of words like Lagunas and that he could speak Japanese just like that. So I heard that. And I was already aware of Aunt Susie's story, her theory, about how we got over to this continent. I wrote that in a letter for the front part of Abe Chapman's book [*Literature of the American Indians (NAL, 1975)*]. I met these Asian-Americans and got to know their concerns and made some more links. Then Phil George, who's Nez Perce, had that Buffalo Dance song, and it's a real Buffalo Dance song, but it's all sung in Japanese. I guess it's something that a Nez Perce picked up in the Second World War in Japan, apparently from some Pueblo person who had picked it up and put Japanese words to it. So when I got to writing the novel about the guys who came back from the war, the ones who were so messed up when they came back from the South Pacific. They were fighting the Japanese. There was one kid around here who bragged that his dad had Jap teeth that he knocked out of the mouth of a Jap colonel and a gold dagger he got from a general. The kids weren't like the rest of the kids. They had grown up in California, and later they went back there. They said their father kept the things wrapped up in a bandana. Well, that made a big impression on me. So, when I started working on the novel and the guys who came back home, the souvenir thing came back to me. Then I started to relate it back to the Black Corn thing, how there are certain objects taken from dead bodies that the counter forces use as their whole stock and trade. You see it just clicks together. Anybody that would bring back that stuff, well, you get what I mean. It became very easy then to see what was really going on with such war souvenirs.

Q: So the oral tradition is anything but dead and buried in dusty reports at Laguna.

S: Yeah, we're going stronger than ever. Even just the good old adultery stories are better than ever and much more intricate because not everyone has indoor plumbing, so that you no longer have that excuse to go out, which was a pretty good one. It's just like what I was saying earlier about the Laguna Feast stories. They just go on and on and on. There's no end to it. The feast changes, but the stories keep right on going with very few differences. The way I end my novel, one of the endings, is to have the old woman say something like "I'm getting too old to even get excited about the goings-on around here anymore. It doesn't even excite me anymore." She said, "It's all beginning to sound like I've heard all those stories before, only some of the names are different." At which point she goes to sleep. That's one of the endings of the novel, probably not the one we'll keep, but that sense of a continuity is just there. You can hear it all around.

Stories and Their Tellers—
A Conversation with Leslie
Marmon Silko
Dexter Fisher / 1977

From *The Third Woman: Minority Women Writers of the United States,*
edited by Dexter Fisher (Boston: Houghton Mifflin, 1980), pp. 18–23.
Reprinted by permission.

This interview was conducted at Laguna Pueblo, New Mexico, on 28
January 1977.

Fisher: What do you think is the relationship between traditional and contemporary Native American literature?
Silko: Well, there are a number of relationships. One relationship that I
see as a continuum, and it's a loose one, is that in Native American communities, especially the more rural ones, there has always been a tremendous concern with language. I think that growing up within a community that has this
concern with language and storytelling is important because you get attuned
to hearing stories. A person who is accustomed to listening, who knows what
a story is, can glean out of all sorts of information the heart of the story.
When I go to the Laguna Acoma High School to talk to Native American
kids, I tell them that storytelling for Indians is like a natural resource. Some
places have oil, some have a lot of water or timber or gold, but around here,
it's the ear that has developed. You have it. In a sense, it's accidental just like
uranium is accidental in a given region. But I want them to know that this
potential exists. There's the possibility for telling stories. I think it has to do
with community, with growing up in certain kinds of communities as op-
posed to others.

F: You would relate your growing up in this community as essential?
S: Yes, I think it's crucial. You can talk all day long about identity, census
numbers, etc. You can be a full blood and grow up in Cincinnati and lose
touch. Their experience is different from the person who is in the community
where there is constant concern for language. The community is tremen-

22

dously important. That's where a person's identity has to come from, not from racial blood quantum levels.

F: Did you grow up at Laguna primarily?
S: All the way.

F: Did you go through high school here?
S: We didn't have a high school. I went to the Head Start school. I went through the third and fourth grade here at Laguna at the BIA [Bureau of Indian Affairs] school. After the fourth grade, everyone had to go to boarding school. Most of the kids went off to boarding school, but my dad had gone to Albuquerque Indian School and he hated it. He used to run away and he didn't want us to have to go, so we and some other families from Laguna used to drive in every day. That was a hundred-mile round trip. I did that until I was sixteen. At that time, my aunt in Albuquerque died and left my mother a house, so we moved into Albuquerque and came back to the pueblo on the weekends.

F: Did you go to the University of New Mexico?
S: Yes.

F: Do you know the Laguna language?
S: Very little. I know very little because we're mix-blooded. I know as much as Grandma knows to get along at the store, but there was an absolute value placed on speaking English. I grew up with my great-grandmother, so I understood a lot more when I was small.

F: When did you first begin to write?
S: I started writing when I was in the fifth grade. A teacher gave us a list of words to make sentences out of, and I just made it into a story automatically. I can just do stories.

F: Why don't you talk a bit about your novel, *Ceremony.* How does the section on Gallup fit in? ["Gallup, New Mexico—Indian Capital of the World" is included in "Traditions, Narratives, and Fiction"—ed.]
S: That piece works in a number of different ways in the overall structure of the novel. My character from Laguna, Tayo, is going with his uncle to Gallup to see a very strange, unpopular, and unorthodox medicine man who lives up in the hills in a very old place in the dumps above the Gallup ceremonial grounds. As they go into Gallup, this piece fits in, though it doesn't have anything directly to do with the story. The section is about the little child and

his relationship to his mother. It also relates to Tayo because his mother comes and goes like the kid's mother. Tayo lost his mother when he was very young, so the child's mother becomes a metaphor for his mother and the mother of creation. The Laguna story that I follow is about the mother creator, and it's uncorrupted by Christianity. The mother in the Gallup section has her own kind of momentum and her own way and that goes without saying. But because she and the other mothers aren't conventional, the assumption is that they are unfit and their children should be taken from them. The idea I was trying to work with is that nobody has the conventional mother, really. If a mother is docile on the outside, she may be seething inside; no one really has the perfect mother. I became intrigued by this. Both Tayo and the child really know they are loved, and when the little boy is waiting for his mother to come back, he doesn't feel as rotten as the outward appearance of his life shows. He's been loved. It all comes together in the end, his being loved, the mother, the creator.

F: Why did you entitle the novel *Ceremony?*

S: That's what it is. Writing a novel was a ceremony for me to stay sane. My character in the beginning of the novel is very sick. He's been in the mental ward in Los Angeles, but he doesn't remember. He doesn't remember being a prisoner of war in the Philippines. A lot of my cousins, a lot of people from this area, were in the same position during the war. They got caught. So my character is very sick, and I was very sick when I was writing the novel. I was having migraine headaches all the time and horrible nausea that went on and on. I kept writing and all of a sudden it occurred to me that he was very sick and I was wondering if he was going to get well, because of those who came back, some made it and some didn't. My dad and uncle were in the war and they did okay, but some didn't. So here I was in my novel working on my character every day, and I was trying to figure out how some stay sane and some don't, and then I realized that the one thing that was keeping me going at all was writing. And as Tayo got better, I felt better. But then he had lapses. These weren't one for one though. I was just telling my creative writing class the other day that when you're writing and trying to describe something you go to your own experience to see how you have felt in similar situations, because that's all you can describe.

F: Have you studied writing formally?

S: I took a couple of classes. I was an English major, but at that time they didn't have a creative writing major, and they didn't have very many teachers.

Now, I'm part of the whole fleet of creative writing teachers. I never could get too much out of the classes except discipline. I had to have papers in on time, but with my fiction, I just sort of did it. I couldn't just change one section because then the whole thing would unravel.

F: What do you like to read?

S: Everything! I love Milton and Shakespeare, especially the tragedies. I don't have much patience with a lot of contemporary literature, because there's a lot of crap going around.

F: Has there been any one major influence on your writing?

S: The major influence has been growing up around here and listening to people and to the way the stories just keep coming.

F: Let's go back for a minute to the notion of context. It is obvious from your short stories that environment, particularly the landscape here at Laguna, is important. What do you think people should know about context before they read your stories?

S: Well, nothing really. I don't know. Maybe if there are words like *arroyo* that aren't clear, those could be explained. That's irritating. I used to get irritated with T. S. Eliot and all his Greek. I would wish that people would have a little bit better understanding of place, that in geography classes they would teach how people live in Bethel, Alaska, and Laguna, New Mexico, or Iowa City, etc. It's as if what you see on television takes the place of a geography class. Instead, in Bethel, people live without indoor plumbing, and there's one truck that comes around to deliver water and another one to pick up the waste products. What I would ideally wish for is that people had just a general familiarity, a sense of the history, when the Spaniards came in, just American history, for Christ's sake, but they don't. It can be turned around on us; for example, I don't think people here know much about New York subways. I think what's horrifying is that we're made to believe that the television lifestyle and geography are one, and we're really so diverse. It's said. Anyway, that's all my stories really need. Included in geography should be the way people live, some of their attitudes, their point of view, so if you have even just a smattering of Pueblo point of view, that helps. It's not much.

F: Is there such a thing as a "Native American" perspective? Or would you say there's a tribal perspective?

S: As far as perspective goes, there's mine. Leslie Marmon. And insofar as I've grown up here and learned things here and loved people from here, the perspective I have involves very definitely Laguna and Laguna people and Laguna culture. What I write about and what I'm concerned about are relationships. To that I bring so many personal things that have been affected by where I come from, but I don't think one should oversimplify and say this is a Laguna point of view. It's my point of view, coming from a certain kind of background and place.

F: Would you distinguish Native American literature from other literatures, like black literature or Jewish literature, for example?

S: Those definitions are okay, if you have to begin to break things up into groups. It's better than talking about Group 1, Group 2, Group 3. If everyone wants to talk about the same thing, it's useful to say that this will be the group that's to talk about Ezra Pound, but I think what writers, storytellers, and poets have to say necessarily goes beyond such trivial boundaries as origin. There's also the danger of demeaning literature when you label certain books by saying this is black, this is Native American, and then, this is just writing. That's what's going on now, and I don't like it.

F: The other side of that coin, equally insidious, is the whole notion of universals, that literature is good only if it is universal. What do you think?

S: I would say that good literature has to be accessible. It's incredibly narcissistic to be otherwise. Artists can't work with a chip on their shoulders, and that's what has happened to a lot of feminists. Politics can ruin anything. It will ruin a picnic. Politics in the most crass sense—rally around the banner kind. I'm political, but I'm political in my stories. That's different. I think the work should be accessible, and that's always the challenge and task of the teller—to make accessible perceptions that the people need. Sometimes, it's not even that clear. Sometimes, it's just the storyteller uncontrolled. There are these stories that just have to be told in the same way the wind goes blowing across the mesa. That's what the teller used to have to do anyway, make accessible certain ways of seeing things. This is the beauty of the old way. You can stop the storyteller and ask questions and have things explained. And what's going on is an experience or perception being made accessible to those people. And it isn't too difficult to move from that setting into a wider and wider audience. That's why I like to talk about accessiblity. That doesn't mean that you won't learn more and more as you go on, and that takes us back to the context—depending on how familiar you are with the context, you'll get more or less. Like with Hopi country. I'm from Laguna and I know a fair amount about Laguna and Acoma things. I have good friends up at Hopi, and the more I go up and hang around the more I can get into it.

F: What would you say are some of the things you want to make accessible to people?

S: Things about relationships. That's all there really is. There's your relationship with the dust that just blew in your face, or with the person who just kicked you end over end. That's all I'm interested in. You have to come to terms, to some kind of equilibrium with those people around you, those people who care for you, your environment. I notice things about feeling good about meeting a certain animal when I'm out walking around the hills. I'll come back after a wonderful day, and someone will say that place is full of snakes. And I just had the feeling there wouldn't be any problem with snakes and there wasn't. As a matter of fact, snakes know when people are afraid of them and when to get upset. It's just like a horse. And people are the same. If you come into a room all mad and upset, pretty soon you get everyone else all mad and upset. Relationships are not just limited to man-woman, parent-child, insider-outsider; they spread beyond that. What finally happens in the novel, for example, is that I get way out of the Southwest in a sense and get into the kind of destructive powers and sadism that the Second World War brought out. Yet, it is all related back to Laguna in terms of witchcraft.

F: What is your favorite piece of the things you've written?

S: My favorite story is one that isn't set in the Southwest, but I love my characters in it. It's called "Storyteller," and it's set in the tundra of Bethel, Alaska. It's a long short story, and it sets out what the relationship of the storyteller to people is. The story is interesting to me and I like it, perhaps because the landscape is different, because I find a common point where I can relate to the land, regardless of whether it's land I'm from or not. That's a big step for me, to go to a completely alien landscape. I managed. What I did in that story finally was to get the interior landscapes of the characters, and yet they are still related to the tundra and the river because that's how she does the guy in. I love the story just because I like the characters and how she does the guy in.

F: How does humor fit in with your own writing?

S: It's generally double-edged. It seems with humor, there's always something beyond just the laughing—that when you're laughing, you have to think beyond to greater considerations. I think of a lot of the stories that happen around here. Something happens to someone and you just laugh and laugh, but generally while you're laughing, you have an awareness of something great. You get a sense of history insofar as you remember all the other stories like that. Sometimes they were funnier, and sometimes they weren't so funny at all. My next novel is going to be about the function of humor. I got to thinking about funny stories. Whatever just happened, it would be related to other things that had happened, and finally the function of the stories would be to keep you from feeling that God had just dropped a rock on your head alone or that you had been singled out in some way, which is really dangerous, because the stories remind you that this isn't the first time. Or if you feel everyone is laughing at you, someone can always tell a story where something worse happened. So pretty soon, after the whole thing is over with, things are back in perspective. The function of humor is very serious and very complex.

F: Do you think there are any contemporary myths emerging?

S: I don't see that there has ever been any end to the stories. They just keep going on and on. So far, I haven't seen that there are any new ones. There's a need to have a multiplicity of perspectives and tellers. I tell some stories. Simon Ortiz tells others. We need certain tellers to look after certain myths. The ones I'm looking after have always been around. It's part of a continuum. I see it more as a matter that certain people come along and work with the myths that have always been there.

F: How do you relate to the women's movement?

S: I feel I've benefited by it just generally in the sense that anything that undermines the stereotypes perpetrated on all of us by white men is helpful. What it does is take some of the pressure off those of us who have never lived very close to the stereotypes. I've always been the way I was. Here at Laguna, a lot more is expected of women; women are expected to be strong, to manage the property. Children belong to women and to their families. Women do the plastering. It's a relief to have the stereotypes knocked down. It's just made it easier for me to do what I want to do.

F: How would you characterize your literature?

S: I would say that a good story is really important and that's what I work for because with a good story there is no end to the possibilities. . . .

Interview with Leslie Marmon Silko

Per Seyersted / 1978

From *American Studies in Scandinavia* 13 (1981): 26–33. Reprinted
by permission.

Oslo, September 12, 1978

PS: What time is "The Man to Send Rain Clouds" set—is it very recent?

LMS: Yes, it is very recent. It's perhaps in the middle 1960s. It's a quite
recent story. The reason I am so sure of this is because it's based upon
something vaguely similar that actually happened.

PS: Yes, I believe you had some special inspiration for this story?

LMS: Well, it's like most of the inspirations for my stories. One weekend
I drove to Laguna from Albuquerque, as I often did to visit home while I was
in undergraduate school. When I would get to Laguna I would hear all the
news, all the stories of things that had been happening that week, that month,
since I had had my last visit. And one particular weekend I went home, and
they said, "Did you hear that old man Sorsino died?" and I said, "Oh, oh no,
I didn't know that," and they said, "Yes, they found him out at the sheep
pen. He'd been dead for a day or so, and the sheep were scattered all over by
the time they got there." And then my grandmother said, "And the Catholic
priest was very angry," and I said, "What about?" "Well," she said, "they
buried the old man without telling the priest. They just did the traditional
ceremonies and had a traditional funeral and they didn't tell the priest, and
the priest was very upset." And I said, "Oh. Well." And that was all, and I
didn't think more of it because visits, if you know Laguna and the way the
people tell stories, that was only one of many things I heard that weekend.
And I went back to Albuquerque where I was attending the University of
New Mexico, and that semester I was taking a creative writing class, and one
of my professors, the following week told us we had to write a short story.
And I thought, "Well, I'll just write about poor old man Sorsino." So I wrote
about him, imagining how it must have been when they found him, and also
I tried to imagine the Catholic priest and his feelings. So that's how this story
came.

PS: In *Ceremony,* you make a very interesting combination of the fact that
your pueblo or the pueblo close to it, Acoma, is very old, as age goes in

America, together with the fact that close to Laguna you have had the various uranium and atomic installations.

LMS: That's something that for a long time I suppose I didn't really appreciate, the irony. The Pueblo people have always concentrated upon making things grow, and appreciating things that are alive and natural, because life is so precious in the desert. The irony is that so close to us, in Los Alamos, New Mexico, scientists began the scientific and technological activity which created the potential end to our whole planet, the whole human race. The first atomic bomb was exploded in New Mexico, very close by us. To me it is very striking that this happened so close to the Pueblo people, but I suppose it is just one of those accidents of history.

PS: Have you by any chance read Frank Waters's book where he makes that connection between the old and the new culture?

LMS: No, I never have. I think it was easier for me to make the connection, because as a child, people still talked about that day when the bomb was exploded. It was done early in the morning before sunrise, and people at Laguna, some of the old people that got up before sunrise, as was their practice, remembered that the whole sky in the southeast lit up, and it was a remarkable sort of thing and people remember it. So I think that's where I made the connection.

PS: I understand that when you came to visit us now, Norway wasn't entirely unknown to you.

LMS: When I was just a schoolgirl, I had a teacher in the fifth grade, and she was of Scandinavian background. Very early, she read us some of these Scandinavian or Norse tales, and so I learned about Tor and Odin and Loke, and all the wonderful stories of Vulcan, and she read those stories to us, and as a little girl, coming from Laguna, I love stories, we have a great appreciation for stories. And I thought these stories were quite wonderful, and so after she read to us—she only read us a few—I asked her where I could get the book, and—well, tonight we were talking about this—the most sad thing for me is that at the end of this book of Norse tales is a chapter which in the book I read was called "Twilight of the Gods," and I had to read that all these gods would die and that this time ended, and it was very upsetting. It was tragic for me, because at Laguna, we believe that those times did not truly end, but that things only change, and so I was quite horrified to read that for some other people in this other place, that there was this twilight of the gods. So I, years ago, already loved these characteristic deities from the Norse country.

PS: Wouldn't you say, coming from Laguna, from these old Pueblos, that storytelling is not only a way of life, it is also as a sort of continuation of past life in that community, and therefore important to you also for that reason?

LMS: Oh yes, very much so. In fact, one of the older women—we called her Aunt Susie—who told me a lot of the stories, and who in some sense trained me, if that's what you want to call it, helped me to love the stories and learn them—she always said when she told the stories that there was an old custom, long ago, where the storyteller would say to one of the persons in the room, "Go open the door, go open the door so that they can come in," and it was as if "they," being ancestors, can come in and give us their gifts which are these stories, and that through the stories, somehow, even though people may be dead or gone or time is gone a long way in the past, that through the storytelling there was a belief that it all came back very immediately, that it came right back in the room with you. And so the storytelling in that sense was an act of . . . so that there wasn't anything lost, nothing was dead, nobody was gone, that in the stories everything was held together, regardless of time. And so, when I read the story about "The Twilight of the Gods" it was very upsetting, you see, for a person who was taught to believe that "No, these things go on and on and on." As long as we tell the stories, you know, then these things continue. The stories will only—these things will only die if we neglect to tell the stories. So I am still telling the stories.

PS: You also told us today an instance of the healing effect that stories can have. You mentioned a veteran who forgot to put on the brake when he parked his brand new car so that it rolled into a ravine and was wrecked, and who was then comforted by his fellow Pueblos who told him of similar accidents . . .

LMS: Yes, the stories are very important in many different ways. There are the usual ways that people find stories important in terms of history because, of course, the term in English is a combination of the word "story"— "his" "story," but at Laguna, the stories also serve to help the individual feel constantly a part of the group so that a person will never feel remote or lost no matter the time or situation. The way this functions is that, if something happens to you, as soon as something terrible happens to you, people come to you—and first of all, things are not kept private, I think that's important—so as soon as something terrible happens, people hear about it, and people come to you, whatever it might be, and the first thing people begin to do is they begin to tell you stories about other people and this has a very soothing effect—they don't talk about what just happened to you, but they'll say, "Well, now, that happened to my uncle, that happened to my uncle many years ago, the same sort of thing." And then, they will either tell you stories about the same sort of tragic thing, or, if this tragic thing that just happened to you took place in a certain geographical location, they may not tell you a story about a similar incident, but they'll say, "Well, bad things always happen at that place," and then they'll begin to tell about some kind of other terrible thing that happened at that place. And so people will come to you with all these other stories, and of course, the obvious immediate effect is they are taking your attention away from yourself, because you are hearing about other people and other incidents. It helps put things into perspective. We human beings have a tendency to think that we are the only ones that have ever experienced loss or sorrow. We're so self-centered. With the stories you begin to realize that what has just happened to you has happened before to different people. People will recount incidents worse than your own, so that by the time they get finished telling you all these other stories you realize you are not alone. You realize there are many people who have had the same thing happen to them. The best part is that you realize that for many years, in the future, even after you're gone, your story is joining all these other stories, and some day when something terrible happens to somebody else, they'll mention your story, too. So it is not as if it just happened to you or that there is nothing to be gained from your tragedy or loss. You have this sense that there's this ongoing story and your story has become part of it.

PS: You can still be of use to later generations . . .

LMS: Right. Through the story.

PS: You mentioned earlier today the feeling of self-worth. Do you feel that the so-called ethnic revival of the last 10 or 15 years has meant the same to the Indians as it has, for example, to the American blacks?

LMS: Yes, I think it has meant a lot to the people, both for the people who had their feeling of self-worth somehow undermined, or wounded, by schools, and also, I think, it has helped the older people who always believed—who always believed in the worth and the value of the Pueblo culture. I think it made them feel free to talk about the culture. The older people always felt that the Pueblo ways were as valid as the non-Indian ways which their children and grandchildren were being forced to learn, but they were afraid to say so, or they were afraid that maybe they would hinder their children or grandchildren if they tried to encourage them toward Pueblo language or toward Pueblo ways. This ethnic revival was freed them to teach things about the culture, the old stories, and things about the language which they might not have done so freely. They might have died without saying some of the things which are now being said. And in the religious ways, this revival has encouraged some of the older priests and religious persons to ask the younger people to come with them. And younger people, because of this revival, are not afraid or not ashamed. They want to come. So I think it has come in time for us, for the Pueblo people.

PS: Not too late, you'd say, but just in time . . .

LMS: Not too late, but *just* in time, just barely, which isn't to say that it's all going to be easy or that it's all going to be just perfect, or that no real damage was done by all these hundreds of years. I only wish that for some other Native American people it might have come sooner, because I suspect that perhaps for some groups, certainly for some individuals, it might be too late, but we make the best of what we can.

PS: Has there been a development among the Indians, as with the blacks after *Roots,* to try to find out who were your grandparents and so on?

LMS: A kind of research such as Alex Haley had to undertake isn't necessary, thank heavens, at Laguna. One of the things which is passed on from generation to generation among all the stories that are told, are stories about grandparents, great-grandparents, their great-grandparents and their great-grandparents, and on and on and on. And the people have a great deal of patience with the naming of these ancestors, where they came from and which clan they were from and so forth. And so this was one of the things that's just second nature to the people, keeping track of these things. And of course, it is very easy because we have been living in this same area for so long. It's very easy even if some of your ancestors have gone from Paguate village to Laguna, or from Laguna to Seama—we are only talking about 6 miles at most. If someone were to die suddenly and not pass on a certain amount of information to you, it's still possible to get those things. Again that goes back to everyone knowing so much about everyone else. It's as if each person were a source, and so it's all right here.

PS: You have named your novel *Ceremony.* What does the word "ceremony" stand for for you?

LMS: Well, for me, it's the term we use when we refer to certain religious activities. I first heard it connected with the activities which the Navajos participate in in order to cure, healing, medicinal sorts of activities. And the Navajos would say in English, "Old so and so has been sick, so they're giving him a ceremony," or "They're having a ceremony for him." And so that's where I first heard the term, and that's how it will be used in English. Basically it refers to those kinds of activities. It can also refer to other sorts of activities, not necessarily healing ceremonies, but celebrations or giving thanks, those sorts of ceremonies.

PS: Could you say a little about how you feel Tayo is cured, how the ceremonies worked for him?

LMS: Well, it's fairly complex, I think, in the novel. He is first visited by Ku'oosh, and this old medicine man from Laguna is familiar with the scalp ceremony which was a purification ceremony which was done for warriors, or anybody that might have killed another human being in battle, because of course killing another human being was not taken lightly, it was a very devastating sort of thing, a tremendous thing—

PS: And at the same time American Indians joined up to take part in the war—

LMS: Right. The people at home were very, what you would say, patriotic.

PS: Patriotic Americans—

LMS: Patriotic Americans. They were some of the first people to join up. So very many of the Pueblo men went, joined up and went to the Second World War. And also in later wars, the Korean war, the Vietnam war, many American Indians went. So, in the beginning, then, of the novel, certain Laguna rituals have been tried, to no avail, with this particular character. And he is sent, then, to this Navajo medicine man, who is a little bit notorious. The other Navajos don't agree with what he does.

PS: A somewhat questionable character—

LMS: Yes, a questionable character, questionable in terms of the purity of his ritual. Some of the other Navajos would say that he's taking liberties with the ritual; they didn't trust him. But the people in Tayo's family had heard that this medicine man was particularly successful with individual suffering from the effects of things connected with Anglo-Saxon culture. Alcoholism, and those sorts of things. They were willing to try, and so Tayo goes to this medicine man. But truly, the thing that heals Tayo is not only that particular ceremony which involves the sandpainting, it is the greater ceremony which helps Tayo to get well. Tayo's healing is connected to the faith which this old medicine man had, a faith which went back to things far in the past, the belief that it's human beings, not particular tribes, not particular races or cultures, which will determine whether the human race survives. But all people have to constantly be working, otherwise we will manage to destroy ourselves—

PS: Working at being sane—

LMS: Yeah, working at being sane, and taking care of each other. And so, it's because this medicine man reminds Tayo of humanity, of something larger than just the individual and the individual community. He puts Tayo in touch with this larger feeling.

PS: That he is part of humanity—

LMS: Right, that he is part of humanity, and feeling a part again, not just of the tribe, but of humanity, is a very healing sort of thing, and that as human beings we need that. When they say that the human being is a social animal, that's not to be taken lightly; it's almost a spiritual sort of thing. And so once he's joined again, or reminded that he's always been joined—I think that's the important point, that he's always been joined together—once he is reminded of this and can find it again within himself, then the other things he does are acts which reiterate this closeness. They're important acts, but they only help to reiterate this—

PS: This closeness to the integrity he has in himself and has always had in himself—

LMS: So nothing happens, nothing is given or put into him that hasn't always been there. The only thing that changes is his awareness, his perception of himself in relation to the rest of the world.

PS: And wouldn't you also say that it's an important part of the healing process, and thus of your book, to see that evil is everywhere, not just in the Anglos, but also in the Pueblos, and for that matter, in Tayo himself, that it is—again back to your word humanity—it's common humanity?

LMS: Right. That's terribly important, I think, because it's especially easy to blame oneself and say, "It's only me, this evil, this bad is within me." That's too easy, too simple. And so is the opposite, which is just to blame others—to say, "It's white people," or, "It's those people, it's not me," and thereby withdraw in the same way. Either way isolates us from other human beings. If we say, "It's all just me," then we're isolated. If we're saying, "It's everybody else but me," it's the same sort of isolation. Radical Indian politicians like to say, "Well, it's all the white people's fault, you know; we didn't do any of this." That's such a simplistic view, because from the very beginning, the betrayals of our people occurred through deeply complicated convergences of intentions and world views. And there were persons, full-blood Indians, who cooperated with the enemy, or who cooperated with the invaders, and there were mixed blood or "half-breed" people who did—that's human nature.

PS: As you had with the blacks in Africa during slave trading times—

LMS: Right. Sure. It's something about us as humans, not about us as any particular race or group. It's nice to think that none of our people have the capability of doing anything treasonous. But unfortunately, as long as we're all human beings, there are certain human traits which turn up, and so it is important that Tayo discovers that the Destroyers and the destructive impulse don't reside with a single group or a single race, and that to manipulate people into war or other conflicts again is a human trait; it is a worldwide thing. It's not just one group of people, that's too simple.

PS: Yes, this was just what I would like to end on, this note that your book is not only about some American Indian people, but very much about Everyman who could have been in somewhat the same situation. Thank you very much.

LMS: Thank you.

Teller of Stories:
An Interview with Leslie
Marmon Silko

James C. Work and Pattie Cowell / 1980

From *Colorado State Review* 8.2 (1981): 68–79. Reprinted by permission.

The following interview with Leslie Silko took place at Colorado State University on February 2, 1980, when she visited the campus to read from the manuscript of her latest book and to participate in a writer's workshop. We took the opportunity to talk with her about her earlier work, about *Ceremony*'s creation, and her feelings about being the novelist she is.

Ms. Silko began the interview by telling us about "Tony's Story," her first significant piece of fiction. We asked her if she had based the story on her own research.

Silko: No. That's really hair-raising. It's an incident that actually happened in 1951. I was born in 1948, so when I was just a real little kid I heard people talk about it, and the one thing I remember clearly about the incident is that after the state policeman was killed, the guys who killed him burned the body in the car. And my dad said all that was left of him could be put into a shoe box. I remember that so clearly, and it stayed with me. I was in this creative writing class; the first assignment was to do a story and that story came back to me. I tried to imagine how they saw what they did, and so I took that particular point of view. Simon Ortiz has a story about that same incident, but it's from a very different perspective. Anyway, I wrote it and didn't think any more of it; it was just a piece of fiction using this real incident. But years later Larry Evers of the University of Arizona did research on the case and went back and read the Albuquerque newspapers, looked at the court transcripts, and discovered there had been a sanity hearing at the Menninger Clinic, that these three guys had been taken to the Menninger Clinic and that George Deveraux, who's an anthropologist and a psychiatrist, had evaluated them. In a way he saved them. They would have been taken to the electric chair, but he said that they were paranoid schizophrenics. The psychiatrist's report was part of the court transcript and open to the public, so Larry was able to get it. The real hair-raising thing is that he sent it to me, and I felt chills all down my back because they told Deveraux that the state cop was a witch and that the car flew through the air at them and they had seen pieces of bottles and paper rolling through the air in places where they shouldn't have been. In my story I don't have the state police car flying through the air, but I was horrified to find out that that was exactly how these guys had seen him and exactly what they had done. I tried to figure out, well, how did I know this, because no one had ever really told me the story. Simon knows the story much better, but sometimes I think in fiction writing it's better to know less of all the little details. Simon knew a great deal more than I did because he was older, and they were Acoma people who did it, not Lagunas. But I realize that the key, the clue that worked in my subconscious, was burning. Burning the body was a kind of extra touch in the story that stayed with me, and that's what people do with witchcraft. That's the way to dispose of it. That must have somewhere been recorded, and I put it together on some other level, because when I was writing the story I really was just trying to write a story for my assignment.

Work: Is there a word in Laguna for paranoid schizophrenic?

Silko: No. I think Devereaux—I wonder if maybe he didn't just do that to save their lives. Maybe he wouldn't be so insensitive to the culture as that, but called them paranoid schizophrenics to save them. I don't know. Or maybe he really studies the people as an ethnologist and looks upon all that as an aberration. I don't know.

Cowell: You've talked about getting a story from an incident when you were a young child or taking stories from legends. What process do you use once you have this germ of an idea for a story?

Silko: Well, it's a lot of hard work. It's sort of scary; it's not really inspiring. You get the idea, and you know what you want to do, and you just sit down and you just—like the Coyote in last night's reading—keep trying and trying. It's like a steep hill and an old car—you have to make a run at it. You get almost up to the top and you roll back down. The Coyote story, for example, took about three drafts to get to the point where the fourth time it was finished. The material in *The Man to Send Rain Clouds*—in fact the title story I can remember cutting and editing. I know what I want to do, but it's like I just have to keep working at it and keep playing around with it. I'll start it out with an "I" narrator and if I feel myself getting into a corner that way, I'll throw it out and start out "she" or "he." Sometimes I start out with one point of view and I don't like it. In other words, with one story, how to tell it? You've got the story, but how to do it? There's no way I know except getting in it and just seeing if it's going to go. It's pretty tedious and it's scary. It means you don't instantly, once you get a story, have command to make it turn out. You just don't know.

Cowell: And sometimes the stories you begin won't turn out?

Silko: Right. They won't. I think almost every writer—fiction writers have more of them—have stacks and stacks of things that just don't quite go. You can't quite part with them, you know, but at the same time they didn't quite make it. So you hang onto them . . .

Cowell: Hoping they'll go at some future time?

Silko: Right. What I always tell students is not to worry about that. When I tried to write *Ceremony* I got two, what I call "stillborn," novels. They're stillborn at about sixty-five pages. That's a real frightening experience. That's why I use the term "stillborn." After *Ceremony* came out I was going through some books and papers, and I glanced through these two "stillborn" pieces. Part of one of the "stillborn" pieces is in *Ceremony*—the part about the kid in Gallup, the little boy that has no name and doesn't call his mother "Mother." Everything I was trying to work out and trying to do and wanting to get out of those two—what I wanted to say *in* those two "stillborns"— came out in *Ceremony* and came together just right. It wasn't like they were lost causes or a waste of time. Jesus, you know, I spent six months working on this and now it's "stillborn." There's a temptation to feel really defeated. But it's not. It's part of the process; it's taking you someplace, and sooner or later those things you're trying to say and trying to work out are valuable. You have to do that, you have to write these things that don't work out. You *have to,* and if you don't I think you should be more worried than if you do and have boxes full of things that don't work.

Work: Tayo does that in *Ceremony* . . . dead end after dead end until he finally wills himself to live and finish.

Silko: Yes. Well, in a lot of ways some of the things he goes through turn out to be the kinds of things, as I was writing the novel, that I was going through. Like the part where Ts'eh warns him that they want the story to end with him being killed out there. With the way of American writing and violence and the Bonnie and Clyde mentality of American art, I realized that the book predictably would end that way. That was how it was going, that was how it was set up, that's how an Indian character in this situation in modern American fiction would be expected to end. I realized that, and I hated it. So I had her say to Tayo, "Don't let this end like that." Basically it's me saying that to myself.

Work: I put it down and said to my wife, "This is going to be the greatest novel to come along in so long, just because of the ending." It's so optimistic. It sounds as if he discovers a new ceremony. We are not left with that bi-social man, that half-White, half-Indian that Jim Welch gives us. It sounds like you've got the answer.

Silko: Well, I was really determined. I'm interested in survivors. In Jim Welch's new book, *The Death of Jim Loney,* Jim has wonderful control and beautiful skill with language. Some of his supporting characters—like the guy who owns Kennedy's Bar—are survivors and they have a vitality to them. They might not have survived quite intact, but they survived. I'm interested in those kinds of characters. Jim is aware of it but he seems more interested in the sort of existential figures, which is fine. Very soon for me the character becomes a living person and I know the things that are possible for him or her and I know the things that aren't. It's like trying to help a real person out of a situation—how are we going to do this?

Work: Is it kind of hard to write in the male persona?

Silko: Not at all. In fact, the frightening thing is that I just start with a persona and a point of view, and I go with it. When I was writing this book in '73, '74, and '75, I got about halfway through it and realized that feminists and people who focus on women's writing might be very angry that I had written a book with a male persona and a male point of view. I thought to myself that male writers have been doing this all along with women, so I just decided to go on with it. This is the way the story had to be told. I didn't consciously choose to say that I'm going to write a story from a male point of view. It just happened that he was the one, and I don't know why. It could as easily have been told from another point of view, I suppose. Anyone could argue that, but when I start working with a point of view, if it's the right one for the story, there's no question. In fact, that's how I know that I have it all together—I can feel it go with the character.

Cowell: Unlike the earlier novels you call "stillborn" that don't?

Silko: Right. In fact, the two earlier ones that were "stillborn" were told from female points of view. One was a woman my age and one was an old woman. For a while I was afraid I couldn't write from that point of view. But then I did "Lullaby" and "Storyteller," two later stories not in *The Man to Send Rain Clouds.* In "Lullaby" we have an older woman's point of view. "Storyteller" is an outrageous story from a young woman's point of view. I decided I could do any point of view I need to. It's up to the story, not up to me.

Cowell: Could we explore in more detail why those narrators were not appropriate for *Ceremony*—why the female narrators just didn't seem to work?

Silko: Well, first I should explain, I had two "stillborn" novels, but they weren't *Ceremony* and they weren't about soldiers and war or anything like that. The first female narrator was a young woman who was going through a lot of the kinds of things that Tayo's mother did in the novel and the Ute woman—Helen Jean—the woman who hooks up with Harley and Leon and then runs off with a Mexican. The first novel was about a woman's life, and I felt really uncomfortable with it because I started to identify too closely with her and that will limit sometimes, if you start getting involved with your character, what you'll let her do. The next one was intriguing. It was an old lady, from Laguna, who was going to California to see her grandchildren who were growing up out there, not at Laguna. She goes through Gallup; that's where you get the Gallup section in *Ceremony.* Her story was that when she was a young girl she helped smuggle Geronimo to California. The person they said was Geronimo back in Oklahoma wasn't really Geronimo; they had gotten him away. I had never read or heard anything about Geronimo, and I had him having special powers. Later I found out that he did. They had taken him away to Baja, California, and the seagoing ships of the Haidas from up in Alaska had come and taken him away. It was a very strange, spacey story. It didn't work out, I didn't like it. Just sitting here and telling it, it's too far-fetched for me. Then one day I sat down and started to write a short story about this guy—Harley in the novel—a funny story. It just kept going and going, and I discovered Tayo. It wasn't that I tried to use a woman to tell this story. This story and this narrator are like one.

Cowell: You call your new book *Storyteller,* and you have spoken about the stories in the oral tradition that you find are important to your writing. Is there another literary tradition that's important to you as well? Are there other traditions that you find your work developing from?

Silko: I think the primary source is just growing up in that community and learning to know a story. Very early, the one thing that saved me in school—

because basically school wasn't a very good experience for me—was that I discovered stories in books. Up until that time you had a person tell you a story, and it was very pleasurable and secure and loving. It's a very generous thing to take the time, you know, whether it's a sort of gossipy story or whether it's a story to a child, it's a very generous and beautiful thing. Then I discovered that when I was away from people and that kind of security, I could open up a book and there were stories. I discovered that for me a story is a real place to be and so I loved reading. By the time I was a junior in high school, I had read almost all of William Faulkner. I had read John Steinbeck when I was in the seventh and eighth grades. I read *Lady Chatterly's Lover,* I read *Lolita.* I had the notorious books, because my dad believed in reading and he had those books around hidden under the bed. I love Shakespeare's histories and tragedies very much. I love Proust, I love Henry James. I wrote a piece in the new book that goes round and round with the pronoun "she" because James in his later work, notably *The Ambassadors,* plays with the beauty and the ambiguity of how in conversation we say "he" and "she" and "he" and by a nod of the head or an inflection of tone we keep straight who he and she—who these different people—are. James played with it in *The Ambassadors* because he'd spent hours sitting, I guess, in these private clubs and at parties listening to these conversations. He got fascinated with English as it's spoken and what happens to spoken English on the printed page, which is exactly what I'm interested in. Sometimes when I say I'm interested in Henry James, especially his later works, everyone thinks, "God, how can she be interested in James? He's so literary." But no. All of his later novels were dictated. I had a wonderful professor, George Arms, who said when you have trouble understanding or getting hold of a piece of James, read it out loud, because Henry James dictated it. Anyway, in this one story in *Storyteller* I didn't consciously set out to play with pronouns, but I realized what happened after it started to happen and then I made that connection to Henry James. Borges is very interesting to me; Flannery O'Connor—I love Flannery O'Connor.

Cowell: Are there other women writers than Flannery O'Connor that you might feel are important, or just writers whose work you admire?

Silko: With women, most of the people I admire are poets who are living right now and are friends of mine who are very key persons, Roberta Hill, for example. Roberta's a wonderful Oneida country poet. Those people mean a lot to me. There's a lot of writing by women nowadays that you can get your hands on. The publishers have picked it up because there's a sensationalism. Publishing is like the record business; it's capitalism and big business. There's a lot of hype in marketing. For me, I'm not interested in a lot of the things that are being pushed as important books by women because I don't think they're going to be that important over the long haul, just like there's lots and lots of things by men on different subjects that won't last. Publishers are looking for things that will sell. They're cashing in—exploiting and cashing in—on the women's movement and women's consciousness, and I resent that. There are a lot of important women who have gotten published, but I think there are a lot more that were just publishers exploiting the women's movement.

Cowell: Do you think that a similar thing happens with Native American literature?

Silko: Sure it does. There's this real romantic notion that if you're an Indian, whatever tribe or whatever background you grew up in, somehow you have this magical power with language. That's not true at all. There are more and more Indian writers coming into print, and we should be treated just like any other American writer. I like to think of myself as being a pretty good *American* writer; I like to think of Jim Welch as being a pretty good *American* writer. I don't like to think of him as being an *Indian* writer. I think I should also be included as a Western writer, that I shouldn't be excluded from that. That's how people should read the books. It's okay to have courses that focus on a particular group of writers, but the attitude which the books are dealt with should be the same as with other books.

Work: Let's relate that to your novel. Would I have to know all about the chants and songs and history of the Laguna to read/teach *Ceremony?*

Silko: No, not at all. In fact, you shouldn't have to know any specific details, but there are a few general attitudes that you should have going in. Most of what's been written and published in America, right up until today, has been really European writing. There are very few true American writers and poets. It's almost all aping of European usages and styles and so forth. Galway Kinnell is a wonderful poet, but I don't call him an American poet in that sense of really using an American English and American form. One of the things I hope you would have in approaching *Ceremony,* or any other pieces that are consciously working with an American English and an American experience and American personae and struggles, is that openness, to realize that you're going to see different structures and different emphases, on colloquial English and so forth, and not to throw it down and say, "Oh, this doesn't look like Charles Dickens, or Nathaniel Hawthorne." It's that kind of openness that people need to go into *Ceremony* with.

Work: Why is *Ceremony* centered on World War II? Why not Korea or Viet Nam? Does World War II have some . . .

Silko: Sure. Because of the atomic bomb. Because of how World War II was ended. After the Second World War, the Korean War and the Vietnam War are just a part of the big slide—the human race's big slide into the big abyss. The world was never the same again. That morning which I recount in the novel was at Trinity site near Alamagordo, New Mexico. The first atomic bomb was detonated, and it was seen at Laguna. An old blind woman with cataracts really did see the flash. I have that in the novel but that's true, and the world was never the same since then. I did have a lot of the experiences of Korean veterans and Viet Nam veterans in mind. You couldn't live through the sixties and not. I focused on the Second World War, but I had a Viet Nam veteran, a guy from Laguna, say, "You don't know how much this book meant to me." I know that somewhere in the back of my head Viet Nam and something of that must have been there. But why the Second World War? I'm sure it must have to do with the bomb and the impact. The people were never the same after the Second World War. I mean the Laguna people. Going away to fight that war was a real big break, and it marked the end of a time. It isn't just the end of time for Indian people, but marked an end of a kind of time in life for everybody.

Cowell: Do you see that break in time as making a difference in the kinds of stories or the functions of stories that are told now? The storytelling tradition goes far, far back. Is there a breaking point where the functions of stories become different?

Silko: Right. *Everything,* not just our stories—stories of Laguna or Indian tribes—*everybody* has to re-examine what they're about as human beings in terms of culture and so-called advanced countries. If it isn't a change in storytelling, it's like diplomacy, to keep us from destroying ourselves if that change should come. And if it doesn't come, we're as much doomed as the people in the novel who won't change. But we all, from that time, have to change the way we look at things and how we do things; otherwise that's the end of us.

Work: Perhaps the novel can help. We appreciate your having come to talk to us today about *Ceremony,* and we thank you for the book, for the story.

Silko: Well, I thank you for listening and for reading the book. It's sort of lonely work if you think there isn't somebody out there. In the old days, the storytellers had the people right there with them. You could see their faces; if they didn't like something, you could start trying to shift things around. That's the difference between storytelling and writing, which is really lonely and solitary. It's very important for me to get that kind of feedback. So I thank you.

The Novel and Oral Tradition: An Interview with Leslie Marmon Silko

Elaine Jahner / 1981

From *Book Forum* 5.3 (1981): 383–88. Reprinted by permission.

Leslie Marmon Silko is one of the three best known American Indian novelists writing today. The other two are N. Scott Momaday and James Welch. All move with calm authority through literary perspectives previously unexplored in American fiction. Of course other writers have used Indian settings and characters; and other Native Americans have written good novels; but no other novelists have shown so compellingly how the definite geographical horizons of a tribal homeland mark spiritual boundaries which, in turn, enclose places of transition and healing. To do that requires a carefully trained awareness able to hear and then orchestrate the many voices in oral traditions which dramatize how time has shaped people in one particular homeland.

Although today's American Indian novelists share a remarkable capacity for conveying a sense of place, there is otherwise considerable diversity of theme and technique among them as they skillfully combine a zest for the pleasures of a well-told tale with a feeling for the tensions and strengths inherent in tribal life today. Perhaps none is more completely preoccupied with the life of tales in oral tradition than Leslie Silko whose love of what a story can do for people is evident in all her work.

Before publishing her novel *Ceremony* (Viking, 1977), Silko was known for her carefully crafted short stories and poems. Her narrative skill is fully realized in *Ceremony,* a novel about a shell-shocked veteran of World War II who can find healing for his terrified mind and sick body only through learning of his place in a story "great and inclusive of everything." Because of her diverse accomplishments and interests, I felt an interview with her was central to this issue of *Book Forum.* But what began as an interview turned into several informal discussions as I realized that the freshness and the excitement of her thought emerged most clearly through the spontaneity and reciprocity of conversation.

Talking to Leslie is like taking a casual walk with a friend and using the visual details as reminders of shared concerns. It is quite a different matter from moving directly toward a goal with no attention at all to the passing landscape. In fact the image of an imagined walk became the point of reference for an entire conversation.

We began by talking about her current work (more short stories and a filming project). I asked about the carryover effects from film to writing.

"Film," says Silko, "is a way of seeing very like the oral tradition. It operates on a highly refined, simultaneous, personal level. It makes me aware of the visual signals in the language and helps me realize a way of seeing, of organizing as a whole instead of through fragments of experience. Film gives the feeling that we get going for a walk, experiencing many things at once in a simple, elemental way.

"On a walk we see something; we experience it. Insight is in that instant. It can't be bought or sold or even given away. The nearest way to reproduce it is through film or perhaps fiction which can help us see a whole experience.

"The oral tradition with its cycles of stories creates whole experiences too, a foundation of experience on which to build. It presents all these different possibilities that affect how we see the structure of things. The transition from oral tradition to film with its juxtapositions is a natural one.

"People often ask me about my use of the novel; they assume that the novel is not a natural form for the Indian. But the cycles of stories in the oral tradition were like a novel. I just continue the old storytelling traditions."

Her remarks reminded me of the way one of my students summed up her work. The student had written, "I feel that her stories are the result of collecting life through time."

"That kind of reader," she said, "is the kind that jogs us and makes us see things; they bring about the mutual exchange we constantly need."

The notion of mutual exchange led to talk about non-Indian critics and their approach to her work. Once again we returned to the image of a walk. Two people going along the same path stop and notice different things. One will marvel at the shape of a leaf while another will look at light through trees. So it is with critics. The simple image is a good one, promoting a feeling of companionship that Silko knows is not always present. For, as she says, "Modern American consciousness is still one-way; their way is the only way." I thought of her description of the destroyers in her novel. Their purpose is to "destroy the feeling people have for each other."

Because in some tribes English is still a second language, the question of the adequacy of the English language to express the consciousness of people whose primary language is not English arises frequently. In our discussion,

Leslie brought it up herself in a way that shows her love of language and its possibilities. "English is a bastard language, inherently open and expansive. I love its expansiveness and inclusiveness. The nature of English is to defy academies. Look at the many people who have created a form of English that is their own, the Jamaicans for example. You can arrange and rearrange the language."

In *Ceremony,* Silko tells about one reason why Native American writers and their ways with English are so important. Describing a character's desperate efforts to reconcile her family and her community she writes, "the old instinct had always been to gather the feelings and opinions that were scattered through the village, to gather them like willow twigs and tie them into a single prayer bundle that would bring peace to all of them. But now the feelings were twisted, tangled roots, and all the names for the source of this growth were buried under English words out of reach. And there would be no peace and the people would have no rest until the entanglement had been unwound to the source."

Writers like Leslie Silko who are untangling old feelings by giving expression to them find that when they follow feeling to its sources, it is not so much what language is used that matters as it is what patterns can be found both at the sources and in contemporary life. "The ear for the story and the eye for the pattern were theirs; the feeling was theirs; we came out of the land and we are hers."

Clearly the landscape of Laguna Pueblo attains the force and importance of a character in Silko's novel and in many of her short stories. But the character who helps the protagonist in *Ceremony* realize the meaning of this relationship with the Laguna landscape chooses to live in the city of Gallup. He has traveled to the large cities of the nation bringing back old telephone books and calendars. He has all these precise memorabilia in order to keep track of what he has seen and to understand the important patterns of today's life. It was my fascination with this character, living in the Gallup slums and touching the names of people from all over the United States, that led me to ask Leslie how she viewed the urban setting and its spiritual possibilities for Indian people. Her answer pointed toward the style in which she wrote about Gallup. The reader sees most of the action from the perspective of a small child watching people as they come and go.

"I haven't spent that much time in cities. I can enjoy them but I am a wide-eyed visitor and when I write about cities, like that section about Gallup, it is from the standpoint of going in and going out again. I think that is as far as I have gotten. Right now I don't know if I'll get any further into the question or not. If it goes by any parallels with how much time I've personally spent in cities, there isn't much hope for I have been spending less time in urban settings during these last ten years than I did before. I think the question of life in cities is a real important one. I think about it a lot. There is a whole urban psychology; but writing about it is not for me, now."

Finally we talked a bit about the way *Ceremony* has been treated by the literary community. Among those directly concerned with Native American literature, the novel has received careful attention. A recent issue of *American Indian Quarterly,* guest edited by Kathleen Sands, is devoted entirely to its study. Many university courses throughout the country use the novel as a text. But outside that group, the work has received little attention. This does not particularly trouble Leslie who says that what she wants is the right kind of attention rather than uncomprehending but general notice.

The novel itself teaches the right kind of attention. It involves "the ear for the story and the eye for the pattern," both of which link peoples unknown to each other and events far apart in time and space. Far more than most novels, *Ceremony* engages the reader as a participant in shaping the story. Its transitions are sometimes unexpected and a willingness to go along with the protagonist in seeking the connections between place, time, and event is a preconditon for experiencing the novel's particular impact. *Ceremony* is an experience of sharing. It accomplishes its commentary on art's ancient function of healing and of shaping human community primarily because Silko maintains descriptive contact with the concrete physical details that make a story work. The reader can *see* with the protagonist—the people, animals, landscape, all that is part of the novel and the ceremonies within it. As the title suggests, such seeing makes the novel itself a ceremony of participation for the reader.

My record of conversation with Leslie Silko is not the first. Several have been published. A far longer and more extensive interview, conducted by Dexter Fisher, is the first article in *The Third Woman,* a book of writings by minority women in the United States. In that interview, Dexter Fisher asked about the ideas that Silko wanted to make accessible through her writings. The answer, perhaps, explains why the use of conversations and interviews seems an appropriate way to convey Silko's ideas. Conversation springs from a relationship and the meaning of relationships is what concerns Silko most.

"Things about relationships. That's all there really is. There's your relationship with the dust that just blew in your face, or with the person who just

kicked you end over end. That's all I'm interested in. You have to come to
terms, to some kind of equilibrium with those people around you, those people who care for you, your environment. I notice things about feeling good
about meeting a certain animal when I'm out walking around the hills . . .
Relationships are not just limited to man-woman, parent-child, insider-outsider; they spread beyond that. What finally happens in the novel, for example, is that I get way out of the Southwest in a sense and get into the kind of
destructive powers and sadism that the Second World War brought out. Yet it
is all related back to Laguna in terms of witchcraft."

In describing her novel, Silko herself relates to an ancient pattern of going
out from a central point and then coming back with new insights that keep
the home place vital. "It is all related back" and somewhere in it all we find
points of convergence as we participate in the ceremony of her art.

Clearly Silko's work carries on the best of the Laguna Pueblo artistic heritage just as it participates simultaneously in many other traditions as it makes
its universal statements. Each such realization of tribal and universal themes
adds to an emerging tradition of American Indian novels. Healing, the land,
and the place of traditional knowledge in the modern world are also themes
used by N. Scott Momaday in his novel *House Made of Dawn.* When it won
a Pulitzer Prize in 1969, critics were confused by this work of literature that
has clear echoes of Faulkner and Melville while depending wholly on southwestern Indian aesthetic traditions for its basic meaning. Since that time,
critics' fascination with what seems constantly elusive has led to numerous
articles in scholarly journals about Momaday. It has also directed attention
to other Native American novelists.

As we seek for ways to approach these novelists on their own terms, we
are developing a more finely-tuned awareness of the impact that a particular
setting can have. In his autobiographical book *The Names,* Momaday wrote
that "one does not pass through time but time enters upon him in his place."
In Momaday's thought, literature and ecology are linked developments, dependent on each other. "We Americans need now more than ever before—
and indeed more than we know—to imagine who and what we are with
respect to earth and sky. I am talking about an act of the imagination essen-
tially, and the concept of an American land ethic."

It is easy to select statements like this one from his now famous essay
"Man Made of Words" and use them as a starting point for discussing not
only his work but that of other Native American writers as well. In all of his

prose, there is that richness of texture which usually belongs to poetry. Read aloud, passages of his novel and other prose works are as intricate with motion and meaning as the experiences of which he writes. The making of art leads to wonder and delight which, according to Momaday, are important emotions to bring to our considerations of art or history.

In sharp contrast to the poetic styles which characterize both Momaday and Silko stands James Welch. His patiently realistic novels are written in a spare and direct style. His most recent book *The Death of Jim Loney* is even more closely crafted a work than his previous novel *Winter in the Blood.* Welch reminds us forcefully that tribal identity does not automatically attune a person to what is best about a tradition. Jim Loney, his hero, is a man who "somewhere along the line had started questioning his life and he had lost forever the secret of survival." For Welch's hero questioning the past can be devastating because so much of it remains mysterious, so much knowledge has been lost. Welch's heroes exist on the frontiers of human possibility. Little is given them. To salvage from their bleak lives even the traces of hope and dreams they have to learn that the very struggle to find something to look forward to is the life-force of the dream and the bit of hope that one can build on.

There is a touching scene near the end of *The Death of Jim Loney* which exemplifies the kind of hope which people of all cultures can find in American Indian literature. On his way to an encounter that he knows will result in his death, Jim Loney meets a friend and asks him to carry a message to a child. "Don't tell him you saw me with a bottle and a gun. That wouldn't do. Give him dreams. Tell him you saw me carrying a dog and that I was taking that dog to a higher ground. He will know."

Give dreams to those who follow. The struggle to meet that command is at the heart of many novels written by Native Americans. In the nineteenth and early twentieth centuries, novelists wrote about the struggles of assimilation. Now the effort to convey the dream often involves rediscovering how to be at home, truly at home in the tribal homeland. That isn't easy anymore. In the terms suggested by Leslie Silko's novel, it means finding the place that home has in a pattern "great and inclusive of everything."

Leslie Marmon Silko

Laura Coltelli / 1985

From *Winged Words: Native American Writers Speak,* edited by Laura Coltelli (University of Nebraska Press, 1990), pp. 135–53. Reprinted by permission.

Leslie Marmon Silko was born in Albuquerque in 1948. Of mixed ancestry— Laguna, Mexican, and white—she grew up at the Pueblo of Laguna, not far from the Los Alamos uranium mines and Trinity Site, where on July 16, 1945, the first atomic bomb was detonated.

From earliest childhood she was familiar with the rich cultural lore of the Laguna and Keres people through the stories told by her grandmother Lillie and "Aunt Susie" (her grandfather Hank Marmon's sister-in-law). Both women had a deep influence on Silko, passing down to her "an entire culture by word of mouth."

She attended a Catholic school, commuting to Albuquerque, and in 1969 she received a bachelor's degree in English from the University of New Mexico. In her college years she wrote a short story, "The Man to Send Rain Clouds," based on a real incident that happened at Laguna. The story was published in 1969, and she was rewarded with a National Endowment for the Humanities Discovery Grant. She enrolled for three semesters in the American Indian Law Program at the University of New Mexico, but she rejected a legal career for writing. In 1974 she published a book of poetry, *Laguna Woman.* That same year, seven of her stories appeared in one of the first anthologies on contemporary Native American writing, *The Man to Send Rain Clouds,* edited by Kenneth Rosen. Later she taught at Navajo Community College at Tsaile, Arizona, and then went to Ketchikan, Alaska, where she wrote her first novel, *Ceremony* (1977), which received enthusiastic praise both from critics and readers. In the past few years Silko has taught at the University of New Mexico and at the University of Arizona. She has two sons and currently lives in Tucson.

Her short stories have been included in *Best Stories of 1975* (1976) and *Two Hundred Years of Great American Short Stories* (1976). In recent years she has been awarded a National Endowment for the Arts Fellowship and a MacArthur Foundation grant to complete the novel, *Almanac of the Dead.*

Owing to this work in progress, she announced, "no more travel for lectures, readings, or conferences, and no more interviews over the telephone, in person, or by mail." But in spite of her declaration, when I called her from downtown Tucson, she agreed to a meeting at her home on September 26, 1985.

Leslie's house was on a mountain covered with saguaro stylized shapes. A few horses stood in a little corral at its side, and two dogs bearing marks from coyote bites barked furiously at my arrival. Newspapers were stuffed under the back door to keep out snakes, although Leslie soon proudly introduced me to a small, exotic serpent. The interview took place in a room filled with purple light, huge Indian masks, pueblo pottery, and Leslie's art of storytelling.

A Note from Leslie Marmon Silko

When my friend Professor Laura Coltelli sent the transcription of our interview, I was horrified at how crude and convoluted and wild my answers and comments about time-space and particle physics looked on the page. I made attempts to edit the transcription of the interview so that I would sound slightly more coherent. But the longer I looked at the interview, the more awkward and unsatisfactory my responses seemed.

Now, months later, suddenly I understand the source of my resistance to this interview: in the process of writing my novel, *Almanac of the Dead,* my subconscious had cannibalized this interview to create an important character, the Mexican Indian woman I call Angelita. I realize now I could not edit or salvage this interview because the character called Angelita had already taken possession of all my notions and ideas about particle physics, space-time, and European thought. The character, Angelita, comes up with wild and strange notions about Europeans, their history and cosmology, but Angelita is funnier and more articulate than I; and Angelita doesn't sound as pompous.

The novel is a voracious feeder upon the psyche; *Almanac of the Dead* has dominated my life since 1981. The following interview has interest and value insofar as it illuminates the evolution of certain characters and themes in *Almanac.* As for interviews in general, I think novelists should write more and talk less.

Leslie Marmon Silko
November 23, 1988
Tucson

LC: In *Ceremony,* Thought-Woman thinks and creates a story; you are only the teller of that story. Oral tradition, then: a tribal storyteller, past and present, no linear time but circular time. Would you comment on that?

Silko: The way I experienced storytelling as a young child, I sensed that people—the person you know or loved, your grandma or uncle or neighbor—as they were telling you the story, you could watch them, and you could see that they were concentrating very intently on something. What I thought they were concentrating on was they were trying to put themselves in that place and dramatize it. So I guess as I wrote those words, Ts'its'tsi'nako, Thought-Woman, and the Spider, I did not exactly mean in the sense of the Muse, at least as I understand the Muse with a capital *M.* What was happening was I had lived, grown up around, people who would never say they knew exactly, or could imagine exactly, because that's an extremely prideful assertion; they knew what they felt, but you could try those words and all that follows about Thought-Woman, the Spider, as being a storyteller's most valiant—and probably falling short at the same time—attempt to imagine what a character in a story would be like, and what she would see, and how in the logic of that old belief system, then, things would come into creation.

LC: As is said of some archaic societies, there is a revolt against historical time. What about the concept of time?

Silko: I just grew up with people who followed, or whose world vision was based on a different way of organizing human experience, natural cycles. But I didn't know it, because when you grow up in it, that's just how it is, and then you have to move away and learn. I think that one of the things that most intrigued me in *Ceremony* was time. I was trying to reconcile Western European ideas of linear time—you know, someone's here right now, but when she's gone, she's gone forever, she's vaporized—and the older belief which Aunt Susie talked about, and the old folks talked about, which is: there is a place, a space-time for the older folks. I started to read about space-time in physics and some of the post-Einsteinian works. I've just read these things lately, I should tell you, because in Indian school, in elementary school, I got a very poor background in mathematics and science. So it has only been recently that I've ventured, because I'm so curious. And why am I interested suddenly in the hard, hard, cold, cold (something I thought I would never be) so-called sciences? Because I am most intrigued with how, in many ways, there are many similarities in the effect of the so-called post-Einsteinian view of time and space and the way the old people looked at energy and being and space-time. So now I am doing reading and what I am finding is that if the particular person, the scientist, is a good writer—can write in an expository manner clearly—then I'm finding if I read along doggedly, reading it as you would poetry, not trying to worry if you're following every single line, I'm starting to have a wonderful time reading about different theories of space and distance and time. To me physics and mathematics read like poetry, and I'm learning what I try to tell people from the sciences: you know, don't get upset, don't demand to follow it in a logical step-by-step [fashion]. Just keep reading it. Relax. And that's what I did. I just went with it. I would get little glimmers of wonderful, wonderful points that were being made. I got so excited. I told somebody: "I'm only understanding a fifth of it, because I never had very good mathematics or physics or anything. But, you know, I really like to keep on learning." That's what I'm doing right now. In some ways you would say what I'm reading and thinking about and working on is many light-years away from the old folks I grew up with, and how they looked at time. But not really. Really what I'm doing now is just getting other ideas about it. Although you might not notice it from the books you would see around, I am working on just that right now. And of course this new book I'm working on is also about time, so it's very important to me.

LC: *Ceremony* has a male protagonist, but it is a story created by a woman, told by a woman [but a story] already known by another woman, Tayo's grandmother, whose words conclude the novel. Does it stress women's role and importance in the Pueblo society?

Silko: Certainly, that's part of it, just because women hold such an important position in temporal matters—the land-title, the house, the lineage of the children; the children belong to the mother's line first, and secondarily of course to the father. There is not any of this peculiar Christian, Puritan segregation of the sexes. So there is very much wholeness there. Women remembering, listening, hearing the things that are said and done. There's no prohibition against a woman repeating a funny story that's basically about the copulation of say, two coyotes, any more than a man. There's no difference, but you do find that in different cultures. Therefore, a girl has as much of a chance, as she grows up, to be a teller, to be a storyteller, as a boy-child. And as we always like to say, the women are tougher and rougher and live longer, so chances are we'll live to tell our version last, because of course we all know that there are different versions. I can say I will outlive so-and-so and then I will tell that story one time when she cannot be around, or later whisper it to somebody. But the viewpoint in the novel wasn't intentional; I mean, I didn't sit down and say, "This is what I'm going to do." About two-thirds of the way through I was pleased for what I knew then; I was pleased with those characters. I'm not really pleased with some of them now, especially the women. I think I understand why they're not as fully realized as the men.

LC: There are three women who play a very important role in the novel; Night Swan, Ts'eh, Betonie's grandmother; all associated with the color blue, the color, by the way, which is associated also with the West, yet their relationship with each other is somehow mysterious, even if Night Swan seems to be an anticipation of Ts'eh. Is that correct?

Silko: I am interested in certain convergences and configurations, where many times the real focal point is the time. I'm interested in these things that aren't all linked together in some kind of easy system. For example, the Ute woman, Helen-Jean, appears very briefly. She's in the bar when Rocky's friends, the drunks he hangs around with, Harley and Emo, are there. She is telling herself, "pretty soon I'm going to go home" and she does try to send money back to this poor, poor reservation. She's just there, and she goes. In one way, if you were judging her by more conventional structural elements of a novel, she just sort of comes and goes. But I would rather have you look at her, and get a feeling for her, so that when we make a brief reference to Tayo's mother, the one who dies early and is disgraced and so on, then I don't have to tell you that story. I'm trying to say that basically what happened to Tayo's mother is what happened to Helen-Jean, is what happened to—on and on down the line. These things try to foreshadow, or resonate *on* each other.

LC: Actually, the Gallup story and the Helen-Jean story at first seem to be separate stories within the main plot. Do you relate them to the story-within-a-story technique of the old storytellers?

Silko: When I was writing *Ceremony,* I just had this compulsion to do Helen-Jean. But the other part, about Gallup, is the only surviving part of what I call stillborn novels; and the Gallup section is from one of the stillborns. And you have to remember that when I was writing *Ceremony* I was twenty-three, maybe twenty-four, years old; I really didn't expect anything to happen. So I figured nothing's going to happen with this anyway, and I really like the Gallup section, and in a strict sense it sort of hangs off like feathers or something. It's tied to it, and it belongs there, but its relationship is different. I put that in for exactly the same reason, vis-à-vis structure, as I did the Helen-Jean part. Again, it was important to see a woman caught somewhere—I wouldn't even say between two cultures—she was just caught in hell, that would be the woman who was Tayo's mother, or the woman who is Helen-Jean, or the woman who was down in the arroyo with the narrator of the Gallup section. And the reason I did this—which in a way only story-tellers can get away with, narratives within narratives—is that [the stories] are in the ultimate control of the narrator. But for me there was something necessary about taking a perspective which pulled me and the listener-reader back always. It's tough to write about humans living under inhuman conditions; it's extremely difficult just to report it; one gets caught up in one's own values, and politics, and so forth. And I think I fear too much a kind of uncontrolled emotion. And so it had to be done like that. But it's the old theme, which the old lady at the end articulates: "Seems like I've heard these stories before."

One of the things that I was taught to do from the time I was a little child was to listen to the story about you personally right now. To take all of that in for what it means right now, and for what it means for the future. But at the same time to appreciate how it fits in with what you did yesterday, last week, maybe ironically, you know, drastically different. And then ultimately I think we make a judgment almost as soon as we store knowledge. A judgment that somehow says, "I've heard stories like that" or "I would tend to judge her harshly except I remember now . . ." All of this happens simultaneously. When I was working on *Ceremony,* these were deliberate breaks with point of view. And I agonized over them, because after all I knew that those kinds of shifts are disturbing. But ultimately the whole novel is a bundle of stories.

LC: In a story there are many stories.

Silko: Right. You can get away with it. I was aware of that. What caused those first two attempts at the novel to be stillborn was that I had a narrator who was a young woman, about my own age. And it just did not work. It just becomes yourself. And then you have to look at how limited you are, and so the only way you can break out of your personal limitations is to deal with a fictional character. Fictional characters are very wonderful. They are parts of ourselves, but then you get to fix up the parts that don't work so well for you in your mind.

LC: A young man named Tayo is the main character of a legend tran-scribed by Franz Boas. Is it still a Laguna or Pueblo name?

Silko: I don't know for sure, but I think it probably is. The sound of it was on my mind. I guess in Spanish, Tayo Dolores is like Theodore, or something, but I didn't even think of that. I just liked the sound of it.

LC: It's a familiar name.

Silko: It's a familiar sound. When I say I liked the way it sounded, I mean comfortable, intimate, the person you're going to travel with. As a writer you're going to have to follow this character. You'd better really feel comfortable with him.

LC: In "Storyteller" there is an intriguing association concerning the red and the white colors. The color yellow is very often associated with something connected with the whites: "yellow machines"; "yellow stains melted in the snow where men had urinated"; "the yellow stuffing that held off the cold"; "the yellow flame of the oil stove." What's the meaning of all that?

Silko: First of all, of course, yellow in the Pueblo culture is an important color. It's a color connected with the East, and corn, and corn pollen, and dawn, and Yellow Woman, [the heroine of the abduction myths]. So I don't think we can go too far in a traditional direction, with what yellow means. It's one of my favorite stories, because it's outside of the Southwest. And it's taking myself as a writer, and working with stories, and making radical changes. To tell you the truth, in that particular arctic landscape I suppose to hunters, anywhere except in the town, yellow could be a sign that a herd had freshly been by. In other words, I guess what I'm trying to say is maybe in this particular piece it's fairly insular; how the color works isn't so easily tied to any particular belief system. But certainly up there, just an endless field of white, and that cold pure yellow is kind of an extreme, and when it appears, it's intrusive.

LC: That's the word.

Silko: And it stops things. The rising of the moon, and the way the stars look up there is wonderful, part of that is the color. And certain colors which you can find in the sky, for example, with the aurora, mean more. The key figure I guess is the field of white, if you want to talk about the field of white like a painter, the blank or whatever. Generally yellow, on that field of white, is, in the winter, abnormal—it's just within that story that yellow works like that. It's very much the context of the northern landscape.

LC: How does the oral tradition go on?

Silko: By that you mean at Laguna or any given place?

LC: Among Indian people.

Silko: That's a very difficult question really. One day it dawned on me, I had this sudden recognition that already there were things that I had seen and done, and people that I had been with at home, who had taught me things, that had been gone a long time. What I see is astonishing, on one hand, very exhilarating, and on the other hand very frightening, the rapid change. I was born in 1948; I'm talking about things I saw in 1954 done on the reservation, vis-à-vis the Pueblo people, or maybe some of the Navajo, or even some of the white people that lived on ranches nearby. That part of America, the small rancher, the Pueblo people, the Navajos and the Spanish-speaking land-grant people. It's been such a change, that I would have to be a terrible, pompous liar to sit here and tell you that it's just in my area that I see it. The change in outlook and how the people live in these very distinct racial and cultural communities in New Mexico, and in America, since the middle fifties, is just amazing. It makes me want to laugh at some of the older ethnologists and ethnographers. I would say that most of the material—not most; now I'm starting to use words that are a little too far-spreading—but I think that many of the models that were constructed in the late fifties and early sixties by so-called social scientists, ethnologists, ethnographers, about acculturation, social changes, how humans learn language, how language affects the way you think, and so on, were so incomplete that those models have to be overturned. Not just for Indian people in New Mexico or Arizona, but African tribal people, all of the people who have gone through this period of colonialism. That is, in a sense, what I am concerned with writing about, what I'm working with right now. It goes on.

LC: You said once that we should make English speak for us.

Silko: At that time it hadn't really occurred to me that people who are born English speakers are trying to make English speak for them too. What I was saying was a little naive. The great struggle is to make whatever language you have really speak for you. But I won't back down from it, in the sense that I like to take something that is a given, a given medium or a given mode, and then treat it as if it were a fantastical contest or trick. Here are the givens; you only have this and this; this is what you are trying to describe; these are the persons you are trying to describe this to; we don't want them to just see it and hear it; we want them to be it and know it. This is language and you deal in it. That's the most intriguing thing of all. And of course all artists to one degree or another, whether it's with sculpture or music or whatever, are working with that. And I stand by that. And there are certain things, for example, when you talk about space-time, and all kinds of little insoluble puzzles about time-space, and how it is that we can use language to define language. We have to use language in order to define language. I'm getting more and more humbled, to the point where I think it's a wonder we can express the most simple desire in our given tongue, clearly. And sometimes I wonder if we can even hope for that.

LC: What's the process by which you move from the oral tradition to the written page? How does it work?

Silko: It just happens. From the time I could hear and understand language, I have been hearing all these stories, and actually I have been involved in this whole way of seeing what happened—it's some kind of story. But when it finally happened, I wasn't conscious about mixing the two. I was exposed [to stories] before school, and then I went to school and read what you read in America for literature and history and geography and so on. And then at the age of nineteen, I was at the University of New Mexico. And I had just had a baby—Robert, who's now nineteen—and Robert's father, my first husband, said how would you like to take a class where you could get an easy A? And I said, well, I would like that, you know, becase having this baby and all, it would be nice to bring up my grade-point average. So I took a creative-writing class. The professor gave us little exercises. Then he said one day, "We want a character sketch," even a character, and I thought, oh no! I had thousands. And so I did it. And then he said, "We want a story." I thought, Is he serious? Is this all it is? I just cashed in on all those things I'd heard.

But a more important, fundamental thing happened, probably in the very beginning, which was in the first grade. I learned to love reading, and love books, and the printed page and therefore was motivated to learn to write. The best thing, I learned, the best thing you can have in life is to have some-one tell you a story; they are physically with you, but in lieu of that, since at age five or six you get separated from all of those people who hold you and talk to you, I learned at an early age to find comfort in a book, that a book would talk to me when no one else would. Or a book would say things that would soothe in a way that no person could.

So the fifth grade is when I really started actually writing secretly; but it wasn't until I was nineteen and got to the university, that the two things just fell into place, which was all of my early attitudes and things I'd heard; plus, I'd read Faulkner, I'd read Flannery O'Connor, Henry James, Kate Chopin,

Isak Dinesen. And then this guy says, "Write a story." A lot of people were saying, "I don't know what I'm going to write about." And I thought, I don't know what I'm going to start writing about first. And so the two things just kind of crashed together. What I learned from all the years of reading Thomas Hardy and reading *Julius Caesar* were little mundane things, because Shakespeare has all these clowns and these little underlings who have funny little squabbles but have their little moment when they pipe up and say something that makes the bigger story roll around. That experience from reading helped me realize what a rich storehouse I had. And then, I like to get A's, and I like to have people pat me on the head. So I could just do it. But that's how come I could, because I'd had a rich oral tradition for quite a long time; I mean even now if I go home I can hear all these wild stories about what my family's done, and my cousins and stuff. But also I was encouraged to read. I loved books. And when things were rough, when I was in a bad situation, I could read a book. It wasn't conscious, but it just happened in my life.

LC: Do you feel that as in the oral tradition, the relationship between the storyteller and his or her audience, must be a dynamic one?

Silko: It would be easier on me, in what I have to do in order to satisfy these urges, if there were a place. I really think that it was wonderful during the time when the storyteller could practice her or his art. I went to China for three weeks; the Chinese Writers Association invited a group of American writers. They showed us this teahouse, and there were these two seats, with little wooden chairs with nice little pillows, and they said every night of the week, except Friday and Sunday or something, storytellers come. People buy their tea from us [the writers] and they sit in there, and these two storytellers sit across from them—sometimes it's two old men and sometimes it's two old women—and the teahouse people. This was in Sh'eie, near where all the terracotta warriors were dug up. Anyway, they showed us this room because one of our interpreters said, "Hey look, this is what still goes on in China." And all these people are sitting there listening and drinking their tea. And there's another storyteller there so you can say, "Well, isn't that what you think?" Or you can do routines like, "Oh, you always tell it like that!" I really think that that's wonderful, interacting directly like that, even having another storyteller there who might be trying to catch you on something, which of course means you get to catch them, if you can, with the people there. A wonderful kind of positive energy is generated which you can partake in, and you can get more; I'm not saying I don't get any when I write, or I wouldn't be sitting here a lot. I really think that to me the real, the ultimate moment, is when you have a couple of storytellers and a really engaged, respectful audience. So that I guess in a strange sort of way I'm saying that in Western European culture, the theater, drama, and/or what we have in the United States, mostly it's kind of declined now. The stand-up comedians, someone like Lenny Bruce, that play an older kind of role of the traveling teller or the troubadour, are the storytelling experience.

LC: How do you try to achieve it in your works?

Silko: I'm very aware of a physical audience, whether I'm reading at some distant place, or whether I'm sitting with people. I'm so aware of it, that when I sit down at the typewriter, there's only me. I feel the distance dramatically. Do you see what I mean? At Laguna I have an uncle who's very young; he's only ten years older, he's just like a brother, and his wife and his sisters are very brilliant. They've traveled and gone places to school. They've all come back. They have funny ways of saying things; they like to laugh and tell horrifying stories, but the way they tell them is really funny, and you're laughing. But when I'm writing I have to go into that room, I have to go in there alone, and I'm the one who makes me go in there, day after day. And I'm the one that has to put up with the days when it looks really bad—the words that I write. Then in that area I am just doing what I do, and I have no thought of anyone ever reading it, because I can only relate to someone who's sitting there. I really don't consciously think that much about an audience. I'm telling the story, I'm trying to tell it the best way I can, in writing, but I'm not thinking, Maybe we better have him do this, or Maybe we better not have her do that. I don't think that way.

LC: Humor is one of the main features of modern American Indian literature, central to the real meaning of the story itself. Is there a difference between the use of humor in the old Indian stories and in the contemporary ones?

Silko: You know I haven't really thought about whether there's a difference. I'm so attuned to seeing the many similarities. Same thing, referring to the same incident, especially areas in justice, loss of land, discrimination, racism, and so on, that there's a way of saying it so people can kind of laugh or smile. I mean, I'm really aware of ways of saying things so you don't offend somebody, so you can keep their interest, so you can keep talking to them. Oftentimes these things are told in a humorous way. Even punning—you know, the people at Laguna have such a delight with language, going back to how the Korean people loved language and words. So that in English they like to make puns, and they know a little Spanish, or a little Navajo, or a little anything. So their sheer delight in such things, that goes on and always has—that's an area where I can't see that there's been any big shift.

LC: In an interview in 1976 with Per Seyersted about the American Indian Movement, you said, "It is more effective to write a story like 'Lullaby' than to rant and rave."

Silko: Certainly for me the most effective political statement I could make is in my art work. I believe in subversion rather than straight-out confrontation. I believe in the sands of time, so to speak. Especially in America, when you confront the so-called mainstream, it's very inefficient, and in every way possible destroys you and disarms you. I'm still a believer in subversion. I don't think we're numerous enough, whoever "we" are, to take them by storm.

LC: So is it a matter of how to awaken public opinion to Indian problems, or is it just a matter concerning the very nature of the American Indian Movement?

Silko: No, I think it's more a question of how. You know, I understand the tactics, every step of the way. In a way I'm not even critical of anything particularly that the American Indian Movement has done. I'm just saying that with the givens that I have, with what I do best, and sort of where I found myself, that that isn't where I can do the best work. I certainly understand and a lot of times share the anger and bitterness, and the confusion over certain kinds of policies and attitudes. America is strange; it's very strange for Americans to have to confront whatever color you are. You can be a black American, a Native American, or an Asian American. If you're very upper-middle class and extremely comfortable, you can drive through any city or town home from your job, and if you have a brain that halfway works at all, just driving home you will see things. We can drive from where I drove today up here, and you can see where the distribution method is pretty much unfair toward people with lesser opportunities, and so on. If you're a very sensitive person, it can be real disturbing, just to be around at any time. I understand it, though I also understand, maybe in a more practical way, the conservatism, and the kind of respect yet for order and law that Americans have. And I don't care what color they are. It's kind of heartbreaking, in South Africa, some of the interviews with South African blacks and colored people, these old folks who are in their sixties. My heart breaks. I think about them like the old folks that were around at Wounded Knee, and when that stuff was going on. That isn't the kind of world they saw. And some of their children, and almost all of their grandchildren are doing things, saying things, and having things done to them, and I would say that is not a unique or peculiar experience to those little old people in South Africa. You could have gone to Belfast ten years ago; I mean, fill in the blanks. And that moves me, that moves me. Therefore, I was born in the in-between. I understand why the old folks cry, and don't understand why they have to keep burying. You know, I'm in a strange place. And I don't condemn one or the other. I do understand where I am most effective, if you want to call yourself a tool, which I don't really call myself. I'm better off doing what I do. As a terrorist or militant I'd be good for like one suicide raid, and then that'd be the end of me. Now, you know, if you want to use me like that—and I'm not a good spy.

LC: Could you describe your creative process?

Silko: Well, when I was younger, I figured it was just that certain things that I heard I didn't forget. And then I would have a professor or somebody tell me I had an assignment. So I would just go and I would pull it out, and what I would pull out, of course I would always work on. And sometimes I would just take bits and pieces and make it up, because even when I was a little girl I had sort of a wild imagination. Now I'm beginning to realize that almost everything that happens to me is interesting, and I make notes but I don't really have to make notes. I started just recently though to keep notes and little scribbles here and there, and I do it to laugh at what I thought was important, and what I thought I should remember writing, and then how I feel about it six or eight months later. And what's really, really going to be an important image or theme or character trait stays with me.

And I can remember what some of the old folks said. Years ago these [recording] machines were new, and Dad believed in technology. And he'd go to the old-timers and say, "just go ahead and tell it, and that way if all these kids around here don't remember . . ." And you know, he'd count himself in, "I never listen, better tell it to a machine; you can't trust all of us, we might not remember." And some of the old folks agreed, and did it, archival stuff. But a lot said, "If what I have to say, if my story is really important and has"—they wouldn't say relevance, but that's what it is— "relevance to people, then they'll remember it, and they will say it again, and if it doesn't then it's gone, and it dies out." That's a very harsh point of view, but the older I get, the more I come around to it. And in writing I've discovered that that's how my brain works.

What happened with this novel [*Almanac of the Dead*] now, around about September 1980, I just started feeling parts and places and characters; it was as if you had shattered a two-hour movie. Some of it didn't have dialogue. Like if you took two hours of a feature film and tore it or chopped it up and mixed it all up. These things started coming to me. I began making notes, and I did other things. I finished the *Arrow Boy and the Witches* movie, and still these things came, and they came and they came. I would do extended work on sections, and finally in the summer of 1983, I figured I'd better start. I'd be with people. We'd be at a restaurant, nice people, people I basically liked, or [I'd be] talking to someone and having a fine conversation, and then I would think of something, and I'd have to start saying, "Oh, excuse me," and then I would scribble a note. And so I knew it was there. It was as if I would see things. I have many, many boxes of newspaper clippings, especially about Central America, Nicaragua, politically the rightwing shift in, America. It was as if somewhere else something was going on, and every now and then some would float up to the top. And I'd have to write it down. Then I knew I had to start. By then I even had characters; I didn't have all of them, and I didn't know everything. But it's a very big book and it has very many characters. It literally just imposes itself upon me. I find that it's predictable—predictably, there's certain interest and areas. It has a lot to do with where Tucson is, because the U.S. military is very nervous about instability in Central America, and of course Mexico. The day of the earthquake, the bankers who were so glad to lend them money, the serious American bankers who wanted to make money off those people, found out that the International Monetary Fund said no to Mexico, and then the earthquake came. Anyway, there's a bunch of military generals all along this border, who full-well believe that the economic situation in Central America and Mexico can only get worse, that it will be destabilized; there will be basically a kind of movement to try to shift around. Whether we can dare call it a revolution, I don't want to say. This is the first place and the only place I've lived in six years— but the CIA base for helicopters and training is right over there. That is a part of right now and my life and what's happening right now. And also I find very much has blossomed out in this novel. But my process is mostly, not totally, subconscious, not conscious. The reason I write is to find out what I mean. I know some of the things I mean. I couldn't tell you the best things I know. And I can't know the best things I know until I write.

LC: Could you speak a little bit more of your new novel [*Almanac of the Dead*], still in progress?

Silko: Well, you know it's about time, and what's called history, and story, and who makes the story, and who remembers. And it's about the Southwest. But this time I have purposely, deliberately, taken Indian characters, one in particular, and I've dumped him off the reservation early. He's an older man, too; he's a man and he's retired. He spent years working on the railroad in California; he was away from the reservation. But many people of my grandfather's and even of my father's generation, when the time comes, they're going to retire back home. Well, he does. And he's quite a lady's man and a little bit of a show-off. He gets into some trouble, and he's told he has to leave. And he intends to go to Phoenix, but he accidentally ends up in Tucson. And who he meets up with are Mexican Indians, some of whom are Yaquis from the mountains. But others are remnants of other entire cultures and tribes that were destroyed, early on, after the Europeans came in. And it [the novel] is ambitious because it's saying, "Well, suppose we get rid of the reservation; let's even get you from any of that when you're seven; let's do that." And different groups: "Let's tear you from Yaqui history, and let's form something more indefinite, you now, and let's add this guy who got kicked out. So then, should we say that these people aren't living on the reservation, or never had a reservation, or were there but never really believed?" So what does that mean? And to watch them as characters, and see how they behave; and that's where we pick up. So that's what it's about. So it's really ambitious. It goes back in time.

It's called *Almanac of the Dead,* which is a reference to the Mayan almanacs which are not only used for planting, not just for auspicious planting, but it would also tell you about famine and death, revolution and conquest. They are fragmentary manuscripts, and of course what have I done? I have created a character who has a fragment that nobody else has. So I get to say what it is. So there's only four Mayan codexes. There's the Madrid, the Paris, the Mexico City, and the Dresden copies of Mayan almanacs. And they're just fragments. They're written in Latin or Spanish by Indians, Mayans, fullbloods. They are the first generation of young children, Indian children, young boys, that the priests put in schools. And they could read and write. When they went home, the elders saw that the oral tradition could not be maintained, where you have genocide on this scale. We have no guarantee in this new world of the European conquest, we have no guarantee that the three of us [my two sons and I] will still live.

The old folks thought about it, had people explain to them what writing was. It dawned on them; it's a tool. It's a tool. So in my novel, they call in a person who is trained in the omens. And the old people, men and women, sit down and say, this is how we see it: we've got to start writing. In fact, they theorize something similar to what actually happened, except that my characters have a fragment that no one else has.

Another thing that happens is, I have caretakers of these few pages. At different times they've had to change them around, so they won't be found. Because you do know that the priests would destroy those materials. Some of the keepers have been well-meaning, but they have encoded, they have made a narrative that isn't really the entire narrative. They made a narrative that's a code narrative. And so it makes it extremely strange. What the characters end up with in the contemporary times is a strange bundle, a few fragments of which are originals, but many have traveled and been hidden and stolen and lost. In the novel, there's not that many pages where you actually get to see much of that. But that's in there too.

So I can do anything I want in pre-Columbian times. I'm not even going to call it Mayan. And then because the people believe that these almanacs projected into the future, I can write about a dream I had, which is that the helicopters come from Mexico en route to Tucson, full of American soldiers; that a great battle in this hemisphere will come down. But I connect it to hundreds of years of exploitation of the Native American people here. And I see Marxism as being here, but no better than Christianity. Certainly there are some Marxists, as there are some Catholic nuns and priests, who do some very good things. And I even have a character who actually assassinates—I haven't done it yet—but he's going to assassinate a sort of intellectual Marxist. He's an Indian, and he's very primitive, sort of wonderful, because he just says, "These guys don't want to listen to those guys." Back to the old thing, which is very simpleminded in a way, that it's "our land." And of course, he's a politician; his name is the Ugly One. He says, "We're not interested in any fucking ideology that these outsiders have, we're interested in love." And I don't know about the rest of it, but I'm working hard.

I definitely identify much more with that older generation—so maybe I am a leftover. In terms of the evolution of an ideology, if you want to look at political ideology, I have an awful lot of the old folks' point of view left in me. And I find that in my attraction for the stories, and places, and things I read. There's a lot I don't know. But as a writer and as a person, I like to think of myself in a more old-fashioned sense, the way the old folks felt, which was, first of all you're a human being; secondly you originate from somewhere, and from a family, and a culture. But first of all, human beings.

And in order to realize the wonder and power of what we share, we must understand how different we are too, how different things are. I'm really intrigued with finding out similarities in conditions, and yet divergences in responses, of human beings. I'm really interested in that. Without forgetting that first of all, before we can ever appreciate what's the same, we have really to love and respect and be able to internalize freedom of expression.

A Leslie Marmon Silko Interview

Kim Barnes / 1986

From *Journal of Ethnic Studies* 13.4 (1986): 83–105. Reprinted in Melody Graulich, ed., *"Yellow Woman": Leslie Marmon Silko* (New Brunswick, New Jersey: Rutgers University Press, 1993), pp. 47–65. Reprinted by permission.

KB: The first question I want to ask you is, who do you consider to be your audience? Who are you writing for?

LS: I've never thought too much about an audience per se. When I first started writing, I wasn't sure that anyone would want to read or listen to the work that I did. I didn't think about it at first. In a way, it's good not to think about an audience. If you start thinking about the audience, it can inhibit what you do. When I was younger, there was concern about what will Grandma think, or what will Mama say or something like this, and that in a sense is being concerned about audience and can really inhibit a writer. Initially, I guess I assumed that I wouldn't have to worry about an audience because there would not be an audience. I didn't think about it, and I didn't even worry too much about what Mama would think or what Grandma would think or what Uncle So-and-So would think or what the people would think because at first I didn't think that I would ever have to worry that they would see what I had written. Now, I'm working on this new novel which is long and complex to the point of being foolhardy. Who knows, a polite way would be to call it an ambitious project. But I'm so caught up in trying to see if I can make it happen. It's sort of a personal challenge, and again I'm not thinking about an audience. I've been quoted in other interviews as saying that I want this novel to be a novel that, when you shop at a Safeway store, it will be in the little wire racks at the check-out station and that I don't want to write something that the MLA will want. I want something that will horrify the people at the MLA. Mostly, I'm teasing, but in another way I'm not. I'm sad to see that so little serious fiction gets out into the world. I was amazed that Umberto Eco's *The Name of the Rose* and Mark Helprin's book *Winter's Tale* made it to the wire racks at the check-out stands in the United States. So I'm probably only part-way serious when I say that I don't think about an audience.

KB: So you didn't write a book like *Storyteller* for a particularly white or Indian audience.

LS: I don't think about Indian and white. What I wanted to do was clarify the interrelationship between the stories I had heard and my sense of story-telling and language that had been given to me by the old folks, the people back home. I gave examples of what I heard as best I could remember, and how I developed these elements into prose, into fiction and into poetry, mov-ing from what was basically an oral tradition into a written tradition. The way I figured it, there would be some Native American people who would be interested in it and some Laguna Pueblo people who would be interested in it. There might be other people who are working out of a different cultural tradition but still working with oral material and working on their own art to bring the two together who would be interested. The book is for people who are interested in that relationship between the spoken and the written.

KB: Do you consider yourself a storyteller in a traditional sense?

LS: No, not at all. My friend Mei-Mei Berssenbrugge, the poet, spent some time at Laguna Pueblo a few years ago, and she sat in on a kind of session. I hesitate to call it a storytelling session because they're real spontaneous. It was at my uncle's house, and my uncle's wife Anita and her two sisters were there and some other people. It was in the evening and everyone was feeling jolly and talking. We might have started out with some kind of notorious incident that had happened recently, and pretty soon Mei-Mei was sitting there listening to the way people would relate something that happened, and we'd all laugh and then one of Anita's sister's would say, "Well, you remem-ber the time," then the other sister would take over. When the whole session was over, we all went back over to my grandma's house where Mei-Mei and I were staying, and Mei-Mei said, "They really have a way of telling these stories and incidents and kind of playing off one another." She was really impressed, and I said, "See, I'm not in that class at all." I suppose if I didn't have the outlook of a writer, I might get better at storytelling, but I always say that I'm not good at giving off-the-cuff presentations. Oh, sometimes I have a fine moment. If you really want to hear people who can get rolling in telling, you have to go down to Laguna and kind of fall into the right situa-tion, right feelings and right time.

KB: Was a storyteller a spiritual leader? Was he or she someone who was born into or inherited that role?

LS: It's not like that at all. There is a period of time at the winter solstice when people get together for four days and four nights, and they re-tell all the stories connected with the emergence and the migration of the People. There are people who have to learn and remember those stories and people who have to participate in that telling and re-telling once a year. Those people would probably be designated persons, but they would not be specially designated in any kind of ceremonial or religious way. They wouldn't be called storytellers; they would be called ceremonial religious leaders. The key to understanding storytellers and storytelling at Laguna Pueblo is to realize that you grow up not just being aware of narrative and making a story or seeing a story in what happens to you and what goes on around you all the time, but just being appreciative and delighted in narrative exchanges. When you meet somebody at a post office, he or she says, "How are you, how are you doing?" At Laguna, people will stand there and they'll tell you how they are doing. At Laguna, it's a way of interacting. It isn't like there's only one storyteller designated. That's not it at all. It's a whole way of being. When I say "storytelling," I don't just mean sitting down and telling a once-upon-a-time kind of story. I mean a whole way of seeing yourself, the people around you, your life, the place of your life in the bigger context, not just in terms of nature and location, but in terms of what has gone on before, what's happened to other people. So it's a whole way of being, but there are some people who are willing to be funnier or better storytellers than others, and some people because they are older or they remember better, have a larger repertoire of the *humma-hah* stories. It's not at all like the Irish idea of the bard or the chosen one.

KB: Why are you writing these stories? Are you trying to put the oral tradition in a more stable or lasting form? Do you think anything is lost in the writing down of these stories?

LS: Well, no, I'm not trying to save them, I'm not trying to put them in a stable or lasting form. I write them down because I like seeing how I can translate this sort of feeling or flavor or sense of a story that's told and heard onto the page. Obviously, some things will be lost because you're going from one medium to another. And I use *translate* in the broadest sense. I don't mean translate from the Laguna Pueblo language to English, I mean the feeling or the sense that language is being used orally. So I play with the page and things that you could do on the page, and repetitions. When you have an audience, when you're telling a story and people are listening, there's repetition of crucial points. That's something that on the printed page looks really crummy and is redundant and useless, but in the actual telling is necessary. So I play around with the page by using different kinds of spacing or indentations or even italics so that the reader can sense, say, that the tone of the voice has changed. If you were hearing a story, the speed would increase at certain points. I want to see how much I can make the page communicate those nuances and shifts to the reader. I'm intrigued with that. I recognize the inherent problem; there's no way that hearing a story and reading a story are the same thing; but that doesn't mean that everyone should throw up his hands and say it can't be done or say that what's done on the page isn't catching some of those senses. When I read off the page and read some of the *humma-hah* stories that I wrote down or go through some of the Aunt Susie material, then of course, I think it's more persuasive. In a way, that's not fair; because I'm reading it out loud, I've gone back again. But I think there are some instances where I've been successful so that the reader has a sense of how it might sound if I were reading it to him or her.

KB: In a work like *Storyteller,* are you actually creating something, or are you simply re-telling a myth?

LS: Every time a story is told, and this is one of the beauties of the oral tradition, each telling is a new and unique story, even if it's repeated word for word by the same teller sitting in the same chair. I work to try to help the reader have the sense of how it would sound if the reader could be hearing it. That's original. And no matter how carefully I remember, memory gets all mixed together with imagination. It does for everybody. But I don't change the spirit or the mood or the tone of the story. For some stories, I could just hear Aunt Susie's voice reverberating. The challenge was to get it down so you could have a sense of my Aunt Susie's sound and what it was like. Earlier you said something about writing the stories down in some way that they would be saved. Nobody saves stories. Writing down a story, even tape recording stories, doesn't save them in the sense of saving their life within a community. Stories stay alive within the community like the Laguna Pueblo community because the stories have a life of their own. The life of the story is not something that any individual person can save and certainly not someone writing it down or recording it on tape or video. That's a nice little idea, and in some places where they've had these kind of archival materials, younger people can go and see or listen to certain stories. But if for whatever reasons the community no longer has a place for a story or a story no longer has a life within that particular period, that doesn't mean that the story no longer has a life; that's something that no single person can decide. The old folks at Laguna would say, "If it's important, you'll remember it." If it's really important, if it really has a kind of substance that reaches to the heart of the community life and what's gone before and what's gone later, it will be remembered. And if it's not remembered, the people no longer wanted it, or it no longer had its place in the community.

People outside the community are often horrified to hear some old timer say, "No, I won't tell my stories to the tape recorder. No, I won't put them on video tape. If these younger folks don't listen and remember from me, then maybe these stories are meant to end with me." It's very tough-minded. It flies in the face of all the anthropologists and people who get moist-eyed over what a good turn they're doing for the Native American communities by getting down these stories. I tend to align myself with the tougher-minded people. The folks at home will say, "If it's important, if it has relevance, it will stay regardless of whether it's on video tape, taped, or written down." It's only the western Europeans who have this inflated pompous notion that every word, everything that's said or done is real important, and it's got to live on and on forever. And only Americans think that America, which has barely been around 200 years, which is a joke, what a short period of time, only Americans think that we'll just continue on. It takes a tremendous amount of stupid blind self-love to think that your civilization of your culture will continue on, when all you have to do is look at history and see that civilizations and people a lot better than people building the MX have disappeared. The people at home who say the story will either live or die are just being honest and truthful. But it's a pretty tough statement to make because it freaks out western people who follow the western European notion that something just has to live on and on and on. People at home say some things have their time and then things pass. It's like Momaday when he writes about the Kiowa, how the horse came and they became masters of the Plains. He says their great heyday lasted one or two hundred years. It passes and it's gone, you know? You could feel sad about it, but that's the way it is.

KB: In your article, "An Old-Time Indian Attack," you say that the notion that the writer has the power to inhabit any soul, any consciousness, is an idea restricted to the white man. In "Humaweepi," the warrior priest believes that human beings are special, which means they can do anything. If we see the artist as a kind of priest, and this may once again be a white notion, why can't the artist, like Humaweepi, transcend his own experience? Does a person necessarily have to experience something to write about it?

LS: I think that it's possible that the most deeply felt emotions, like the deepest kind of fear or loss or bereavement or ecstasy or joy, those kinds of deep, deep, deep level feelings and emotions, are common in all human beings. But to have a sense of what sorts of things, what sorts of outside stimuli, if you will, or situations or occurrences, will trigger what in whom, then that becomes trickier. That essay was written at a time when there were all of these writers, white male writers, who wanted to be the white shaman. There was a whole white shaman movement, and it was so bogus, it was such a complete joke and a kind of con game. These were like followers of Snyder. They weren't even working; they couldn't have gotten to a deep level of fear, love, hate. They didn't have the artistic capacity to ever reach that level, even if they'd been writing about themselves and out of their own cultural experience. Again, it was that kind of superficiality, that materialistic notion that if you take the person's line break, or if you take the kind of scanning pattern of the reoccurrences of the bear image or something like that, then you have written something that's equivalent to the healing ceremony of the Chippewas. My friend Geary Hobson, who's a writer—he's a Cherokee—had been savaged by one of these nitwit white shamans, and so the essay was written under those circumstances. The main notion was that those people who were calling themselves white shamans no more had a sense of the deeper level of feeling or what is commonly shared between human beings; they had no more idea than a dog or a cat has an idea of deep levels of human feeling, and yet they were prancing around thinking that they could appropriate that level of experience. The essay was a reaction to that superficiality, and the fact of the matter is that a lot of these so-called white shamans who were kicking around at that time weren't even able to write about themselves or from their particular cultural perspective.

KB: In *Ceremony,* you write about a man's experience. Do you feel like you were going outside of your experience in doing this? Is the Native American male's experience much different from the female's?

LS: Well, I don't know if it is or not since I never was a Native American male, you know. But what I do believe is that again, on that deep, deep level, that deep level where we're moved to fear, sorrow, loss, joy, camaraderie, on that deep level, men and women are the same, just like all human beings are. The way the heart pushes in the chest feels the same, whether a woman or a man is experiencing terror. What would trigger it will differ. A woman walking alone at night can be terrified by the sound of other footsteps; it wouldn't necessarily terrify a man, unless an hour before some guys had said, "Look buddy, we're going to get you." Then I think the same physiological response would be there. In *Ceremony,* the male character was dealing with grief and loss and rage and a kind of sickness at heart and loneliness; I have great faith that my consciousness and experience on that level of feeling is true for him.

People have noticed that I write about men and what they did and how they hung out together and so on. That's more complex. In Laguna Pueblo, little girls aren't kept with the women, and little boys aren't kept with the men. Children sort of range freely, and men and woman range freely. The division of labor at Laguna Pueblo, especially when I was growing up, was much more flexible. Whoever was strong enough and ready to do a certain task would do it. And it wasn't according to gender. If something needed to be lifted, if there was a big strong Laguna woman, she would be the one that would help lift and not the old shrimpy man. Labor wasn't divided into men's work and women's work. When I was a kid, I got to hang around wherever I wanted to hang around. Of the women in my family, only my great-grand-mother was not actively involved in working. Women work very hard, and they work very hard outside of the kitchen or outside of the home in Laguna. Even Grandma Alma, my great-grandmother, who is 90, would go out and get her own coal and wood.

I had this ominvorous appetite for watching people do things. And I watched how my great-grandmother got down on her knees even when she was old and feeble, but I also watched how men built things. Nobody shooed me away, no one told me girls couldn't watch men build a shed. In the Pueblo, men don't go off as much. It's not like your middle-America, white middle-class man who goes off to work, and work is far away from where the women and children are. In the Pueblo, the men are around. There's all kinds of stuff going on, and people are very busy. I spent a lot of time listening and watching men from the time I was a little girl. And I think that more people, women and men, could write about one another if there wasn't this kind of segrega-tion of the sexes that we have in America. Men can handle writing about women only insofar as they are getting them into or out of bed. But, you know, that isn't because it can't be done, that isn't because only men know what men do, that's because in this particular stupid, great middle-America society, men and women really don't know very much about one another. But that doesn't mean that it is inherent and that it has to be. That's just this one particular place in time.

KB: I'm sure you've been asked this numerous times, but how do you feel about being classified as a minority writer? Ed Abbey recently said that to get published today, you need to be three things: female, minority, and preferably lesbian. How do you react to this?

LS: Oh, well. That's just Ed Abbey. Ed's always going around poking at hornets' nests, and then he likes to see if he can still run fast eough to get away before he gets stung. What do I think about that? I think you should ask a lesbian ethnic minority woman, who's just trying to get her first novel published or her first book of poems published, if she thinks that that's necessarily true. I disagree. Actually, right now in these Reagan years, Ed Abbey is a little bit off the mark. Right now, the mood is Reaganism, and the emphasis is back on the white male. Actually, there haven't been that many lesbian minority women who have gotten published. You'd have to ask them what they think about that opportunity. That was the signal of a really bad trend in literature, the bad trending being hopping on a particular bandwagon in order to market books, and so, unfortunately, it would be nice if what Ed said was true, but it really isn't true. It might have been true for a really short period of time, except I tell you, go back and look at the period of time before Reaganism and the supremacy of the white male returned and see how many ethnic lesbians got published, and I'm afraid that's just something that Ed made up. Well, no, he didn't make it up, but it's one of those myths like Indians get a stipend each month from the U.S. government, that all Indians are being paid off for the stolen land each month, and we're not being paid for the stolen land each month. The land's stolen and we're not being paid, but there are a lot of these things that people believe, and I don't even really think that Ed probably believes that.

KB: Do you think that being a woman and being a minority helped you get the MacArthur Fellowship?

LS: Look at how few women have been chosen. If you looked at how few women and how few ethnic women have gotten the MacArthur, you might conclude that it is just the opposite.

KB: You don't feel it was tokenism?

LS: No, because there have been so few. There's so few women and ethnic women that have gotten MacArthur's, you couldn't even call us tokens. We're not even tokens!

KB: I find the Yellow Woman, *Kochininako,* particularly interesting. Do you see the myths concerning her as having arisen from the need for escape on the part of the women from a kind of social and sexual domination?

LS: No, not at all. The need for that kind of escape is the need of a woman in middle-America, a white Anglo, the WASP woman. In the Pueblo, the lineage of the child is traced through the mother, so it's a matrilineal system. The houses are the property of the woman, not the man. The land is generally passed down through the female side because the houses belong to the women. One of my early memories was when our house needed to be replastered with the traditional adobe mud plaster. It was a crew of women who came and plastered the house. Why? The women own the houses so the women maintain what they own. The kinds of things that cause white upper-middle-class women to flee the home for awhile to escape or get away from domination and powerlessness and inferior status, *vis-à-vis* the husband, and the male, those kinds of forces are not operating, they're not operating at all. What's operating in those stories of Kochininako is this attraction, this passion, this connection between the human world and the animal and spirit worlds. Buffalo Man is a buffalo, and he can be in the form of a buffalo, but there is this link, and the link is sealed with sexual intimacy, which is emblematic of that joining of two worlds. At the end of the story, the people have been starving, and the buffalo says, "We will give up our spirits, we will come and die for these people because we are related to them. Kochininako is our sister-in-law." She's a . . . what do you call it in anthropology or sociology, one who shatters the cultural paradigms or steps through or steps out. She does that because there's a real overpowering sexual attraction that's felt. The attraction is symbolized by or typified by the kind of sexual power that draws her to the buffalo man, but the power which draws her to Buffalo Man is actually the human, the link, the animal and human world, those two being drawn together. It's that power that's really operating, and the sexual nature of it is just a metaphor for that power. So that's what's going on there. It doesn't have anything to do with, "Things are really bad at home, so I think I'll run off for awhile." That's not what it's about.

KB: I wanted to ask you a question about the mother figures in some of your work. I was trying to look for a word to describe them. I couldn't quite come up with it. Ambivalent is the wrong word, but you never know quite how to feel about them. For instance, in the very first story in *Storyteller,* the little girl wants corn to eat, and she drowns herself in the lake because her mother won't give it to her. And there's the mother in *Ceremony* . . .

LS: And then the aunt and the mother's sister. I know what you're talking about. People, women especially, ask me about that and men too. It's a real tough one. The story about the little girl who ran away, that's a story which is very clear in *Storyteller*. It's a story that Aunt Susie liked to tell. In a matrilineal society, in a matriarchy, and especially in this particular matriarchy, the women, as I've already said, control the houses, the lineage of the children, and a lot of the decisions about marriages and so forth. In a sense, the women have called the shots pretty much in the world of relationships and the everyday world. While the Pueblo women were kind of running the show, buying and selling sheep, and of course the Navajos are the same way too, the women making many of the business decisions, the Pueblo men would be taking care of ceremonial matters or maybe out hunting. Although there have been a few Laguna women who were great hunters also. So the female, the mother, is a real powerful person, and she's much more the authority figure. It's a kind of reversal. Your dad is the one who's the soft-touch, and it's the mother's brother who reprimands you. If you're really out of hand and she can't deal with you, it will be your mother's brother, not your father, she goes to. When a man marries, he goes to his wife's house or household or whatever, and his position is one you can feel more of an alliance with . . . more of an alliance with the father because he, in some ways, has less power in that household. So when you have a story like that one, that explains it. But then, how do you explain Tayo's mother who is kind of a lost and unfortunate figure, or how do we explain Auntie? And people have talked about how my male characters have vulnerability and all kinds of complexities and the women . . . they're not as vulnerable. You have to have some vulnerability in a character for readers to be able to establish some kind of link with them. So why don't we see that in my female characters? We have to go back, I suppose, to the women I grew up with. I grew up with women who were really strong, women with a great deal of power, let us say, within the family. And I think about that, and I try to think about my mother: is there something about the way she and I have gotten along, or how we related to one another? But, just remember what the position of the father and the mother would be in Pueblo society. If someone was going to thwart you or frighten you, it would tend to be a woman; you see it coming from your mother, or sent by your mother.

KB: I want to ask you a little bit about the form of your writing. Joseph Bruchac in his interview with Momaday notes the blurring of boundaries between prose and verse in *Ceremony*. Do you write what you think to be prose poems? You seem to be bucking traditional form, and we've already

talked about how you want it to look on a page to give the sense of storytellers. Are you working with anything new or unique in doing this type of
writing? I mean, this blurring between verse and prose. And why, as in *Ceremony,* where it will break in?

LS: Well, in *Ceremony* the breaks would be the parts that ideally you
would hear rather than read. As far as what I'm doing with the blurring of
the two, Virgil and the old dudes, the old cats back in the old days, or the
Greeks, they didn't worry so much it seems to me, although I'm sure some
of the genre definitions and stuff came out of that period of time. In some
ways, I feel that it's more valid to have a checklist or a discussion of what
constitutes tragedy or comedy than what constitutes poetry or prose. I don't
decide I'll take a stance. For my purposes, it's just useless, it's stupid, it
doesn't interest me at all. What I'm interested in is getting a feeling or an
idea that's part of the story. Getting the story across. And I'm really not
particular how it's done. The important thing is that it goes across in a way
that I want it to go. I don't waste my time on it. But if other people want to
worry over whether what they've just written is a poem or a prose poem, if
they want to worry about that or if literary critics want to worry about that, I
don't like to tell people what they should spend their time on. I don't spend
my time on that.

KB: Have you ever had people say that to you that your poetry isn't poetry
at all?

LS: Well, certainly not to my face, but in 1973 I sent five of the Chimney
poems to the *Chicago Review,* and that year they gave a prize for all poetry
published in all the volumes for the year, and in 1973 I got *Chicago Review*'s
prize for poetry, which I was really astonished to receive. Then I got the
Pushcart prize for poetry, which is even better than the *Chicago Review*'s
little poetry award. I must say, it gave me more confidence in what I was
doing. The way the Pushcart prize works is all the small magazines nominate
one writer's poem that has appeared in their small magazine, and then the
Pushcart judges select one piece. I won that over all other poems published,
or at least nominated and published, that year. Because of that, if someone
says it's not poetry at all, then all I can say is don't argue with me, go fight
with people who hand out prizes for poetry.

KB: One of my favorite poems of yours is "Deer Song." There's this line
which I really like, "the struggle is the ritual." It seems to me that this line

somehow takes in the essence of cooperative existence in the culture. Could you explain that line a little bit more?

LS: Well, on a literal level, there's some intimations that the wolves get the deer. The western European attitude towards things like this is, "Oh, I don't want to see an animal have to die, I don't want to see the blood. Oh, I can eat it, but oh, no, I couldn't kill it!" Well, I've always said if you couldn't kill it, then you better damn well not be eating it. It's sort of puritanical abhorrence of blood and a tremendous fear of death that western European people have; Americans especially. That's why everyone is out jogging and not eating salt because he's so scared of death; those are like amulets to keep death away. So on the literal level, it's not something nasty or awful or horrible or something to avert one's eyes from: *look* at it. It's actually almost like a sacred or ritualistic kind of thing, that giving up of the life. Of course, I also mean for it to transcend that and for people to be able to see that in a struggle to survive, it is again that you will be able to look and see things that are a part of a kind of ritual. Not ritual in a sense of following a set pattern, a form that can never vary, but ritual in a lighter sense that expands our senses. One should be able to see one's own life and lives of other beings as a part of something very sacred and special. Just because it isn't codified or put in a psalm book or a prayer book or just because it isn't a part of a ceremonial chant or something doesn't mean that it isn't valuable, moving, special.

KB: Have you read Galway Kinnell's "The Bear"?

LS: People always ask me that, and I never have yet. But someday I will. Everyone always thinks about that. Momaday is real interested in bears, you know, and his new novel is about a boy who turns into a bear.

KB: I understand that you took a trip to China.

LS: Yes, I was invited to go with a delegation of American writers who were invited by the Chinese Writers Association and the People's Republic. We were in China for three weeks, and we spent a week in Beijing, having a kind of exchange, questions and answers and comments between the Chinese writers of the Chinese Writers Association and ourselves.

KB: You read your poetry over there, then.

LS: Most of the time it was dialogue. It was exchanging questions. Allen Ginsberg asked them about sexual freedom and when was the People's Republic going to say that homosexuality was just as valid as heterosexuality. I

think Allen amused the Chinese very much from that regard so it was more
dialogue than anything. But one day we did go over to the Beijing Institute,
and each person could read for six or seven minutes. You have to remember,
especially with poetry, that it is difficult to translate English to Chinese and
keep any sense of the music or the whole thing of images and imagery. I
think doing very much poetry reading would not have been particularly re-
warding. It's real difficult. Some of the material had been translated. But
there again, some of the graduate students from the Beijing Institute, who
were also assigned to be our interpreters, were studying to be simultaneous
interpreters for the U.N. so they had a real good command of going from
English to Chinese and Chinese to English. They said they felt that a lot of
the translations of poetry were real tough and that they weren't sure that
everything was coming across. Of course, you hear that complaint, it works
both ways.

KB: Several people have mentioned that the parts you have read from your
new novel sound like Toni Morrison's work. Have you thought about that at
all or felt any influence?

LS: No, not at all. I had never met Toni before we went to China, and I
had never read much of her work before, never. What's funny is I'm always
managing to do something that reminds someone of someone else, and he or
she will come up and say, "Did you know this and this? Did you read that?"
I always say no. I always try not to seem like I'm doing something like
someone else. But then that's kind of an inhibition.

KB: I know that you have said in the past that the greatest influence on
your writing has been your surroundings. Has there been a single novelist or
poet whose work you find particularly inspirational or informational?

LS: You mean working right now?

KB: Not necessarily. I know you have talked about Milton and Shakespeare.

LS: Well, lately, the one person that's meant a lot to me is Wittgenstein. I
think his remarks on color turn into some of the most beautiful poetry I've
ever read. People call Wittgenstein a philosopher and I call him a poet. I
really like reading Wittgenstein right now.

KB: How about influences on your style?

LS: That is for style. You can see the clarity of his remarks on color in one
of the last pieces he wrote before he died. With style, I'm like a sponge. I

don't consciously look towards anyone. The poetry of my friend Mei-Mei
Berssenbrugge, I think, influences me. Her writing influences me, my ideas,
and some of the things I write about influences her. And I think in terms of
my prose style something of what she does with her poetry filters into me
and has influenced me, but I couldn't say how exactly. What she does is real
important, and so are some of her ideas about her connection with the so-
called avant-garde in New York, and so forth. And the kinds of musicians, a
lot of her interests have kind of filtered through to me, and I in turn have
picked up and taken off with that in my own directions. My friend Larry
McMurtry is a rare book dealer, and he comes across wonderful books in
looking for rare expensive books. He's been breaking me out of the mold of
just reading fiction or poetry. For example, H. D.'s tribute to Freud is wonderful. I like H. D.'s tribute to Freud about a million times more than I like any
of her damn poems. I would really not mind if some of H. D.'s magical prose
rubbed off on mine; I would not mind that at all.

KB: Paula Gunn Allen has said that reading Momaday's *House Made of
Dawn* was a turning point in her life. Has Momaday had the same effect on
you as a writer?

LS: I'm trying to think. Turning point? Where was Paula headed before?
I don't quite understand. No. I like *The Way to Rainy Mountain* very much,
but I would have been doing what I was doing regardless of what Scott had
done or not, written or not written.

KB: You've mentioned your novel in progress, *Almanac of the Dead.*
Could you tell us a little bit about that?

LS: It's a very long complex novel, so it's hard to even tell about it. It's
got five or six distinct narrative lines, sort of intertwined through it. The
"Almanac" in the title refers to the Mayan almanacs or Mayan codices. There
are four manuscripts that survived the on-going inquisition and persecution
of the Mayan Indian people and all Indian peoples once the Spaniards and
the Portuguese arrived. Apparently what happened is early on the priests
chose, recruited, captured, whatever, promising young Mayan men, and
taught them how to read and write Spanish. This happened very early after
the Spaniards went into that area, and these anonymous Mayan people or
men used their new knowledge to try to write down what had always been in
more an oral state or what had been kept with the glyphs, the Mayan glyphs
that were carved into stone. Although memory in passing down from person
to person had worked before to hold these things, I think they realized that

with the cataclysm of the coming of the Europeans, they could no longer count on human memory if humans themselves were being destroyed. So anyway, they wrote down what had, up until then, been kind of the knowledge of the various priests.

The almanacs were literally like a farmer's almanac. They told you the identity of the days, but not only what days were good to plant on, but some days that were extremely dangerous. There were some years that were extremely unfortunate with famine and war. There were other years, even epochs, that would come that would be extremely glorious and fertile. The Mayan people were obsessed with time and knowing each day. They believed that a day was a kind of being and it had a . . . we would maybe say a personality, but that it would return. It might not return again for five thousand or eight thousand years, but they believed that a day exactly as it had appeared before would appear again. It's a view that basically denies a lot of western European notions about linear time, death, simultaneous planes of experience, and so on. Anyway, the Mayan Almanacs or the Mayan codices exist. There's one in Dresden, one in Madrid, one in Paris, and one in Mexico City. I've seen what the fragments were like, and decided that I would like to use the structure of an almanac; it would free me to indulge in different narrative lines. Most of the action takes place in the present day. You get a few glimpses of the remaining fragments. You see, my characters in my novel have a fifth manuscript. There are in fact only four that are known to exist in the world now, but for my purposes, I say there's a fifth fragmentary manuscript, and my characters have it. Every now and then, the reader gets to see a bit of the fragment. The novel centers in Tucson and encompasses Mexico and kind of the edge of Central America. It not only runs through the days when the Spaniards and the Portuguese were taking slaves from the Mayan area and dragging them up to northern Sonora to work in the silver mines until they died, but also, because the Mayan Almanacs were believed to be able to foretell the future, my novel will go a bit into the future. It goes to a time when the struggle which the indigenous peoples are having now in Guatemala and Honduras and Nicaragua spreads north into Mexico. The United States, of course, intervenes and sends troops and tanks and so on into Mexico. And that's as far forward in time as it goes.

KB: You're thinking 1600 pages?

LS: I was thinking 1600. It could be longer. I've got 800 right now.

The Boss I Work For
Dialogue: Leslie Marmon Silko &
Rolando Hinojosa

Rolando Hinojosa / 1987

From *Puerto del Sol* 22.2 (1987): 112–27. Reprinted by permission.

The Company of Writers

Leslie Silko: Well, a few years ago, I used to think it was real important. I was living in Alaska and I was 750 miles from any other writers. I think it was, like from '73 to '83, maybe. I thought it seemed like it was important. Now that I'm really caught up in this book, it seems less; of course I'm also older, too—I'm thirty-seven now—it seems less important.

H: I think my case is similar. When you start young, you want to test certain things you've been thinking about, that you've been writing about, or would like to write about. And, if someone agrees or disagrees, it doesn't much matter since you're still going to write anyway. And, I don't know whether we need people as much as we need time. I'm convivial, I like to drink, but I don't kid myself that I'm doing much homework when I'm having a good time.

S: And also I do have some friends, some dear friends, who also happen to be writers. When someone asks me what I need as a writer from another writer, I think of those friends, but, you know, they're more friends to me than they are writers.

Yeah, and when a group of writers is together it's like, let's get together every week and I'll tell you how good *yours* is, and you tell me how good *mine* is. That kind of went on a bit in New Mexico when I was there. It made me very uncomfortable, and so that was a question I wanted to bring up, because it's a hot one. I've been in places where people think that I'm stand-offish or something and I just don't want to get caught in those little cliques and these little things that go on when people are together, not because they really like one another, or would be spending social time together . . . who are groups just because they're writers. And they really don't like one another and they kind of wish things on each other.

H: Tomas Rivera and I were very close for some thirteen years, and we worked together for numerous readings. We didn't talk much about literature to one another. We talked about what people talk about: music, books, family, and so on. But not literature. We did close to fifty readings as a team, and the last thing we'd want to talk about when we returned to the hotel or airport was about literature.

S: I think that's pretty much the way I feel, except with my friend, Mei-Mei Bersenbrugge (she's my wild poet friend). We haven't seen as much of each other as we used to. But there was a time when she'd be cooking breakfast for me if I was at her place, and she'd say, "Here, (I love the way she keeps her books—she sort of pushed them through the mustard, and the spilled coffee or wine). Here, look at this, what do you think of this?" And what's wonderful for me about Mei-Mei is she really brings back what's worthwhile bringing back from the East Coast, and I mean in everything, in post-modern music or sort of the different, extreme directions that some of the non-linear, language poets are doing and so forth. She brings it back, and she'll say, "What do you think of this?"

H: It's the only way to work. The other thing that I find about writers is that they're grumpy and they're not very happy; they say, my agent did this or my agent did that. Or my publisher did that or my publisher did this . . .

S: Or the *New York Times* has a grudge against me and they never review my books.

H: And I don't like that. I mean, I've got about sixty-five years, I've got fifty-six under my belt—nine more to go before I die. I don't want to spend it with that type of person. You know, I really don't. And so when I find someone grumpy like that, I say, "Oh, hell, I'd rather be drinking."

S: We're all so different, you know. I offend a lot of my acquaintances who are writers and their friends from the urban East Coast. They're horrified at how I like to shoot and all the guns I own. And that I hunt and shoot, blast little doves out of the sky and then eat them. We're all so different, and I think, where I've ever seen groups, they're splinter groups. You have real conservative values represented there. You have almost every, every kind of philosophical and cultural and personal and psychic prejudice and all these things going on. That's what makes a literature, and that's why access for all groups and all points of view is so important. To expect us to get into some kind of union—it's almost a contradiction in terms. We shouldn't all be upholding the same kinds of values and even morality. I mean, one of us should want to have guns and blast away.

H: And you have to be independent. I've only been to one American PEN thing, and I enjoyed many things about it. But, some of the conversation I heard by other people (and this is at the Lotus Club in New York)—I just didn't like the things that they were even saying about each other, about other people, whom I know, by reputation only, not by name. And I said, "I don't need old men gossips no more than I need old women gossips, you know." And I'm pretty democratic and I'll admit almost anything, but I've got other things to do, you know.

S: The reader that I have in mind is a real jerk and a real bitch and that's me. I'm the one that I'm writing to and I'm this mean, mean reader. Every year the reader is getting meaner and meaner. The readers who really read out there are dear people, so forgiving and loving of my work. And I think, why couldn't it be for those dear people out there. But, no, I write for a very unforgiving and cruel boss. Sometimes people say something about their bosses. And I'll say, "The boss I work for is a son-of-a-bitch."

H: Well, me, I don't know who the reader is, because I happen to think that five readers are going to read five different books. It's the same book I'm writing, and five guys who bring in all that information and five women who are going to bring in all that experience. I don't know how the hell they're going to read it. So, if I'm happy with the way it's coming out that's the bottom line for me right there.

There was a critic who really liked this last book. Really liked it, he said, "But sometimes some of that stuff is nonsense." And I said, "It is to you. To some reader it isn't, and it sure as hell ain't to me. So it's two to one, huh?, and in a democracy I win." So, that's it. You don't know how people are going to read it. You don't know how a college kid's going to read it, how a forty-five-year-old used car salesman who surprisingly is a good reader.

So I don't have a specific audience in mind. Readers are readers, by the way. And there are damn few of them.

S: I was really gratified one year; I was invited to do a reading at the University of Iowa in the Writer's Workshop and the Women's Studies Center got in a fight with the English Department who got in a fight with the Writing Department who got in a fight with the Native American Club over me and money. And by the time I got there and did my reading, no one showed up except the chairman of the department of English to introduce me. Nobody there. All mad. And what was so wonderful was these people came up later and they'd be kind of apologetic and they'd say, "Well, I don't go to school here, I live out at such-and-such, but I read about this in the paper." And I said, "Oh, oh, how nice."

H: Isn't that a nice thing?

S: To have people who are just readers, not because there is some kind of fucking academic atmosphere or program.

H: What you've been describing happens too often.

The Effects of National Recognition

S: Ten years ago when I didn't know any better, I thought it would be a lot of fun to be recognized. Oh, you say you want recognition and you think it would be neat to have people writing to you and calling you about your work and things you're doing, until, until it really happens and I think if you're working, you really are caught up in the work and or your family and then real quick it becomes an intrusion and real quick, you realize that a lot of the recognition's for the wrong things, do you know what I mean?

H: Sure.

S: [Now] sometimes I don't open my mail for a couple of weeks and, you know, I avoid the telephone now and that's what national recognition has done to me. I don't open my mail and I don't answer my telephone.

H: I've been writing since I was fifteen, and I first published something when I was forty to forty-one years old. And, I liked what I published and I liked the $35 I got for it. That hardly constitutes national recognition, but then came the prizes, one in '72 and the one in '76, an international prize. I'd written both novels in Spanish, and the second one was well-received in Mexico and other parts of Latin America, but it didn't mean beans in the United States. At least that's what I thought at the time, if I thought about national recognition. But I was wrong, I soon found myself doing readings on both coasts and the Midwest.

S: So in a way you went to the top. The ultimate is to be "world class."

H: Right. So, I was quite gratified and I liked the niceties that went with my limited recognition: being picked up at the airport, and my hosts being kind, too. And then? Well, it was back to the airport, and I would stand in line just like anybody else. After this happened a few times, I realized that being famous was relative. The matter has to do with popularity and that type of recognition.

S: Well, let's talk about something that just occurs to me. Let's talk about how America might be one of the few countries where some of the best writers have to have *international* recognition before our own nation recognizes us. Let's talk about that.

That is closer to the truth. When I went to Norway, I had interviews with the equivalent of *Time* magazine. In Norway, there's only 4 million of those Norwegians and what do they know? What they know is what interests them about America. And *they* think that the Latino writers, that the Afro-American, the Native American, that's America to them. And the East Coast establishment is a very pitiful sort of imitation of Europe. So, what was interesting was to go to Norway and have people say, "These are *the writers,* you, these are the artists and writers of America."

And they can quote what you wrote.

H: For many of us, European recognition came before national recognition. Similar, in part, to what happened to those Black American entertainers after World War I, and to other American expatriates, as we know.

Literary Education

H: Leslie, I remember you had an interview with Dexter Fisher. And you used a phrase that caught my eye. Maybe you can correct the wording, but the subject was creative writing, and you said there was "a fleet of creative writing programs . . ." and I could see thousands of ships loaded with writers . . .

S: And guns. See the guns, too?

H: Do you remember you said that?
S: Yeah.

H: I did. When I read the interview, I said, "Fleet. And good God, they're coming at you."
S: I think creative writing programs, both undergraduate programs in cre-

ative writing and graduate programs are good because they provide jobs for those of us . . .

H: For the shut-ins . . .

S: Right. For those of us who have no other way to support our habits of writing fiction and poetry. Insofar as they provide employment, jobs, keep me out of trouble, keep me from crime—which, believe me, I would turn to if I couldn't get a job teaching—I think they're good. Can you teach someone, do we do any good with the students?

H: I don't know if we do. I do enjoy teaching, though, whether it's literature or creative writing.

S: Me, too.

H: But I don't teach it as a critic, a Marxist or a structuralist, a formalist. I teach it as a writer, but I can't explain what that means, unless I'm in the class working with the book and the students.

S: I warn my students in my literature classes. I warn them, I say, "Look, I do not have graduate degrees in literature. The reason these people hired me is because I can write."

Who encouraged you? Teachers?

H: I don't know, I don't think so. I think I encouraged myself . . .

S: Parents?

H: Maybe. I don't remember them encouraging me to write. Both were great readers, though, and this had to be an influence on me.

S: But you didn't know that until you were fifteen?

H: Yeah, that's when I started to write. As for my parents and their reading, that was an example, and I just followed it. I do remember that I had a drive and a desire to write. Wanting to show off is also part of it. The thing is, I wanted to write.

S: From the time I was this tall, at Laguna, when people talked, it was like this major thing. When someone said, "How are you doing?" they really expected the other person to really *tell* them. I don't know what it was about me, but I was real sly and I used to listen if adults were talking. And people would really go into these very detailed, kind of wonderfully dramatized stories, and as a little girl I used to watch and watch and watch.

And when I was in the fifth grade, I had a big change. I went from Indian school to a school in Albuquerque. And I got there and found out that I was behind in everything, that at the Bureau of Indian Affairs school they didn't teach us times tables or multiplication or anything. And I had always tried very hard in school. My fifth grade year was very difficult, it was very unhappy. I also had to go a hundred miles round trip everyday to school. One day the teacher gave us a list of spelling words and she said, "Take each word and use it one time in a story. You have to make a story that has all the spelling words in it." I could find the kind of warmth and comfort of a story which I connected with home. And I could evoke it by writing words down on paper.

From then on I sat in the back of the room and I was not there. I was no longer there. But what I was doing was reverting back to the stories that were told and the feeling, the good feeling you had when someone was telling you a story. 'Cause people at home don't tell really wonderful, detailed stories to people they hate. You know, a story is something you give your friend. When you see your friend at the post office and they say, "Well, hey, you know, what've you been doing?," you think, "Oh, golly, what have I been doing?" And then you really try to think of something if you care for that person.

H: Was there a next important step?

S: Oh, you mean, where I started liking to write? Oh, well, I didn't understand about writing and stuff, so I just did it secretly and did it at the back of the classroom. And what's strange is, the one nun that was really the meanest, most Nazi-like nun, after this one school, Sister Mary Agnes, she could pick you up and her fingers could go through this part of your arm. I swear to God.

She gave us an assignment—we had to write a ballad in iambic pentameter. And I wrote about a stabbing that had happened around Laguna. And there was snow on the ground and it was through this grapevine where everyone says, "God, did you hear what happened last night?" And you get this whole story, all in iambic pentameter. And it just freaked the nuns out, and I didn't understand, 'cause where I came from, the most revered and pure-hearted and fine people—it's a cultural difference—talked about sexual things and violence and death and they were not put down for telling these stories and describing—honesty.

The nuns just about had a fit over me.

H: Much of what I write has to do with my life up to age seventeen, when I left home for the army. Subsequent writing takes up army life, education, work . . . Living, to call it that. The reading was continuous, and I wrote like

Steinbeck and Hemingway, Flannery O'Connor, whoever it was I was reading at the time. I was copying them, feeling my way around. I didn't know I
was feeling my way around, though. It must've been of help, though. But in
the Valley, in the Spanish language part, it was the oral tradition that pre-
vailed. And, I was home with it, and still am.

S: She's my favorite.

H: But it wasn't me. It was copying them. And then when I decided to
write about what I knew, where I was born, it came easily. I was home. It
was oral literature. Things were not necessarily set down.

H: I used to listen as you did—I'd be in the back of a truck just across
from my house and listen to truck drivers, fruit pickers, older men, but I'd
join in too, and I was a kid, not even teenaged. I'd say, "I'll now tell you a
joke," and I would. Probably sexual, even if I didn't know what I was saying.
My father wouldn't hear of it, of course. Now, he was a great storyteller as
was my mother.

So, when I start to write, and with all the formal education that followed,
I find myself going back to where I came from. I'm quite comfortable with
my background; I know the people. It's almost as if what I do isn't creative
writing at all. As if I'm recording, and using my imagination as Leslie uses
hers.

The Land

H: I think that the land has a lot do not only with what you write but also, I
think, with how you write, which is a different category altogether.

S: Well, let me say this. When I left New Mexico, I went blindly, you
know, I went blindly. When you're in a very emotional upheaval stage and
not sure which way you're running, you know, you run, OK? And I was
working on a proposal at that time to try to get money to do this little film
for public television. And I was up here alone a lot and it was a real bad time
in my life. And I had always thought that New Mexico and the kind of higher
terrains around west Albuquerque, around Laguna, the sandstone and lava,
were my mother. I came down here and I didn't come down to like this, you
know. And then it was like I couldn't help it. I don't love it more than New
Mexico. I love it as much. In a sense that's what I always try to do in my

writing is, rather than separate things and break the world apart, I try to figure out how in the world there can be some kind of continuity.

You talk about the importance of land or place. I believe that certain places have in their being, through time and regardless of the people that passed through there, something about them. And, and almost everything that I relate to here in Tucson is kind of apocalyptic.

H: Did you start the novel here, this thing we're talking about, that 1100 page thing?

S: It grew on me, it grew. I came here and I had nothing in mind. And then in about 1981, I began to get transmissions, like from outer space, and little notes and things. And basically what it keys into, though, is what's going to happen in the whole eastern hemisphere. You know, on down the line, I mean.

H: I started publishing when I lived just two hours away from where I was born. I was working at Texas A & I University, and being two hours away, I could drive to the Valley. And if I didn't get ideas (and I didn't have to go looking for them there) I'd go see my mother and my brothers and sisters. Just being there did something. And the more I wrote, the more I got to know the place. And that lasted for seven years.

Then I went up to Minnesota, and I thought I was going to die there, that I'd be buried with strangers. That they'd use a jack hammer to open up the earth, because the ground's frozen up there for so long. And it was cold in Minnesota, and I wrote *Korean Love Songs* there. And then, in the next novel, I took the kids out of Korea, put them in the Valley, and into the university, and finished the novel back in the Valley again.

I live in Austin now, and from the Valley that's just six hours away. I can go down there whenever I want to; I couldn't live there, and I don't need to be there physically. But when I write, I go down there, I mean that whenever I write, I'm down in the Valley.

S: And so you don't have to be there because if you really loved that first place, then, you know, there's a way.

The first of October I was in Alaska, we had forty-two point five inches of rain in thirty-one days. I was living in southeastern Alaska by the Japanese current. It rained a hundred and ninety-two inches the first year I was there and I almost . . . I had a depression and I thought the depression was like, oh-oh, you know, shaky things in one's psyche coming out. Anyway, I wrote *Ceremony* up there. And every square inch of sand, dryness, sun, I wrote in this room with no windows, with the rain beating, I wrote because when I write, I'm there, and I did not want to be in Alaska in all that water. And so I wrote more passionately and in more detail. I made that whole world that I was so homesick for. And I never would have had to have made it in that kind of detail had I been there.

H: And that's it.

S: I mean, there's some point where, where nothing can get you through. And I had reached that point.

H: Tomas Rivera and I were drinking when another Texas Mexican joined us. His name's Raymund Paredes, and he teaches English at UCLA. And Paredes asked, "What are you talking about?" I said I was telling Tomas a story about the Valley, and Paredes laughed and said, "You know. Rolando, that's all you ever write about, but you can't live there, can you?"

I said that was true. That that was the only thing I could write about, wanted to write about and that I didn't have to live there to do it. Then we all talked about place, and I said I could recreate every stream, every person, the mode of dress for the times, whatever I needed. But I also said I didn't have to go there since I was already there, in the writing. Sounds silly now, I guess, but I never left the place.

S: Well, there's a difference. You don't have to.

I think about my friend, Simon Ortiz. I get cut a lot more slack. People at home cut me a whole lot of slack, coming from where I'm coming from than Simon gets cut. I lasted there a couple of years. The thing is, the very thing we love and that nurtures us so much, people getting together and talking, it cuts into what you got to do.

There's a lot of difficulty, especially if you're from a kind of family community thing where they want you right here. *And what we want from you, we want it spoken and we want you right here.*

H: Sure.

S: And the idea of the delay of writing and publishing and all that, it's a conflict. Sometimes, to deal with it—it's real lonesome. And God, the stuff I go through with family and friends over why I do what I do.

Categorization

H: Well, I'm presenting a paper in Sacramento in a couple of weeks. It deals with regional literature, and with minority writing, also. I'm a minority in another way, too: I'm half Texas Mexican and half Texas Anglo.

S: That's right.

H: We're even more minority than they are, right?
S: That's right.

H: The categories make it easier for the publisher to sell. And when they print a catalog, they can put women's lit. People interested in that, the academics, will buy "women's lit." But should we make it easier for any publisher to allow ourselves to be categorized?

When I read Lucy Tapahonso, I look at her as a woman but not necessarily as an Indian woman alone. Not that Lucy denies what she is. She merely prefers to write the way she does, and her talent allows her to do so.

I don't know who could write about the coyote better than Simon Ortiz right now. I don't think anyone can.

But does that automatically categorize him as an American Indian, as a Native American, as a, what, First American? Because true folklore, which is what he writes very well, is as European and as Oriental as anything.

So I am a Mexicano and I'm a Texas Mexican. But if I was born in this country, and I was, I can draw from all over the world for my work. What I'm contributing, what Leslie is contributing, what all of us are contributing is really American literature.

S: That's right.

H: Yeah. Here's Leslie Silko, a kid born in Laguna, goes up to Alaska, freezes her buns off and writes about life five thousand miles away. What Leslie writes is American.

S: Actually the Europeans are more cognizant of that than Americans.

H: They call us American writers.
S: I must say, that after the publishers, I want to point the finger at something like the Modern Language Asociation and say that they have a very large stake in saying that you're the finest "Chicano writer."

H: Or the first.
S: . . . or the first.

H: I love that too.

If it suits Simon and Schuster, Random House, et cetera, to categorize, it suits them, but it sure as hell doesn't suit the rest of us . . .

S: No.

H: . . . who are Americans, writing American lit, you know.

Politics and the Writer

H: I think that what every writer writes is, in one way or another, political. I can write something and a critic will say, "That's not political enough." The same article comes out, the same book, novel, story—the very same one—and another critic will say, "A very highly charged political statement." Well, who is one to believe. . . .

The writer has an obligation to tell the truth. If the writer has an obligation and it happened to be political, that writer had better adhere to the truth or he's not a writer.

S: I'm a believer in human language. I don't care what language it is but I'm a believer in language being loaded with almost everything that's necessary. And that it's a political act to choose whether you go into a New Mexico–sounding dialect, or whether you choose to obey certain syntactical or grammatical rules.

The most radical kinds of politics are not in harangues given at stupid rallies. I mean the most earth-shaking kinds of shifts occur when language is plain truth. So that even in translation we might lose some truth or the other. But I believe that in every careful, caring use of language is already a political statement. Our best statements for some of us happen with our fiction. Some other people are better as essayists and some are better as haranguers. OK. But I will not back down to these people who say, "What good are you to the movement, blah, blah, blah?"

The Influence of Family

H: My wife has not read one complete novel of the eight or nine I've done. My daughters have read parts of some. They're not fans of mine. I'm married to one and am the father of the other two. To the girls, I'm not a writer, I'm their dad.

S: It's a different relationship.

H: Right. Completely.

S: I couldn't stay married to a person who . . .

H: Who would criticize?

S: I couldn't.

H: Now, one of my sisters—I have two—one of my sisters reads everything I've ever written. And she's a fan. The other reads, but I don't know how much of mine she's read. My brother and I are very close, and I think he reads my stuff. I've not asked him what he thinks of my writing. I think it's favorable, he's always asking me for my stuff, but my family's reaction to my writing is not important to me. I'm going to write and will continue to do so. No writer can afford the luxury of seeking approval.

S: Well, I think this is where we're going to probably have our greatest divergence in opinion, Rolando.

I found that what was expected of me was extremely difficult and, of course, what's expected of me is in part what I expect of myself in certain roles.

It's no accident that I'm not married and I haven't been married in a while. We're still on the kind of frontiers of what happens to a woman in American society, a woman who pursues the arts and who's relatively successful. And it's been real difficult for me and not just with husbands, but with my family in New Mexico. They're real proud of what I do. They want me to do it. When I was pregnant and I was seventeen and in college at eighteen, they helped me to stay in school and they babysat. They wanted me to and yet they still can't understand why, like right now, in the middle of this long novel, I don't want to see them or I can't go there. It makes me very sad. I don't say it with any kind of bitterness. I just say it as a fact that, that's been the whole area of my life where the greatest conflicts have come, between what they and I expect of myself.

I can remember when my youngest son was just a little toddler. He sensed something about the typewriter; he knew a certain kind of attention and energy from me was going in there. And as a little toddler, he'd toddle up and stick pencils in to jam the keys.

In certain interpersonal battles, inevitably I've had people throw this, "You care more about the writing than you care about me," which is real unfair. And I say, "Look, you're way off base to say that in the first place. But if you press it, you'll be real horrified if I answer. Don't ever ask that one." I've had that thrown at me and I think women get that thrown at them a lot more than men.

The Past Is Right Here and Now: An Interview with Leslie Marmon Silko

Ray Gonzalez / 1991

From *Bloomsbury Review* Apr/May 1992: 5 + . Reprinted by permission.

In this year of debate over the Columbus Quincentennial, it is appropriate that Native American writer Leslie Marmon Silko emerges before the public eye after years of seclusion in Tucson, Arizona. Her reputation as a recluse is off the mark; she has been working and struggling for ten years to write *Almanac of the Dead,* one of the most important novels published in the U.S. in more than a decade. The book has enormous scope as Silko experiments with narrative and retells five hundred years of American history. For Silko, 1992 is the culmination of centuries of genocide, mass migration, family tragedy, and triumph—timeless stories encompassing tribal myths, legends, and personal sacrifice and vision. To produce this epic required that Silko leave her sense of community and her literary commitments behind. For years, her readers had little to go on except Silko's earlier novel, *Ceremony,* a critically acclaimed, almost legendary novel; a few poems in journals; and *The Delicacy and Strength of Lace* (Graywolf, 1986), a powerful collection of letters between herself and James Wright. Two other books, *Storyteller* and *Laguna Woman,* are now out of print. Silko admits it was risky to reappear with a 763-page book, but she also feels this is the right time for *Almanac of the Dead,* a book that alters the reader's sense of time while it offers true histories and stories that affect millions of Native peoples.

Silko is a Phi Beta Kappa graduate of the University of New Mexico and has attended the University of New Mexico School of Law. In 1981, she received a John and Catherine MacArthur Prize for her work in fiction, poetry, and film. She has also received grants and fellowships from the National Endowment for the Arts. Currently she lives in Tucson, Arizona. This interview was conducted in October of 1991 in San Antonio, Texas, during the Inter-American Bookfair and Literary Festival, where Silko read as part of a national promotional tour for *Almanac.*

The Bloomsbury Review: Snakes play an important part in *Almanac of the Dead.* Your characters Yoeme and Zeta talk to snakes and know a great

deal about them. And of course, there's the giant stone snake near the uranium mine. How did you begin to approach the mythology of snakes in such
a massive book?

Leslie Marmon Silko: When I first moved to Tucson from Laguna, New
Mexico, going from the high mountain plateau country into the Sonoran Desert, it was a radical change. I had a sense of leaving the Pueblo country
behind, and I was leaving an unhappy marriage. In a sense, Tucson was an
arbitrary destination. I really didn't know too much about it and had been
there only once. I also went there because I was working on an NEH film
project, and the other people involved were there. There were, of course,
rattlesnakes in New Mexico where I had grown up, and there were rattlesnakes by my house up in the Tucson mountains. They were friendly rattlesnakes because my house is near the National Monument, and people hadn't
hunted them and killed them. They were gentle. My mother was never afraid
of snakes, and I'm not afraid of them.

I was in the hills alone a lot and started to feel very sad about how people
treated snakes. I started to pay attention to them. I like to see them and am
amazed at how forgiving they are, how they really don't want to bite or harm
things—you know, they only eat when they're hungry. The early stages of
the novel started in 1981. In those fragments, I had an old woman, who was
the prototype for Zeta, talking to this old snake. The one scene in the book I
stole was something we really had to do—build a corral. The snake was so
gentle, but he was in our way; we just scooped him up with a shovel, and he
didn't get mad or strike. It was almost like he understood when we moved
him. I don't plan or outline, so that was how the rattlesnakes and talking to
the snakes got into the novel.

I then came up with this character, Sterling, who got into trouble at Laguna
by showing the movie company the stone snake. He was supposed to super-
vise the film company. I made an NEH film in 1981. In 1980 I saw the stone
snake. It came back to me. Again, I appropriated that, so the stone snake was
the reason that Sterling got sent away. Then the snake comes in again. But
still, I wasn't planning at that time, at least consciously. It wasn't until about
three-quarters of the way through when I was struggling with how to end it
that the snake figures in.

I was having trouble, and I went out on the side of the building on Stone
Avenue in downtown Tucson, where I worked, in desperation. I had sold the
novel, not just because I needed money, which I did, but the MacArthur
Fellowship was finished, and I thought if I sold it, it would force me to finish

it. I put some graffiti on the side of the building. The landlord was uneasy with all the anti-Mecham stuff and political stuff. I bullied him into letting me keep the graffiti up there until we got rid of Mecham. By God, we got rid of him. When Mecham was gone, the landlord hurriedly painted the wall white.

Anyway, I was having a struggle. After the wall got painted blank again, I left my typewriter and all my notes and went outside and painted a great big snake on the side of the building. I started working on this mural. I just said to myself, "I think I'll just paint for a while, and maybe it will let my mind settle so I can gather myself." As I painted I didn't think about the book at all. The mural got more and more elaborate. And finally I said to myself, "If I can bring this off, I know I can finish this novel." It's a great big huge snake. It's got skulls on its stomach, and then it has this slogan in my broken Spanish, "The people are cold, the people are hungry, the rich have stolen the land, the rich have stolen freedom." The last line is "The people demand justice, otherwise revolution." I put it up on top, and I wrote it in Spanish because no one in Tucson understood it. The police and asshole power figures don't—they're completely ignorant of Spanish. It's in a neighborhood where it's very mixed, Hispanic, African-American, and poor students, poor Whites. So I put that on the side with the big snake and went back inside. The painting really worked. The longer I was in Tucson, it became clear that town was crooked and racist. When I painted that snake, I knew what it said. He had the skulls on his stomach and the reflection in his eyes got a skull too. And there was the spider, and she weaves the web and the plants. And there's rain and night and day. The snake's coming out of night into day. I realize now that it was a unifier. It always was a unifying figure or image.

I went to China in 1985 and went to this museum where they had old pottery from a 6000 B.C. Chinese site. They had painted black and white pottery with the black paint on it like Mesa Verde and Chaco Canyon. It's just like the 1200 A.D. pueblo pottery from the country where I'm from. What the Chinese call the dragon was the water serpent figure on the pottery. I was so amazed that I even copied it in a little sketchbook. So, I think I've always been fascinated by the power of snakes. And that giant stone snake at Laguna, when it appeared, there were all kinds of rumors about what it might mean or not mean. I was consciously able to figure out that the snakes are messengers from the Underworld where the Mother Creator is. The Stone Snake is a messenger. That's sort of how it all fit together.

TBR: Can you tell us more about the Stone Snake? Is it still accessible to the public?

LMS: Well, I don't want to get into trouble myself like Sterling did in the novel, because it is a very sacred shrine, and it's very private. The people feel it's really private and special. I want to make it clear that people shouldn't come driving in from Washington, D.C., or New York City, or something and stomp all around looking for this snake. First of all, they would be accosted politely by people who would tell them not to. I don't want to draw people to it and have them get into some kind of trouble.

TBR: Did your relationship with the snakes influence the isolation you felt over the ten years of writing the novel?

LMS: Absolutely, in every way. The Sonora Desert is a new kind of terrain. The more I wrote, the more I isolated myself. There's something I learned writing this that scares me about novel writing—the self-imposed isolation and solitude, the way I turned away from the world, a person who likes to have parties and see people and eat, drink, and make merry. I isolated myself, even when I was teaching at the University of Arizona. The isolation was necessary for the novelist, I guess.

A lot of time I felt closest to the snakes in a spiritual way. They were the reminder that what's good is in the earth and the animals, not in the people who have trampled it, in the people who have appeared overnight, invaded that country, trying to destroy it with what they do with water and subdividing. I had to look for what was good and positive, because I saw political evil going on—the way the Tucson police killed people and beat them up. I had to struggle to find something that I could relate to and still connect with that was positive. There was so much that was negative. That's one of the reasons I ended up writing that book. What was it about that place that so many people had been sold out, sold down the river? The violence. It was something about Tucson.

TBR: You say you realized the snakes were messengers and that the novel was going to work. Did you reach a point where you accepted the snakes as messengers and felt that finally, after all these years, you were going to finish the novel?

LMS: Yeah. When I figured it out, it came out in the characters that are down in Mexico, that huge sort of Mexico narrative line. I knew I wanted to show the people dying in the desert, trying to come north. I kept watching how the International Monetary Fund and the World Bank would tell the

Mexican government, "Raise the prices more on beans. Raise the prices more on milk. Starve the people down to come into line with these Western European capitalists." That's all the International Monetary Fund and Bank is, a tool to control people. I understood what the message of the snake was, and that I had it. But then I had to go ahead and write the scene. The whole thing that inspired it, the people coming across, was the character of Ría. Originally, she was supposed to die, but I just couldn't let her die. She's real tough. She just couldn't die. There are also a lot of characters who aren't necessarily good at all, but the forces are loose. At the end of the novel all these characters living on bothered me a little. Alegría makes it, and she's around. She's going to be doing stuff. It made me think about the other Native American prophecies about the gradual disappearance of Europeans. The snake messengers were really important.

TBR: In your notes about writing *Almanac of the Dead* you mention a dream about helicopters flying over the desert in Arizona, and you seeing dead and wounded U.S. soldiers. You saw Tucson as another Saigon and a war with Mexico. How did that dream influence the direction of the book, and how did you decide to focus on the political situation in Arizona, the crime and injustice that are such forces in the novel?

LMS: The dream was really early, in 1981. It was so vivid and so horrifying. The dream was triggered by the Air Force helicopters on these small bases behind my house in the Abra Valley. The Air Force base in Tucson does maneuvers over there. I'm afraid to think where I got the intuitions I finally had to write about, like the torture. There are facilities at those bases to train army officers from down south. I had the dream right before I woke up early one morning. The helicopters were going over my house. In the dream I see them coming very low. And I knew from that dream there would be war, someday, for whatever reason. There was saber rattling by one general at Fort Huachuca in Arizona—*New York* magazine ran a piece about it. He said, "Today we'll take Tegucigalpa and tomorrow Tucson." I cut out the article because I had that dream. He was basically talking about Fort Huachuca in Arizona, and why we were there.

There was also talk that terrorists from the Middle East might come across the border and come into the United States about that time. And I thought, "Wow, I'm not the only one who dreams or thinks that way." I started reading the *Wall Street Journal* and the *New York Times* to try to understand economics. Before that I didn't know what the World Bank was and what happened to the people. I started to understand what that one crackpot general said, and his fear and the domino theory. And this was even before the Maquilladoras and the big corporations of America were moving toward Mexico for cheap labor.

There's also the attitude of Tucson towards anything from Mexico or anything brown or indigenous—they hate it. The whole situation within the city of Tucson with the police and the people made me see that Tucson wasn't any better than Argentina when there were disappearing people. Amnesty International has reports about the torturing of eighty percent of the people taken into custody in Mexico. They were doing that in Tucson, too. There's no boundary, there's no border. I'd also run into people who were telling me about the Papago people and Yaqui people. The Treaty of Guadalupe Hidalgo allows the Papago to go back and forth across the border because their time of crossing predates any kind of boundary line. So I started to think about imaginary boundary lines, real boundary lines.

TBR: The concept of time is a key metaphor and element in *Almanac of the Dead.* How did your interest in the astronomical knowledge of tribal people weave itself into your work?

LMS: I think it's impossible to really understand how tribal people, say the Maya, personified time, how they experienced a spirituality and the individual identity of the days. Post-Einsteinian physics is sort of laughable because of its beginning, middle, and end. They can shoot quarks and subatomic particles in the face of linear time. I read about that for a while, interested in how one can see the future and the past. When I was working with narrative, there was something very difficult about what I was trying to do. I wanted to tell this story in a certain kind of way. I was doing it to destroy any kind of sense of linearity. It's done in a way that narrative can have a narrative within a narrative, and where past/present/future can really be experienced. It is actually the way in which a lot of tribal people see and measure time—past, present, and future at once. Where I grew up, everything was always in the present. The past was in the present, and the future was in the present. And the old people just lived that way. When someone died, they still referred to Joe's store or Ray's horses, and he'd be long gone. This is a feeling that no one ever left. At the family table in Laguna, little pinches of food are taken and put in this little jar for all of the family members who are around but have gone. It's like a spirit world or dreamtime or spirit time. No one who ever lived was lost or gone forever. I had experienced that growing up at

Laguna. I relied on that experience of hearing narratives that would have inner narratives. In the narratives I was exposed to at Laguna, people didn't worry about linearity at all. There were no edges or ends to it. I can't explain it. But it was all one. I had experienced that when I was working on *Almanac.* I wanted it to be an almanac. But it's an almanac made of narrative. At the same time, I like the idea of the later kinds of advertising almanacs and medicine show almanacs, liniment almanacs, the farmer almanacs. I tried to keep dates out except in the parts that talk about slave revolts or rebellions. That was done deliberately along with the fragmentary nature of the things that were included. That's the way almanacs are, too. I carefully put references to dates and times just in those inner sections because I *did* want to destroy this idea of 1492. Because people are always saying, "Well, we can't do anything about it. All that happened a long time ago. We weren't the ones that went to Fort Grant and massacred the Apache women and children. That was a long time back." My poor character Sterling didn't get into so much trouble just because the Hollywood movie crew went and photographed a stone snake. It was for all those other things in the past just as critical as what happened to him. Past history or the stories are critical to what happens now. The past is very much right here and now. That was another reason I consciously didn't want *Almanac* to be this thing that started over here and went over there, because I don't think that's a valid expression of how we humans experience history. Something that happened five hundred years ago will damn well impinge sharply on right now. And it's very stupid to think, "Oh, no, we left it way behind." For the people I grew up with, it was only yesterday that the land was taken. The king of Spain gave the Laguna Pueblos and Rio Grande Pueblos land rights, so we didn't seriously have bad trouble and real conflict and land stealing until the Anglo Americans came in the 1840s. I decided, I'm going to suit myself with this almanac; it's my almanac. The Western European rules about the form of the novel don't apply. Hell, the nice thing about the novel is that it's wide open. I decided I would go ahead and raise hell with linear time. In a sense I was trying to work with that in *Ceremony,* the idea that things aren't lost, the dead aren't lost. I was trying to imagine how the complete Maya almanacs might have worked, in my own idiosyncratic way.

TBR: Do you think it ironic that *Almanac of the Dead* appears just as everybody is looking at 1992 and Columbus and the Quincentennial is getting so much attention?

LMS: Yeah, I think it's kind of ironic. It scares me that something in my subconscious made me create *Almanac.* I scares me to think that I might be on track about our people's history. When I was writing this, I sometimes felt I was being controlled by a spirit, not by spirits, but by a spiritual story-teller and narrator. The one who tells, the one who remembers the stories to be sure they're not lost or silenced. What's really scary is that I meant for this book to be short. I didn't mean for it to be this length at all—just kind of a cops-'n'-robbers dope-smuggling novel set in Tucson, really, really sim-ple. And I meant for the novel to be finished within five years because of my MacArthur Fellowship. I kept thinking I would be finished in 1987. I never consciously thought that it would finally end up coming out now. It makes me wonder. I didn't plan it that way. And it's sort of dicey.

TBR: The only other book of yours that appeared during the whole time you were working on *Almanac of the Dead* was *The Delicacy and Strength of Lace,* your letters to James Wright. Do you think the relationship you had with Wright affected your work on the novel or had anything to do with it?

LMS: I don't know. I wrote those letters to James Wright, and sometime after he passed away, Annie Wright, his wife, contacted me, saying she thought the correspondence was beautiful and she wanted to make a book of it. I accepted her judgment totally, and if that's what she wanted to do, it was OK with me. Annie sent me the manuscript, and I couldn't read it. I still can't read it. My friend Larry McMurtry happened to be there, and I said, "Larry, would you please look through and see if there's anything that should not be, you know, either something I mentioned about my ex-husband, my son, you know, please read this, because I can't." And to this day I've not read the whole book. So I don't know. Did you see some possible connection between *Almanac* and the letters?

TBR: Yes, I saw the connection in the earth and the landscape. The image in the letters that I come back to, and that led me into reading the novel, is when you write that you saw the owl in the Saguaro on the day Wright died.

LMS: Oh, that's good. Yeah, I wasn't aware of that. He was very impor-tant. The time of our correspondence was during one of those difficult times. I guess that comes out in the letters. And writing has always saved me when I'm really unhappy or when I'm just at the very end of my rope. When I wrote *Ceremony,* I was really having a struggle way up in southeastern Alaska. It was such a radical change. I was trying to write my novel and things with my marriage weren't going so well. As I wrote *Ceremony,* I got better as I went along. It really saved me. So the correspondence between myself and James Wright helped keep me together enough so that I could survive to write this book. I see the connection, too.

TBR: You mentioned *Ceremony.* Did you ever go back to that book, or refer to it in any way while you were working on *Almanac of the Dead?*
LMS: Not at all.

TBR: Do you see the two novels as being very different?
LMS: I thought they were very different until recently. The further I get away from *Almanac,* I hope I haven't written the same book twice. But in a sense, I probably have because I'm still trying to figure out where injustice comes from. Injustice I pretty much equate with evil, an imbalance and un-wellness. In my mind, I was probably thinking back to *Ceremony.* If people though that vision of good and evil ended with *Ceremony,* then what I was seeing around me in Tucson told me I could define it some more. Once I delivered *Ceremony* to the publisher, I don't think I ever read it all the way through again.

TBR: Most people are used to reading 150-page novels. The same writer can come out with a novel once a year. How do you expect the public to respond to a book of more than 700 pages, and how do you go beyond those ten years of working on such a project?
LMS: My editor from Simon and Schuster was pretty worried about that. When I delivered the manuscript, it was just a monolithic narrative. It wasn't broken up. He said it would be too much for the reader. One of the first things we did was try to make it easier. At the same time, I thought it made it more like an almanac. It began breaking into the little chapters. I went ahead and named them because I thought that might be helpful. I started having fun. I wanted to keep linearity out of it. I realized what I had done defied linearity anyway, so it was OK. The other thing we did for the reader is the map. There's the 500-year map, and it shows characters this way and that way. But as far as what I expect from the readers, I feel I wrote it and it had to be that big because it really is about five hundred years. I think I did a fairly good job of putting some impressionistic five hundred years in the Americas into the book. I wouldn't blame people for being put off by it. And you could almost read it like a long, long poem. You're not supposed to be able to remember. It's not a linear experience. As soon as the reader can begin to figure that out, it isn't so intimidating.

TBR: Where do you go after ten years of struggle on one book?

LMS: Some voice just says, "Oh, go out and paint on the side of the building. It will be OK. It will work out. Go do something different." So for right now, this voice says, "Ah, go on the promotional tours, go to the book signings. Take a little break." You know, it was ten years. And then I think, "Yeah. Ten cruel years, you spirits," or whatever that caused this. If I do contemplate it consciously and seriously, I think it is scary. While I was waiting for my editor to go through the manuscript, I still was in that mode and I went to my writing office every day. I spawned a violent, scary, little novel that began as a kind of child of *Almanac.* I stopped working on it. I haven't decided about my relationship to it yet. It's sort of scary because I begin to wonder if *Almanac* wants to rule the rest of my writing. I don't know. I'm trying to teach myself how to write Chinese. I read Zen Buddhism. I'm trying to remove myself as far away as I can from *Almanac* because I'm still under its spell. I have to just have faith.

Narratives of Survival

Linda Niemann / 1992

From *The Women's Review of Books* 9.10/11 (July 1992): 10. Reprinted by permission.

I first met Leslie Marmon Silko [writes Linda Niemann] early this year in San Francisco, halfway through her tour for *Almanac of the Dead,* her new novel about the history of the Americas since the conquest. The first thing she told me was that it was hard to be away from her macaw since it was just home after being kidnapped and she was worried about it. Within five minutes we were talking about water politics in Tucson, where she has lived for the past ten years. Leslie's wells were dropping due to the deep-well pumping for yet another golf course, developed in spite of environmental laws forbidding it. We had met briefly in a crowded room, and yet I found myself confiding in her instantly, telling her about my own vagabond life on the railroad. Storytellers listen. "Well," she said sympathetically, "Maybe the train is your home." "Yeah," I thought, "Maybe it is. Maybe I have one, after all."

In *Almanac of the Dead,* the meting out of justice to wrongdoers is swift—but often very, very funny. The mainstream press, however, has focused exclusively on the angry aspect of Silko's work, never even mentioning the humor. Can't white elitists take a joke? Are they so "squirmy"—to borrow from *Newsweek*'s review—that they can't even recognize one? Or is the author of *Almanac* so "ferocious," "defiant," "scathing," *(New York Times Book Review),* so "vengeful, very angry, raging, self-righteous" *(Time),* so "mighty angry" *(Newsweek)* that she would just as soon skewer a white person ("In her cosmology there are good people and there are white people"—*Newsweek*) as sit next to one?

LN: Why do you think mainstream reviewers have focused on the "angry" aspect of your work?

LMS: In the beginning of *Almanac* it says that the People believe that their narratives, their stories, have to continue to survive, and that if they do, then the People will. These stories work on unconscious levels that we don't have control of and access to by direct everyday means. When I was working with these narratives, I wanted them to have an after-effect in the unconscious, and I knew that things are present in some narratives, especially oral narratives, that make them just unforgettable.

Then these reviewers came along, certain white male academics—the one who had the hardest time was a political science professor at Yale who did the *USA Today* review, but I noticed the *Newsweek* and *Time* reviewers, both white males, were very up-front about their emotional reactions. They could tell that something had happened in the part of them that writes reviews for *Time* and *Newsweek,* and they say that. In the *New Republic* the guy was honest about how viscerally affected he had been, and you could see it in the language. "Aha," I thought, "Something magical *did* happen." I didn't control it, really, but there was something in those narratives that just forced itself to be told through me.

The guy in *USA Today,* he really lost it, but he wasn't honest about where the emotion was coming from, and so that makes it almost the most obsessed, flipped-out one of all.

LN: What kinds of things did he say?

LMS: Suggesting that I needed psychiatric help because of all the presentations of the male organ. He lost it so beautifully that anyone reading it just had to go "Wow! Look!"—and *USA Today* printed it! And of course, if you're a discerning reader, and you read a review like that—I mean, I would go buy that book so fast. . . . Anyway, I knew I had somehow gotten those narratives pretty much the right way, the way that they wanted to be, for them to have had this power.

LN: The *Time* review criticized you for inattention to character development, but I thought they missed the point. Weren't you doing something different from the usual focus on characters?

LMS: I was trying to give history a character. It was as if narrative spirits were possessing me, like a spell. If time is alive and has spirit and being, and the days enter and leave, and epics seek themselves and return—if you get that sense of spiritual being in time, then . . . I didn't plan this, I didn't do this cold-bloodedly. I knew I was breaking rules about not doing the characters in the traditional way, but this other notion took over—and I couldn't tell you rationally why. I knew it was about time and about old notions of history, and about narrative being alive.

LN: And the storyteller's job?

LMS: In the section of the *Almanac* where I tried to talk about Karl Marx and those narratives of the injured women and children in the factories; in recalling them, in telling their story, he'd hit on what you do to get people to rise up and be focused. It's when someone stands up and declaims, or screams, and says, "This happened to my loved one; this happened to me." One part of my conscious, rational self was increasingly horrified at my task, that my job was to write about five hundred of the ugliest years in world history. But then I saw that all those old folks who had, when I was a little girl, talked to me and spent so much time with me—that was what it was about. In some odd sort of way, I had always been set up for it.

LN: How did you research the Maya portion, the Almanac portions?

LMS: I had always been interested in the stars and astronomy, and there's been all this wonderful work in the Southwest by archaeologists who are into astronomy, like Mike Zeilik, who's a professor of astrophysics at the University of New Mexico. I've always been interested, too, in time, and how post-Einsteinian physics and particle physics render good old linear time. The interest in the stars and in things Mayan got really stirred up when I found a book by Anthony Aveni, called *Skywatchers of Ancient Mexico,* but he really talks about the Pueblo people, too, and the solar observatories that the People made up at Chaco Canyon, which isn't that far from the Pueblo where I grew up.

LN: And when you started writing *Almanac?*

LMS: I got all kinds of books on Mayan culture, I studied the glyphs. What I wanted in *Almanac of the Dead* was for those narratives to be like glyphs in a visual sense—that's why characterization isn't so important, because I was working with these other notions of how things can be codes and glyphs and intertwinings of the visual and the narrative. My life is my research—whatever I happen to be interested in—and for a long time, it was Mayans and particle physics and post-Einsteinian theories of time. Then when I started writing *Almanac,* it just all fell together like that. That's why I write—I don't know what I know until it comes out in narrative.

It's like do-it-yourself psychoanalysis. It's sort of dangerous to be a novelist. I really learned it with this one—you're working with language and all kinds of things can escape with the words of a narrative. With this one, I was especially in danger. It was like someone not knowing what they were doing, or only half-way knowing. You know the old saying that a little knowledge is dangerous. About two-thirds of the way through, I just finally had to stop and read Freud, and I read all eighteen volumes, one right after the other, because I'd been having this debate with my friend Larry McMurtry, and I was always down on Freud, and kicking Freud around. And it's his followers, really, who need to be kicked. Just like I say in the *Almanac,* the followers of Mohammed need to be kicked, and the followers of Jesus need to be kicked around. So I read the eighteen volumes, and I finished the novel, and it was like do-it-yourself psychoanalysis, but at the same time I realized how utterly dangerous doing it was. And for some people I think *Almanac* is kind of a dangerous book. Maybe you shouldn't give it to somebody who's depressed.

LN: I think the humor would rescue anyone who was depressed.

LMS: Oh, good. You saw humor.

LN: *Naked Lunch* kind of humor.

LMS: Well, you know, Burroughs was one of my heroes.

LN: I also like the way you express affection even for the evil characters.

LMS: I loved them all, and I loved the evil ones, too, as only a novelist can love a bad, very evil, wicked character—like Beaufrey. In a strange sort of way, it's like when they say "Oh, it's the mother, and the mother loves the child." Well, it's the novelist. But I think you have to love. You have to be able to be honest. That's the scary part for yourself, for you to admit that the reason you love them is because that's you, too. I'm not a stranger to Beaufrey, really. That's me. That's all of us, in some ultimate way. I don't mean that we're all him, but any one of us could be—you have to watch yourself all the time. We could all get that way.

LN: I wanted to ask you about witchcraft, and how you use evil. I think people might have difficulty understanding exactly what you're doing there, because you don't seem to be labeling people as good or evil.

LMS: No, not at all that dualistic notion of good or evil. It's more of a yin/yang. Too much of anything good can be bad—too much rain can cave in your adobe ceiling, or drown your little corn plants. So rain isn't absolutely good. Nothing is absolutely good or absolutely bad, in that old way of looking at things. It balances. I was intrigued with—worldwide, from culture to culture—people's notions about witchcraft and the evil eye. What I do in *Almanac* is project tribal notions. I like to take different notions about witches and evil and even let my characters make some up that aren't really from any group—they're their own—but I'm really interested in trying to project what evil looks like in the twentieth, or the late twentieth and early twenty-first centuries. Just because somebody like Nietzsche says God is dead doesn't mean that evil left, too.

LN: I thought that *Almanac,* in a certain way, was a kind of a prediction, and in another way, maybe it's a wish, or a vision or maybe just an exaggeration of what's here already. So, let's ask, what's the world going to be like in fifty years—the world you live in?

LMS: Well, I right away can imagine four or five or six answers, and what I try to do in *Almanac* is give you all of those possibilities. I could tell you the one I would hope for—the one I would hope for would be one in which democracy would actually be practiced, and the disenfranchised would actually be allowed to vote—homeless people could go vote, and the people of color who are so alienated. In the future, it's possible that we could have—by getting rid of professional politicians, and people using and somehow seizing the processes—a gradual, peaceful kind of shift, in that in fifty years you would see women, people of color, and not professionals, just ordinary people, not lawyers, in positions of government.

LN: And the scenario in *Almanac?*

LMS: It's like the way the Pueblos would use the ogre Katchina to scare the bad kids. It's like, read this and be horrified, and then don't let it be this scenario—let it be the other scenario, where just through birth-rate and immigration the tide is changing. You can't stop it. The United States is never going to be, it never has been, what they said. We've always had the Third World right here, always.

LN: What about the role of women?

LMS: I think that in *Almanac* I do imply that women and female power are survival. I love Alegría—the one who makes it across the border. She's sort of an awful person, but I love her. She's very bad, very bad. I love her because she made it. And then I like Leah Blue—even though she's polluting the desert and the water, and even though she doesn't love my desert, I love her. She's unstoppable. She's still going to do it! I think that I would want to write a whole other book to talk about what could happen, what's already happening, because of the attack on *Roe v. Wade.* One of the things that I think could happen in the future is just this fierce anger that all of us women are feeling. Push us a little bit further and they just haven't seen trouble yet. That's something that I didn't really run—they wouldn't let me make the *Almanac* any longer—that I really believe in and I only imply this thriving power with these women characters. We just don't want to think about how mad we are, how really angry, and how, when you finally have nothing to lose, what you'll do. By God, they're about to find out.

LN: And in the meantime, how are things for you?

LMS: Right now there's no money coming yet from *Almanac.* I'm sitting here, I don't have a job, they put a hiring freeze on at all the state schools here, and I had resigned my position so I could finish my book, so I'm sitting here going, "Oh, I can identify with all of the unemployed," because although, as a writer, I never feel unemployed because I'm writing and doing things, still, technically I'm unemployed and thinking, "Oh, no!" And this voice is saying, "Leslie, if you'd just written a nice book, like a nice girl . . ." So I need to get praise.

LN: Well, I certainly hope you keep on doing what you're doing.

An Interview with Leslie Marmon Silko

Stephen Pett / 1992

From *Short Story* 2.2 (1994): 91–95. Reprinted by permission.

Stephen Pett interviewed Leslie Marmon Silko Friday, June 5, 1992, during the Second International Conference on the Short Story at the University of Northern Iowa in Cedar Falls. Their primary focus was the teaching of creative writing. The interview took place in the Columbia Room of the Maucker Union, a reminder that approximately five hundred years earlier, Western European culture stumbled upon the native people of this hemisphere, with nightmarish consequences. Leslie Marmon Silko, who grew up at the Laguna Pueblo in New Mexico, is a writer interested in consequences. She is the author of *Laguna Woman* (1974), a book of poems; *Storyteller* (1981), a book of poetry, fiction, and photographs; and two novels, *Ceremony* (1977), and, most recently, *Almanac of the Dead* (1991). She attended the University of New Mexico and is the recipient of a MacArthur Foundation Fellowship. She lives outside Tucson. Stephen Pett is a novelist who teaches at Iowa State University.

Pett: You come out of a storytelling tradition that's very different from the Western European narrative tradition. I'm wondering if that has affected the way you introduce stories to writing classes. Do you ever try to define "story" in an explicit way, or do you just let people—?

Silko: Sometimes we joke around, kick around what makes a story and what doesn't, and say "Well, when I hear it, I'll know it." That kind of thing. I don't usually try to do that. We look at newspaper stories; we do in-class exercises and we try to talk about it, but with the idea that you can never definitively lay down any kinds of rules about narrative. I tell them right away that I think that some of these boundaries between genres are illusory.

Pett: One of the things that strikes me about your writing—one of the things I like most—is that you never seem to settle for the formal traditional structure of any particular genre. I mean you're always pushing—

Silko: Yes, that's just how I experienced language; that it was all coequal, every statement, every expression, every story, it was equally interesting or important; in Western European culture you have so much that's hierarchical, and you're always so busy sorting out and kicking things out and so forth. In my experience, everything was seen as story and worked into narrative and all those distinctions weren't made. When I did encounter genre, that notion of genre and these boundaries and distinctions, it just didn't seem real to me and, indeed, it's not. In the Pueblo language there's just this continuum and they don't make these exclusive classes as in Western European. I think that that's one of the things that's already sort of dissolving. It already started with Joyce and the breakdown between poetry and prose and the different genres; it's started to, you know.

Pett: I'd like to ask you a few questions about how story develops for you and how your work develops, the process. Yesterday, I talked to Joyce Carol Oates and I mentioned my colleague and friend Jane Smiley knowing the last sentence of a piece she's starting. That's very different from the way I work. Joyce Carol Oates said, "Yes, that's how I work, too. I can't imagine writing if I don't know the last sentence. It's like traveling and not having a destination on your ticket."

Silko: That's what I do, set out unsure where I'll end up.

Pett: She said, "Well, there're those two kinds of writers." I'm wondering if you could talk about what sort you are and if you think there is another sort.

Silko: Well, there must be another sort. Another sort uses outlines and outlines chapters and knows exactly what's happening and that's what publishers and people who bank on literature have a definite preference for; the whole notion of control, you're in control, you can see where it's going to go and how long it's going to be. That's one way of working at fiction; it's the safest, least frightening, most reliable way to go. I don't ride that train because it's really boring. In fact, if I knew what the last sentence was, I wouldn't want to write the book in the first place. I write to find out things I don't know. I write to find out what my unconscious knows but what I don't know.

It's almost now to the point where I really am the fall guy, the straight guy. I start out writing and I think I'm writing a short novel about drug smuggling in Tucson and that's all it is, you know. And then as I work and work, I keep thinking well, yes, this still looks like a drug smuggling novel but, gee, it's getting these other things, so that it starts to grow. I have to work that way. If I'm bored, if I know what it's going to be already, I won't write it. What's the point? What's the point in writing something that you already know what's going to happen? And, of course, I'm sure Joyce Carol Oates and people who work like that don't know everything and then the fun is in filling it in.

I guess I'm just not interested unless it's an entire adventure or mystery. And of not knowing the last line? It is like being with a plane ticket without a destination on it. I sort of like that because that way you can get to places nobody else has ever gone and that's what I'm trying to do. I'm not interested in selling books or just writing books so I have another book out, or writing books to keep busy. I write when something stirs, something sweeps across my feelings and my consciousness. It might just be one image or one element, and it hooks me, though.

It's like waking that morning and hearing helicopters going over the house, because I was hearing helicopters in real life. It made me dream of helicopters, but the helicopters were coming. In the dream I could see the helicopters were flying very low and they were coming from Mexico and they were full of wounded U.S. soldiers. It was such a strong impression and such a strong dream and that became then a kind of marker post and I started wondering about that dream, was there something that I knew, that the dream-side of me, my imaginative side, my unconscious side knew that I didn't know about Tucson and where I was? Well, what the hell is it? How can I be dreaming that there's going to be a war in Mexico? Where is this coming from? And so, I was already working on the cops and robbers part of the novel [*Almanac of the Dead*], you know, the beginning part. But then that dream comes in early on and that dream was very important because I couldn't forget it and I knew that the book I was working on was going to have to explain this somehow, was going to have to account for this.

Another dream that I had one morning was the gardens of Xochimilco in Mexico City, the hanging gardens, and there's little canals with little boats and things. I dreamed before morning two human heads floating in a plastic shopping bag and staring up; it was this real striking image again. So I just thought what is this all about? And so then I take that and go to my writing room and begin to wrestle with it because those things rise up out of my unconscious and it's about something that's happening or going on, that the only way I can discover what it means is to write about it. What happens is that you just start working with the material and it will lead you, it takes you. That's the way I work.

Pett: That sounds grueling. Can you put in long hours working like that?

Silko: I'm usually good for four hours, four intensive hours. That doesn't count the first hour where you're sort of floundering around. So that I might spend a total of five or maybe six hours in my writing office in a day when I was working on *Almanac of the Dead*. But it's real clear to me that after about four or five hours you're no good. And then I have a problem making myself stop, even though the conscious one, I don't know which one anymore, some voice in my head says, "You know you've worked five hours. It just isn't happening anymore." It's like a race horse or something. "Stop!" But there's this other impulse which is, "No, look how good. I'm really going." And this other voice saying, "Well, you have been really going but it's starting to get thin now. So stop." And this other voice like, "No, goddamn it, it's so fucking hard to get started! I'm going to write this book, I'm going to finish this book." And this other voice, "No, don't you understand, this book is going to take such a long time, you will have to get up and eat. . . ." You know, it came to that, where some part of me just didn't want to leave it ever, to eat or sleep or to do anything—even when it was real clear to me that it was time to stop, that it was time to rest at the end of a day. So there were these terrible struggles, and then the next struggle the next day, of course, is to go back. There's a great resistance in going back to face that struggle again. To get started again is very hard—every day, every day, yes, for ten years.

Pett: And through all that work, you're discovering the story as it grows.

Silko: Yes, discovering as it grows, that's how I work. It's real. It means that in your first draft you have to work the way a poet follows words and it makes a poem, you know, one word leads to another. It means that you've got to exhaustively give a chance to every possibility—to let lots of little tendrils grow out even though later on they may be chopped off. I sort of strive to have the biggest, most huge mass in the beginning and then cut, cut from there. It's easier to prune than it is to add on. The added-on things also, you can always see the seam, whereas the things that are cut off you can't see.

Pett: That's what I wanted to ask you about next, revision. When you work the way you do, I would think it requires a lot of re-working and trimming or development. Do you go through a lot of drafts?

Silko: On this one [*Almanac of the Dead*] I guess there were probably three or four versions, and they don't differ that much, but yeah, there was a lot of revising, and re-working that couldn't be done until I had gotten it a good two-thirds, three-quarters of the way. That couldn't begin until then and then it was horrible to have to go back through. Then, of course, I'd forgotten. In a book that long, you forget writing whole sections . . .

Pett: *Ceremony* took two years, I think, and this one took ten. Did *Ceremony* go through fewer drafts?

Silko: I wrote *Ceremony* just like you'd write a short story. Each sentence was perfect before I went on to the next one. So there was no re-writing; there was just very little editing. So the way I wrote this book was completely different from the way I wrote *Ceremony.* So that was real hard too. But I didn't write at all the same way.

Pett: You started writing when you were in the fifth grade, and you read a lot. I'm interested in what keeps people moving. What were you writing when you started? Do you remember? What writers were you reading early that came back to you when you started writing again in college?

Silko: When I was in the fifth grade, our house was always full of books. I remember my dad had *Lolita* when it first became legal, *Lady Chatterly's Lover* when it first became legal. People forget how much censorship there was and how there were forbidden books. Of course, we're almost back to that again in America. So I remember sneaking those books out from under my dad's side of the bed and trying to find out what the trouble was. Of course with *Lady Chatterly's Lover* there aren't very many scenes that are very notorious so I was disappointed and I couldn't find what the problem was with either one of the books. So I read what my dad was reading and my dad read the popular fiction of the day, and in some ways a lot of it was better than it is now.

I read. My parents got us all kinds of books, books about dinosaurs. I did all kinds of reading. When I was in junior high, I read John Steinbeck; when I was in high school, I read William Faulkner. This was on my own. I just loved to read.

In the fifth grade, though, I was really unhappy. I had switched from a Bureau of Indian Affairs school to a school in Albuquerque and it was a long drive and we were real strangers there. I had found that I had a real deficiency in science and math because the Bureau of Indian Affairs schools were so bad; so that one day our teacher gave us a list of spelling words and she said take each word from the list and use it at least once in a story and I never can forget that day. I can still see the room and everything. I started to do her assignment. Now in Indian School we had really bad teachers. I had never heard of such a neat assignment before. Isn't this great? So I started taking the spelling words and putting them into a story and something happened. I can still feel it, and it's what's always kept me going all these years. As I did it and as I made the spelling words turn into this story and got each one of them in there at least once, this incredible pleasure and satisfaction and security and even power, a feeling of empowerment, came over me, and all of a sudden none of it mattered—being behind in science and math. From then on, I would take seats towards the back of the room, I would always get my work done, I was a good student, but as soon as I'd get my work done, it was like I'd pull out—and I always had—and so what I was doing when I was writing, I wasn't in that room anymore, I wasn't there, I was in that wonderful state that as a child, as a listener, when my great-grandmother or Aunt Susie or someone was telling the stories, you feel so loved and secure when you're surrounded with the voice of the storyteller telling you a story.

What I had discovered was that when I wrote I could in some way put myself into that mind state or that feeling, that narrative makes you feel good and safe and it's a completely different world than the world that you're in. So from that time on, from the fifth grade on, I'd finish my assignment, sit in the back row, and write.

I can remember my eighth grade teacher, after I got the MacArthur Fellowship, she started corresponding with me—Sister Mary Agnes. Sister Mary Agnes remembers that I would do extra credit. I thought that they were assignments, but she says I was always asking to do extra credit and writing. I wrote a ballad in iambic pentameter when I was in eighth grade about a stabbing near a bar across the reservation line. Once that thing clicked in the fifth grade, and I think even before that, it had to do with the happiness and pleasure of listening to stories. From then on I've been hooked.

Almanac of the Dead: An Interview with Leslie Marmon Silko

Laura Coltelli / 1993

From *Native American Literatures* Forum 4–5 (1992–93): 65–80. Reprinted by permission.

LC: The map is the very first page of *Almanac*. The subtitle is "Five Hundred Year Map." The four boxed texts tell of the past, present, and future of the American continent. Is it a spatial introduction to the novel, but also a temporal dimension, a story-within-a story?

LMS: Yes, I started out with the idea of writing about Tucson and its power to attract criminals of all kinds, and political plot-makers. I was interested in locations which themselves seem to have a spirit, a presence which remains the same over hundreds of years.

I have read about the pre-Columbian trade routes from the Pueblos in New Mexico south into Mexico. Tucson seems to me a crossroad, and as the Native American-African American beliefs of Voodoo religion tell us, a crossroads is a place of intense conflict between all the spirits, and all the forces. So, in the very beginning, I meant to write a novel about the spiritual identity of a place, a location.

Maybe the almanac is a map of the past five hundred years—that is, a "map" made out of narratives. But these narratives themselves seem inextricably bound to certain geographical locations, so I drew that map in *Almanac* as a "glyphic" representation of the narrative. This "glyph" shows how the Americas are "one," not separated by artificial, imaginary "borders." The landscapes, the spirits of the places are known by the narratives that originate in these places.

LC: The map is also the last page of the book. A frame then, or a sequence like past history/prophesy?

LMS: Yes, the map works like that, but also I was thinking of the "vévé"— the Voodoo religion's patterns drawn on the ground during ceremonies. I guess the notion of the sandpainting in a healing ceremony also influenced the drawing of the map, as well as the drawings of the spider, snake, and rainbird and squash flower designs which the book-designer at Simon and

Schuster allowed me to draw myself. (The drawings of snake, spider, etc. are on the title page of *Almanac*.)

I realize now that *Almanac* is not just an almanac, but it is a sort of Voodoo spell, too, and so it was good that the women book-designers at Simon and Schuster asked me to make my own drawings. I have been interested in the interplay between visual images and the narrative for a long time. The map's presence influences how a reader reads the narratives.

LC: Many characters in the novel, both Indian and white, have to deal with maps. Is it a unifying thematic structure?

LMS: Oh, I never noticed this map theme in *Almanac*. I only remember a scene in *Ceremony* where Betonie represents the four sacred mountains in the sandpainting, and is something of a "spiritual map," which breaks down boundaries between the worlds of the animal/spirits and humans.

But Western European maps are used to steal Indian lands, to *exclude,* to imprison, to cut off, to isolate even segments of the human world from one another. Maps are the only physical evidence of boundary lines. Before constructing fences or other markers for a boundary, the map-maker-surveyor is consulted. My great-grandfather was a surveyor for the U.S. government, and some way he mapped the boundary line in favor of Laguna Pueblo over Acoma Pueblo. But one of the Bibo family (Lebanese traders) was also a land surveyor who had married an Acoma woman, and this Bibo surveyed boundaries in favor of the Acomas over the Lagunas.

LC: Sterling is deeply in touch with traditional values. The novel closes with his awareness of the real essence and importance of the snake's message to the people. But all his life he has been very attracted by old Tucson heroes, mostly outlaws, such as John Dillinger, Billy the Kid, Pretty Boy Floyd, and more recently, Mafia Godfathers or famous white sheriffs. Why?

LMS: Sterling has always been curious about "outlaws" because he senses that the dominant culture has relegated Indians to a category which is outside the laws. Sterling is curious about the non-Indians who end up as "outlaws," because Sterling is trying to understand how the white man's law and order work. Sterling knows that "outlaws" suffer injustices in the hands of police and the courts who sell "justice," and he knows intuitively that what passes for "law and order" in the U.S. is actually just injustice and racism. Sterling is fascinated with flamboyant, daring rebels who oppose the unjust system because Sterling himself is so mild-mannered and law-abiding.

LC: Sterling is banished from the Pueblo; he got punished for acts he had no part in, acts related to the Hollywood movie crew seeing and filming the Giant Stone Snake. Why did the Tribal Council members fail to recognize Sterling's innocence?

LMS: Sterling was unfortunate enough to be caught in another episode in the long, long struggle to protect Pueblo culture from outsiders. The stone snake had just appeared and was very special, so the people were particularly emotional about the desecration by the film crew. They were just so angry and upset, they behaved in a human way and they gave in to their emotions, and blame Sterling 100 percent, when, really, Sterling was probably 20 percent to blame. He *was* supposed to watch out, and make sure the film crew did not intrude. If Sterling had not been away from Laguna so many years while he worked for the railroad, then his position with the Tribal Council would have been stronger and he would have avoided banishment. If Sterling had only been romantically involved with someone from the village—that lover would have marshalled aid and support for Sterling. Edith Kaye, his old flame, was angry at him—that did not help.

If Sterling had not been an orphan without close relatives, probably he wouldn't have been banished. His family would have defended him. If the people hadn't been reminded of the stolen stone idols, Sterling would've been spared banishment too.

I wanted to show that Pueblo people are human, and they may *displace* their anger for past and present injustices, and punish one of their own people, even someone like Sterling. Don't believe Sterling when he says he is "so innocent"—he muffed his duties watching that film crew. He didn't deserve banishment though. This is the reason Sterling can return to Laguna. The people will "forget" the banishment order because it was not really merited in the first place.

LC: In *Almanac of the Dead* there are about seventy characters; it encompasses five hundred years, events take place all around the world, and yet the structure of the novel is like a spiral in which every story or single character is somehow connected with the other.

LMS: I did *not* plan the structure of this novel, just as I did not plan the structure of *Ceremony,* at least not consciously.

I thought originally that the stories would *not* interconnect, and so I called the novel "an almanac," because entries in almanacs are often "unrelated" except that they are all together in an almanac or the entries are related only by a linear time-line; that is, Western European almanacs are this way.

I was surprised when the various characters and plot-lines began to inter-connect, and that's what makes my almanac less like a Western European almanac and more like an old Mayan almanac in which all days, all months, and all time are living beings who are interconnected.

I learned a great deal from writing *Almanac of the Dead.* I had very little conscious control over the characters and the stories; I was taken along by the characters and the stories themselves and I merely wrote down what the characters and the stories showed me and told me.

I didn't realize *Almanac*'s structure was a spiral. The spiral is very impor-tant down here with the Tohono O'odham tribal people. Their basket designs feature the spiral. I'm not sure, but I think they represent human creation by showing the figure of a human coming out of a spiral. But of course, the spiral is also the main figure of the petroglyph of the snake which points to fresh water. (See my *Sacred Water*).[1] The spiral snake is a messenger of fresh water which is life itself. A spider web is a sort of modified spiral structure too.

LC: This novel is an almanac in that each day shapes and contains a story which cyclically returns. "It's as if the days were ancestors of themselves, much as humans," if you consider circular time, as Joy Harjo put it in review-ing your book.[2]

LMS: What a wonderful insight from Joy! I don't know if I can add any-thing. I am fascinated with the Mayan notion that days are living beings, and I did try to make that concept come alive in *Almanac*. Living beings must have ancestors, otherwise they would not exist (unless they are gods).

Who are the ancestors of the days that are visiting the people of Bosnia right now? We know only too well that World War I was precipitated in Sarajevo; these days now are direct descendants of those days eighty-some years ago.

LC: What are your sources for the old Mayan Almanac?

LMS: Fragments of old stories I've heard here and there inform my imagi-nation, and to this, I combined what I could recall from reading some books.

LC: Everybody in the novel is a refugee: Sterling from his Pueblo people, Seese from the drug world, Zeta from being a witch, even Tucson inhabitants are refugees from the heat. Would you comment on that?

LMS: When I first moved to Tucson from Laguna in 1978, I had to think about what it meant to be separated from one's tribal land and people. Simon

Ortiz used to call me and ask me when I was "coming home." Laguna is my first and last home. But I have also learned that the Earth is my home, and the dry air and dusty blue mountains northwest of Beijing felt like home, just as these lava rock cerros outside Tucson are home. Now I begin to suspect that in the days before monarchs' maps with boundary lines, the tribal people of the Americas thought of the whole earth as their home, not just one continent. Humans used to feel that way until the rise of the nation-state fiction, which sought to destroy ancient liasons between people on opposite sides of the newly-created borderline.

I wanted to understand how the Yaqui people felt, because they had taken refuge in Tucson after the Mexican army began the genocide of the 1900s and 1920s; of course the Yaqui people had always ranged this far north, so the land here is not so different than the land they fled. Because I was so close to Mexico, I began to think about the Indian people torn out of their villages south of Mexico City, and marched north for a thousand miles to be slaves in the vast silver mines in northern Sonora. The European slave-catchers made entire cultures extinct in the Americas, and I thought about what it might have felt like to be the last of one's tribe and far away from one's land. Ishi, the Californian Indian, might have been the last one of his tribe, but at least he was on his mother-land, with all his clan's people, the trees, plants, birds, and animals, so Ishi's story doesn't seem so sad until the white people grab him and lock him in a museum.

I realized that to be a refugee is part of the human condition, and the urge to migrate, to flee, is stronger than the urge to reproduce. Human beings have been moving and relocating for thousands of years and before the rise of kings and nation-states, humans recognized and tolerated the appearance of travellers and strangers because they themselves had experienced a migration or because their oral history recounted hundreds of migrations by their ancestors. To be human is to have the potential of becoming a temporary and even permanent refugee.

Long ago, to be a refugee was not abnormal, and most communities recognized the right of strangers to take flight into or across one's home territory. Today, nation-states have greatly limited human migration and attempts are being made to stop human migration altogether. But the instinct and urge to flee is stronger than the instinct to reproduce; thus steel walls and armed borders will slow but not stop human migration.

So the condition of migration is basic to the human being because we humans are fragile and flighty creatures that must flee or die from intense desert heat, extreme cold, and most often, disasters of human creation. The minute we humans are born, we become refugees of one sort or another. Yes. I am alarmed at the way the dominant powers and the media that serve the powers have managed to make the status of refugee or immigrant a crime. The sexual urge was criminalized, and now they have criminalized an even more basic human urge, the urge to flee, to move, to migrate for survival.

LC: "Invisibility" seems to be the key word to describe relationships among many characters. Seese is invisible to Ferro and Paulie, or Beaufrey and Serlo, Sterling is invisible to almost everybody, Ferro does not acknowledge the presence of his mother, Paulie has a strong, emotional relationship only with his dogs, Lecha is absorbed in her thoughts, Zeta in her revolutionary plans, the poor Indians in the bus depot simply don't exist for Lecha's father, Mosca has his own theory about invisibility, the medicine man's specialty when he rides with the warriors is invisibility. No sharing then from one side, and the spell of invisibility from the other?

LMS: Physicists say most of the Universe is composed of invisible matter. In our day-to-day life we cannot or will not see most of what surrounds us. Our eyes are designed to focus only on isolated points. We can scan the horizons but our eyes are able to focus only on isolated points. As children we are taught what we are allowed to see; Western European culture does not allow us to see the spirit and being in rocks, water, and trees and other plants. Therefore the spirit and being of rocks and water and plants remain invisible to most of us.

Invisibility is neither good nor bad; it is a result of knowledge or the lack thereof. If one knows how to see, less of the world will remain invisible. The medicine man with his spells of invisibility for the warriors is one example of the positive value of invisibility. The U.S. Army men don't know how to see invisible Apache warriors; if one knows how to see them, it may be done. Medicine people know how to do this. Sterling cultivates his invisibility; he is so frightened of the weird household he's in, he is glad to be invisible. Seese also used her invisibility although she was also denigrated by it; she used her invisibility around Beaufrey to avoid being sent away. If Seese had pushed even a little more, Beaufrey would have got rid of her pronto! Paulie is so crushed by his past and the loss of Ferro's love that any love except dog love is invisible to him. The judge with the basset hounds is not so different except Paulie loves the dog, and the judge doesn't love his dogs. He just likes to have sex with them.

Invisibility may marginalize a person or a group; but with daring and resourcefulness, the invisibility can be turned around and used as a valuable weapon. Most human beings keep dimensions of themselves invisible to all—even to their lovers, and sometimes to themselves. Families and people today talk about intimacy and trust, but human beings are far more complex and secretive than anyone is comfortable to admit.

What is invisible to you may harm or destroy you, whether that thing is part of yourself or someone near you. The starving people who are invisible to the rich someday will destroy the rich.

What does "invisible to the naked eye" mean? What does "visible" mean? The film image gives our brains more bits of optical/light data than does the video image.

LC: In dealing with the characters, you unfold their stories mostly using the flashback technique. Can you talk about your creative process in *Almanac*?

LMS: As usual, I had no real plan or outline when I began *Almanac*. I thought I would write an action thriller novel. Something short, something that could be sold at the book stand in the supermarket. But I had already been thinking about a character like Sterling who gets in trouble because of a Hollywood film crew. I had a funny novel in mind. Anyway, once I began typing, stories and characters that I'd had on my mind since I finished *Ceremony* suddenly began to appear. The anguish of a woman character in one of the stillborn novels before *Ceremony* seems to resurface in the character of Seese. As the storylines and characters emerged, I let them remain and did not worry about putting them all together, I guess because I already had the idea about the old almanac in my subconscious; anyway, I did not expect that all these characters and storylines would intersect and converge, at least not consciously. I was quite worried for a long time as I wrote *Almanac,* because more and more characters kept showing up with more and more stories. But then I understood that this really was an almanac I was writing, and just as the old Maya and Aztec almanacs were full of many people and events, so too must my almanac allow all these people and events or time would not be represented properly. Once I understood that my almanac was supposed to cover five hundred years, then I began to feel a little better about all those characters.

I used flashbacks because I wanted the moments of the past to be as alive as they really are; I wanted the reader to be there and to see and feel the aliveness of the past. The past does not die. The past is alive, side by side with the present. Also, I wanted the reader to know the stories of the different characters from the inside, through the eyes of these characters. I wanted the reader to feel what the characters felt so the reader cannot distance himself from the history the almanac recounts.

The flashback makes a statement about the inextricable relationship between the present and the past. Whoever we are, wherever we may find ourselves at this moment cannot be isolated from what we have been and where we have been prior to this moment. The experience of language itself is not unlike the flashback. When I say "red," your mind flashes back to present experiences you've had with the color red. When I talk about a future dog I hope to have, the word "dog" causes your mind to flash back for an instant to all experiences you've ever had with the word or the concept "dog."

The use of the flashback also prepares the reader for the realization that time is not linear, that the past is not left behind and the past is not dead. All the past goes into the creation of this present moment.

LC: The twins motif and duality in general underline one of the most powerful patterns in Pueblo cosmology. In the first part of *Almanac* Lecha/Zeta are in the foreground, in the second Tacho/El Feo. Would you elaborate on that?

LMS: For a long time I was not really aware of the twins motif; I know that sounds odd, but I forget those things which I am planning to use or "convert" into fiction. I prevent my conscious self from remembering these things so that I can more effectively appropriate them into my fiction. If I were conscious that I was making an appropriation, I might become intimidated by the audacity of my appropriation as in the case of the twins motif. When I thought of Lecha and Zeta, I had no idea that this was going to be an almanac with the Mexico section; I never dreamed that I would have El Feo, and even after I first created El Feo, time passed before I realized he had a twin brother. Even after I had the novel full of twins, I had to look at the *Popol Vuh* a second or third time before it really dawned on me that I had filled the novel with twins and the twins play a really big role in the Maya stories just as the twin brothers in the Laguna Pueblo stories play the roles of heroes. Some of the Maya stories about the twin brothers are even identical to the Laguna stories about the twin brothers. In fact, I did not really spend much time with the *Popol Vuh* because so many of the stories are almost identical to the Laguna stories.

So I was almost finished with *Almanac* when I noticed all the twins who appear. Later, when California suffered those twin earthquakes, I wished I had thought of twin earthquakes to include in my *Almanac*, but when I was actually writing *Almanac*, I wasn't thinking on that level, wasn't saying to myself, "I must use the twins motif because it is a dominant motif in the oral literature of the Americas and Africa." I was excited when I found out about the Twin Brothers in West Africa, thanks to Zora Neale Hurston, but even then, I didn't think about the twin characters throughout the novel. I even made twins out of non-twins; the white men in the wheel chairs at the Veterans Hospital are twins of sorts. Rambo and Clinton are twins of sorts. Liria and her sister are almost like twins for Calabazas. I can look back now and see this, but at the time I was actually writing the novel, I really wasn't thinking at all about motifs or even the importance of twins in the Americas. Too much thinking ruins novels, because thinking is linear and logical and blocks out the imagination and great flights of the intuition. Don't think, listen to the voices in your head when you write a novel.

LC: How could you distinguish Lecha and Zeta's power to transcribe the notebooks and decode the Almanac?

LMS: It is very difficult to distinguish between Lecha's power and Zeta's power to transcribe the notebooks because we aren't told much about the process Lecha uses with the notebooks, although we are told a great deal about her, how she gets "results" for her clients seeking revenge in love affairs. Lecha knows her gift as a psychic comes from old Yoeme and the notebooks are from Yoeme also, but it takes Lecha years of learning, from Rose, from the old Eskimo woman, from Root, from her father, from her sister, and even from her clients, before Lecha is ready to return to Tucson to begin the work on the notebooks.

Zeta works directly on a computer of some sort. Zeta employs a Korean computer hacker to help her perpetrate sabotage on her enemies by computer. Zeta seems to have translated the old notebook fragment she received into action. Zeta seems to follow the philosophy of Calabazas which translates a political philosophy of resistance against colonialism into direct action. The act of smuggling contraband becomes the political action which Zeta and Calabazas take in defiance of a ficticious line drawn by white men on maps.

Zeta seems to have made the same commitment to defiant action that their grandmother, Yoeme, took when she earned her title of "short broad-shouldered woman with deadly aim" during the Mexican Revolution. It is as if Zeta begins to live the Yoeme narrative I call the Great Influenza of 1918 even before Lecha transcribed and decoded it. Zeta is like El Feo who becomes politicized before Tacho/Wacah does because Wacah is distracted by his macaws just as Lecha is distracted by her psychic gift to find the dead. But even these "distractions" actually prepare Tacho and Lecha for what they must do in the future.

So Lecha becomes aware of the necessity of transcribing the notebooks after she sees the effects of the savage violence running loose in the United States, a violence aimed at the bodies of young children and women, but also at the bodies of young men. Lecha sees the connection between "domestic" violence and political violence and colonialism. While she is voluntarily separated from her son Ferro, the clients who contact her are desperately searching for their children.

Lecha's life experiences are preparations for her work with the notebooks. She bridges the imaginary gap Western European culture sees between the "personal" and the "political." Zeta abandons social and sexual contact to commit acts of political resistance; yet she is the one who is the mother to Ferro. Lecha, who seems apolitical, has a "vision" of the assassination of the U.S. ambassador to Mexico City, and subsequent inquiries from the U.S. government are factors in Lecha's decision to retire from the talk show circuit. Lecha has to grow into her role as keeper and transcriber of the notebooks, and so does Zeta.

In a way, Lecha and Zeta are already under the spell of the old almanac even before they settle down to transcribe the almanac because of Yoeme's influence over them. Like Yeome, both women depend on experiences in their personal lives to transcribe and decode the old notebooks. Even Yoeme's way of talking to Lecha and Zeta, Yoeme's irreverent attitude, all were part of their preparation to take over as keepers of the notebooks.

LC: In *Almanac* European, American, and Native histories are seen as having totally divergent trends of the same period. Only one example: the 1929 crash vs. a year of bounty and plenty for tribal people.

LMS: The divergent trends are evidence of the radically different world-views held by Europeans and Americans. The stock market crash of 1929 was a catastrophe, but it was entirely man-made and the losses existed only on paper, at least until investors began to leap to their deaths. In the natural world, 1929 was a good year with plenty of rain, fat game, and good harvests. Where world-views differ so greatly, it is not unexpected that what is good for one will be not so good for the other. But there were similarities too in the history of Europe and the Americas. The riches plundered from the Americas gave the Europeans the ability to wage war upon one another thus bringing suffering and death on Europe for the past five hundred years. Even the potato made the wars in Europe last longer because the potato does not require the intensive cultivation that grains do. So while there are divergences in American and European history, there are also parallels. Today, all living beings in the world live under the same shadow of nuclear holocaust and ecological disaster.

LC: All roads in *Almanac* lead to Tucson, for one reason or another. It is at the very center of the novel, with its past of bootleggers, murderers, corrupted government people who in one generation had become Tucson's fine old families with all their money coming from the Apache wars. Everything in Tucson speaks of decay and death (although in Papago, Tucson means "plentiful fresh water"), even the obscenely luxurious green golf course at the edge of the desert whose cacti have "shriveled into leathery, green tongues" (p.64). The other geographical pole, as in *Ceremony,* are the mountains surrounding your Laguna Pueblo, the place to start the restoration rite.

LMS: The death and decay which pervade Tucson arrived with the colonialists. The water was fresh and abundant before the coming of the Europeans. *Almanac* mainly covers the past five hundred years and so we don't really get to see the Tucson of plentiful fresh water. Perhaps in some future time people will once again see the Tucson of plentiful fresh water.

Death and decay are not so negative if one looks at them from the point of view of the old time Tohono O'odham and Pueblo people. Down here in the Sonoran desert, death means life for some other creature; decay means food for some other creature. How selfish of us humans to always interpret death and decay as negative; we always assume it is us dead and decaying but due to the deaths of many beings, we humans eat every day.

The important death and decay found in Tucson is not in the physical world but in the spiritual lives of the people who invaded here. No new life emerges from the dead decaying human soul of Max Blue or the Judge or the Police Chief.

Tucson has every bit as much healing grace in its mountains as Laguna does in the mountains there. It's just that Tucson has a great deal of burdensome history, many angry spirits that reside there, and which draw kindred spirits to the place. Sterling is from Laguna so he would expect to get healed back at Laguna. In a way, Sterling's personal healing process commences in

Tucson as he realizes that his life hasn't been so bad after all. I did not mean
to imply that Tucson is devoid of spiritual healing power.

Seese has to come to Tucson before she can ever hope to continue with her
life; she may not be able to go on, but at least for awhile she is in the care of
Lecha, and so Seese is a little better off.

Tucson has harsh stories and harsh lessons but sometimes desperate conditions call for harsh medicine.

Death is not evil or bad *per se.* It all depends on when and how one dies.
The spirits of the dead already whisper in the dreams of the living on these
American continents. The prophets of the Ghost Dance on the Plains remind
us in our continuing struggle against the colonialists.

LC: Evil is everywhere just like the dry heat that parches the landscape.
Everything radiates heat and evil. Where's the rain? Is it coming with the
struggle to retake tribal land as well as with reclaiming ourselves as human
beings, with reclaiming our connection to the earth? Would you comment on
what has been said of your picture of white man's culture, not only sick, but
rather, "it is itself a sickness, bloody and metastasizing, in an already "in-
fected continent," as the *Time* reviewer writes.[3]

LMS: The *Time* magazine reviewer became a little hysterical after reading
Almanac. Almanac tries to catalog those ideas and objects from Europe
which do have value. It is difficult to know what to credit to Europe and what
was stolen from other cultures and appropriated by Europeans. It is the *Time*
magazine reviewer's own self-loathing that leads him to interpret *Almanac*
as a condemnation of white cultures; *Almanac* never says that the white culture is a cancer. The cancer is the secret Gunadeeyah clan which has members
all over the world; their worship of suffering and destruction is the cancer
which afflicts all cultures to some degree. But the world is out of balance
now and the forces of destruction seem to be increasing in every place, in
every community. *Almanac* treats Marx and Jesus with respect, though it is
harsh with their inheritors. Eric is white and he is a good-hearted person, but
not strong enough to survive the world of Beaufrey. Seese is white and she
is not evil, she is powerless and self-destructive. The blonde whose car breaks
down in Winslow and who treats Sterling to sex in the back seat of her car
to pay for its repairs is not evil or mean-hearted.

All human beings committed to the protection and love of Mother Earth
are welcome by the Twin Brothers, Wacah and El Feo. They even send Angelita, La Escapía, to the healers' convention in Tucson to deliver that message.

People of all nations are not only welcome, but we are told about the Dutch and German television crews who begin to document the walk North. We are told that once the European television shows are aired, more Europeans arrive and join the thousands of Indians who are walking North.

As for evil, yes, evil is everywhere and good is everywhere also. The balance of evil to good is a balance that seems disturbed on Earth now, but no single group is evil, just as no person is pure evil or pure good, but instead we are differing proportions of evil and good throughout our lives. *Almanac* is quite stern about Montezuma's sorcery and the secret brotherhood of destruction which both Cortez and Montezuma shared. Evil may seem everywhere because *Almanac* is covering five hundred years in which an imbalance occurs between the forces of destruction in the Universe.

Yes, the rain will follow the Twin Brothers with the sacred macaws who lead the people walking North.

LC: Three pivotal themes already treated in *Ceremony* also shape the meaning and structure of *Almanac*: reverence for the earth; the spirit energy of a story, as we can see in the old Yupik woman and in the fragmentary almanac of tribal narratives which have a living power that would bring all the tribal people to retake and redeem the American continent; then the destroyers whose witchery would turn upon itself, upon them. Tayo in *Ceremony* waits for this to happen at the uranium mine, the same site where in *Almanac* the Giant Stone Snake is pointing south.

Can *Almanac* then be seen as a continuation of *Ceremony*, "an exploded version of the same text,"[4] enlarging its range in terms of colonization and exploitation of tribal people, their common fight to retake the Americas, in the light of a new awareness of a global design which will map the beginning of the twenty-first century?

LMS: Yes, *Almanac* might be seen as an "exploded" version of *Ceremony*, but one should beware of over-simplifying *Almanac*. *Almanac* examines time and history in a way that *Ceremony* only begins to approach. In *Almanac*, I go farther with my thinking about the influence of spirit beings as well as animal beings. I go farther with my thinking about the power of narrative in *Almanac* when I consider the writings of Marx. I go farther in thinking about dreams and their influence over human consciousness.

Whereas *Ceremony* is about one person trying to recover his health and well-being, this is about the whole Earth trying to save herself. *Ceremony* barely hints at the activities and thinking of the Gunadeeyahs, but with Trigg,

Beaufrey, the Police Chief, the Judge, and the rest, the reader gets to see what actually goes on in the minds of these Gunadeeyahs, these worshippers of suffering and destruction. And of course, these "monsters" are not so different from the rest of us.

Ceremony emphasizes ancient links between the Americas and Asia, and focuses on the World War II era. *Almanac* is about a far greater expanse of time, and explores the links between Africa and the Americas. *Ceremony* is about illness and self; *Almanac* is about slavery and otherness. Tayo was ill and wanted to get well. Beaufrey, Menardo, General J., the Police *Turtureres* are ill and they revel in their sickness; they don't ever want to get well. The enslaved ones seek to break free before they sicken and die. Greed as a component of evil is also explored in *Almanac*; the use of economics to terrorize and coerce is also more developed in *Almanac*. *Ceremony* doesn't deal much with economics.

The rain will follow the Twin Brothers with the sacred macaws and the thousands of people walking North. Rain will not follow if La Escapía is forced to use her hand-held rockets to protect the Twin Brothers and the people from attacks by the U.S.

LC: How do you value the reviews of *Almanac*? You know that your novel has been criticized for being too violent, with its picture of white society hideously perverted, attracted to, and excited by the spectacle of death.

LMS: The publishing industry looks to a few big publications for reviews which will sell books. The worst fate is have a book ignored. But even the hysterical reviewer in *Time* and *Newsweek* stated that *Almanac* is a book which cannot be ignored. I was actually surprised at how few negative reviews came out in regional and small city newspapers. The Orlando, Florida, newspaper review was very positive; so was the *Detroit Free Press*. These reviewers represent, for better or for worse, the ordinary readers; the big publications represent commercial publishing interests and the profit motive and academic interests as well; after all, the struggle over curricula and the importance of dead white male culture figures was in full swing when *Almanac* was published. (More about an alleged "conspiracy" to suppress *Almanac* later.) So anyway, out of approximately fifty reviews, including the review in the *Village Voice* Literary Supplement, *USA Today,* and the *Women's Review of Books, New York Times, New Republic*, etc., only the review in *USA Today* was really negative, and I found it and the reviews in *Time* and *Newsweek* to be fascinating documents of white male hysteria at the end of the twentieth century. I am quite proud to have written a novel which so disturbed the Yale Professor of political science who reviewed it that he lost control of himself on paper. I was surprised that *USA Today* would publish such a wildly impassioned outpouring, but I was glad too, because it revealed the lasting effects of *Almanac* on that reviewer. The Ivy League professor from Yale (George Bush and the CIA's *alma mater*) totally lost his cool, and suggested that I need psychiatric help because of my "obsession with the male organ." I laughed and laughed when I came to that part of the review. Typical white male's hysterical response to an outspoken woman: lock her in the looney bin. I knew that the kind of readers that would most enjoy *Almanac* would read that hysterical review and then say to themselves, "Wow! I have to read this book!" I think the reviews in *Time* and *Newsweek* also fall into this category, though these two reviews were not nearly as hysterical as the one in *USA Today*; still these reviews also make it clear that the big issue with *Almanac* is a political rather than literary issue.

I had not one but two reports that Mary Gordon on one occasion and Toni Cade Bambara on another occasion held up a copy of *Almanac* during symposiums and stated that within the New York literary world, attempts had been made to "suppress" this book. I am not acquainted with either Ms. Gordon or Ms. Bambara, and I do not know if they really commented on *Almanac*. My editor at Simon and Schuster is also the editor-in-chief; he fought with the Hungarian freedom fighters when he was in college, and I like to think that whatever enemies *Almanac* had, *Almanac*'s friends were equal. Without someone as powerful as Michael Korda, I doubt *Almanac* would have been published by Simon and Schuster. There was some opposition within Simon and Schuster. The head of publicity treated me rudely and Simon and Schuster bought only one book ad for *Almanac* during the book tour and promotion period. When I received a Lila Wallace *Reader's Digest* Writers Award, Simon and Schuster did not acknowledge my award as the other publishers did for their winning author. The reviewer for the Sunday *New York Times* gave *Almanac* a very positive review, but the *Times* did not include an excerpt from *Almanac* as they usually do when a book receives a positive review. The Simon and Schuster book tour was restricted to the west coast. (The publicity person at Viking Penguin, which bought the paperback rights for *Almanac,* was shocked that Simon and Schuster had not sent me to Minneapolis, Chicago, or the east coast.)

If *Almanac* has enemies, *Almanac*'s friends are equal to them, because in the March 18, 1992, *Rolling Stone* magazine Campus Issue, *Almanac* was number three on the college best-seller list. The number four book was *The Autobiography of Malcolm X,* and it had Spike Lee's movie to thank. The number two book was Cormac McCarthy's *All the Pretty Horses,* which has a prestigious book prize to thank for much publicity. The number one book was Norman MacLean's *A River Runs Through It,* which of course had the hit movie to thank. So *Almanac of the Dead* made it to the number three position despite or maybe because of the reviews it received, and despite or because of its enemies who rallied *Almanac*'s fierce defenders.

As for the outcries against *Almanac*'s portrayal of white society as attracted to and aroused by violence, I think the spectacle of Desert Storm, a giant nation attacking a tiny nation, and then the madness and genocide that devour Serbia and Bosnia easily rebut the charges that *Almanac* portrays white society too violently. Yugoslavia was really quite well off, a country that was in the "first world." Now look. They have bombed themselves clear into the "third world."

During Desert Storm, the U.S. was swept by excitement and festivity generated by the bombing of Iraq. People in the U.S. loved the notion of U.S. tanks burying Iraqui troops alive. Nothing in *Almanac* approximates the depravity of the white men leading the U.S. today; nothing in *Almanac* reveals the "lynch mob" mentality of the ruling class in the U.S. today. I finished writing *Almanac* a few weeks before Operation Desert Storm; I could tell that Bush, and the other white men and toadies to the white men, were aroused and were determined to do some killing, so I included references to Desert Storm veterans in *Almanac* anyway. And I was correct.

A hundred or even fifty years from now, *Almanac* will be judged to be too mild, too soft on Western European culture's compulsion for violence.

Notes

1. Leslie Marmon Silko, *Sacred Water* (Tucson: Flood Plain Press, 1993).
2. Joy Harjo, "The World Is Round: Some Notes on Leslie Silko's *Almanac of the Dead," Blue Mesa Review* 4 (Spring 1992): 207–10.
3. John Skow, "People of the Monkey Wrench," *Time* (Dec. 9, 1991): 60.
4. Harjo, 209.

An Interview with Leslie Marmon Silko

Florence Boos / 1994

From *Speaking of the Short Story: Interviews with Contemporary Writers,* edited by Farhat Iftekharuddin, Mary Rohrberger, and Maurice Lee (Jackson, Mississippi: University Press of Mississippi, 1997), pp. 237–47. Reprinted by permission.

Boos: Do you consider yourself primarily a writer of stories or a novelist?

Silko: I've never tried to categorize what I do according to generic lablels. I'm a writer, and I love language and story. I started out loving stories that were told to me. Growing up at Laguna Pueblo, one is immersed in storytelling, because the Laguna people did not use written language to keep track of history and philosophy and other aspects of their lives.

Imagine an entire culture that is passed down for thousands and thousands of years through the spoken word and narrative, so the whole of experience is put into narrative form—this is how the people know who they are as a people, and how individuals learn who they are. They hear stories about "the family," about grandma and grandpa and others.

When I started out at the University of New Mexico, I took a folklore class, and began to think about the differences between the story that's told and the literary short story. I started writing the "literary" short story, and tried to write it as closely as I could according to the "classical" rules which seemed to manifest themselves in my reading. I wanted to show that I could do it. But I've turned away from this since and haven't really written a short story in the usual sense since 1981. From 1981 to 1989, I worked on *Almanac of the Dead,* and so I don't think of myself as a short story writer. Yet stories are at the basis of everything I do, even non-fiction, because a lot of non-fiction reminiscences or memories come to me in the form of narrative, since that's the way people at home organize all experience and information.

I found the rules of the "classical" short story confining. I think you can see why the post-modernist narrative and the contemporary short story went off in another direction. They're trying to escape the strictures of the formal story form.

I've now tasted the freedom one has with a novel, so I wonder if I'll turn back to more structured forms. I've written one short story, "Personal Property," which I'm going to read tonight, and which purposely breaks some of the rules of the classical short story. Maybe I'm not done with making trouble with the short story form!

Boos: How are your poems related to your stories?

Silko: For me a poem is a very mysterious event . . . my poems came to me mysteriously. I started out to write a narrative, fiction or non-fiction, and something would happen so that the story would organize itself in the form of a narrative poem rather than a short story.

In fact, that happened with "A Story from Bear Country," in *Storyteller.* I intended to make a note about a conversation I had had with Benjamin Barney, a Navajo friend, about the different ways our respective Navajo and Pueblo cultures viewed bears. I started a narrative of our converstion, but something shifted abruptly, and before I knew it, I was writing something that looked more like a poem. At the very end of that poem a voice comes in and says "Whose voice is this? You may wonder, for after all you were here alone, but you have been listening to me for some time now." That voice is the seductive voice of the bears. Benjamin Barney and I had been discussing the notion that if humans venture too close to the bear people and their territory, the people are somehow seduced or enchanted. They're not mauled or killed, but they are seduced and taken away to live with the bears forever.

So I don't have control [over whether my tale becomes a tale or a poem]. I set out to narrate something—either something which actually happened or a story I was told—and after I begin the piece sorts itself into whether it will be a poem or a short story. I find a mixing of the two in *Sacred Water,* a piece that I wrote a couple of years ago—a wanting to have the two together—so that there's really no distinct genre. This story also contained a bit of "nonfiction." I wanted to blend fiction and non-fiction together in one narrative voice.

So I am never far away from oral narrative, storytelling and narration, and the use of narrative to order experience. The people at home believe that there is one big story going on and made up of many little stories, and the story goes on and on. The stories are alive and they outlive us, and storytellers are only caretakers of the story. Storytellers can be anonymous. Their names don't matter because the stories live on. I think that's what people mean when they say that there are no new stories under the sun. It's true—the old stories live on, but with new caretakers.

Boos: You present yourself as a narrative writer, but it struck me as I read *Storyteller* that you also think visually. How do you decide where to put the words on the page?

Silko: I'm a very aural person. On the other hand, my father was a photographer, and when I was a child, I would go in the darkroom, sit quietly on the stool, and watch as the images of the photographs would develop. As I've written in *Storyteller,* there was this old Hopi basket full of snapshots. One of us kids would pull a photograph and say, "Grandma, who's this?" or "what's this?" A photograph would be tied to narration. And when I was a child walking in the countryside, I'd see a certain sandstone formation of a certain shape, or a certain mesa, and someone would say, "Look, see that hill over there? Well, let me tell you . . ."

Through the years I've done a lot of thinking about the similarities and differences between the "literary" story and the story that's told. I began to realize that landscape could not be separated from narration and storytelling. One of the features of the written or old-fashioned short story was the careful, detailed description of its setting. By contrast, in Laguna oral stories, tellers and audience shared the same assumptions, a collective knowledge of the terrain and landscape which didn't need to be retold. That's why something an anthropologist or folklorist has collected may seem sparser than a literary short story; sometimes the oral short story can seem "too sparse." I realized that all communities have shared knowledge, and that the "literary" short story resulted when all over Europe—and all over the world—human populations started to move. People didn't have this common shared ground anymore.

Boos: *Storyteller* seemed to evoke a whole context related to your deep kinship with your family. Even the shapes of the stories seemed to arise from your identification with those telling the stories.

Silko: Right. One of the reasons that *Storyteller* contains photographs was my desire to convey that kinship and the whole context or field on which these episodes of my writing occurred. The photographs include not only those of my family, but of the old folks in the village and places in the village. I started to think of translation [from Laguna]. I realized that if one just works with the word on the page or the word in the air, something's left out. That's why I insisted on having photographs in *Storyteller.* I wanted to give the reader a sense of place, because here place is a character. For example, in the title story, "Storyteller," the main character is the weather and the free, frozen land itself. Or in the story I'm going to read tonight, "Private Property," the community itself is a character—although places and communities are not ordinarily characters in the "classical" literary short story. I felt a need to add in these other [visual] components which before were supposed to be extraneous to the narrative, but which existed at Laguna Pueblo as visual cues—a mountain or a tree or a photograph.

Boos: When you advise your creative writing students, what suggestions do you give about choosing topics or about technique?

Silko: Usually I tell them just to think about a good story, not to think consciously about topic or theme. I tell them that their stories should contain something that they don't know, something mysterious. It's better not to know too much, but to have just the bare bones of an idea, and let the writing be a process of enlightenment for them.

I often say, "Well, you can tell me the idea for the story, so why can't you write it down?" There's a large difference between speaking and writing. But when I'm writing, it's as natural to me as if I were speaking, though the results are different. The most difficult element of writing to teach the student is that ease—writing as if you were talking to yourself or to the wall.

Students are traumatized by the writing process. I've noticed the traumatization begins right from the first grade. Usually kids withstand it till around the seventh or eighth grade, and then they experience a real terror of failure and scolding. People who can talk, who can tell you things, freeze when they sit down in front of a blank piece and a pencil. It shouldn't be difficult to make the transition from speaking to writing, and I blame the United States educational system for the fact that it is.

Boos: Though you speak of an oral narrative tradition, you also remark that you speak and write differently. What's different about the writing process for you, and why do you value that?

Silko: I was conscious that I wasn't as good a storyteller as the storytellers at home, for the people at home are so good at this. An oral performance is just that, so I needed to go off in a room by myself to evoke that same sense of wholeness and excitement and perfection that I seemed to hear all around me [during their performances].

Also, when I'm writing I'm alone. When I'm speaking to an audience, by contrast, I'm very sensitive to what people want from me or expect from me, whether the audience are becoming restless or whatever, and I'm anxious to please and to serve, putting the comfort of others ahead of my own. When I write I'm alone with the voices . . . with the people in my memory. Some of the voices that I'm alone with might even be those of people still living, so that I could go and talk to them outside that door, but when I'm alone in the room writing, a connection with the older voices occurs, which cannot happen for me when I'm storytelling.

Boos: Writing isn't just inscription of stories, then, but something that requires solitude as well?

Silko: Being alone allows me to hear those voices. I think it's aloneness to be able to hear Aunt Susie's voice, for example. If I were in a room with her I would only listen, not write or speak, but solitude enables me to hear [and transcribe] her very distinctive voice. I think it was meant to be distinctive so that I could never forget it.

I've thought a lot about this distinction between oral narration and writing. Storytelling was done in a group so that the audience and teller would respond to each other, and be grounded in the present. As I said, I'm not as good at that, but I learned that it's also dangerous to go into the room alone and hear the voices alone, because those voices from spirit beings who have real presence . . . and bring dangers . . . There's a real danger of being seduced by them, of wanting to join them and remain with them. I'm forty-six, and things are becoming clearer to me, things that before I had only heard about and hadn't experienced, so I couldn't judge.

But now I'm beginning to understand. Old Aunt Susie used to say that when she and her siblings were children, her grandmother started storytelling by bidding the youngest child to go open the door "so that our esteemed ancestors may bring in their gifts for us." But when we tell the stories of those past folks telling stories, they are actually here again in the room. It's therefore dangerous for a storyteller to write in a room alone without others, because those old ancestors are really coming in.

In writing *Almanac of the Dead,* I was forced to listen . . . I was visited by so many ancestors . . . it was very hard. It changed me as a human being. I came to love solitude almost too much, and it was very frightening.

Boos: Don't you ever fear that the presences of the dead might view critically something you wrote?

Silko: No, I've never been afraid. I know the voices of the storytellers, and I know that if you tell their truth and don't try to be self-serving, they aren't dangerous—in fact, they bring great protective power—*great protective power.*

Boos: How do you know what is true rather than self-serving?

Silko: I can tell. One method to avoid self-serving is to use a male protagonist, as in *Ceremony*. I wrote two stillborn versions of *Ceremony* now in the [Beinecke] Library at Yale—though I suspect that the rest of the university may have thought I was the Anti-Christ, so maybe they're not even catalogued! If anyone is interested, they can read the two stillborn drafts—each about sixty pages long—that lead up to *Ceremony.* "Stillborn" is of course such a grim term, but before I sold them to Yale University I looked at them again and saw that they're not really "stillborns" at all, but a necessary part of writing the novel. This gave me new confidence in the process of writing, and all young writers should understand that even those things that we throw in the trash can are necessary to get us to where we want to be. The first two stillborns had *female* protagonists.

Boos: Why would changing to a male protagonist have enabled you to transcend yourself?

Silko: When the characters were females, I identified too closely with them and wouldn't let them do things that I hadn't done or wouldn't do. It's not good to identify too closely with [one's own characters]. All this happened when I was very young; I started writing the "stillborn" versions of *Ceremony* when I was twenty-three.

Boos: Did you start to write short stories before you published poems? You published the poems of *Laguna Woman* quite early.

Silko: I wrote stories before I wrote poems, but the poems were easier to get out. That was because in writing stories I found myself too connected to the main character. Even though I wanted [her] to be a separate character, [she] wouldn't be. When on the third draft of *Ceremony,* I created Tayo, and I was so liberated by working with a male protagonist.

Also, in a matriarchy the young *man* symbolizes purity and virginity—and also the intellectual, the sterile, and the orderly. The female principle was the chaotic, the creative, the fertile, the powerful.

Boos: *Ceremony* struck me as a book about the bonds between men, very deep bonds. Why would it be liberating for you to deal with male bonding and the recovery of a man's sense of himself?

Silko: When I was a little girl, I hung around adults. I was always the kid who wouldn't go off and play with the other kids, but liked to watch and eavesdrop on adults. I come from a culture in which men and women are not segregated, and so I had a great deal of opportunity to listen to the men talking. When I was really small, I listened to World War II and Korean War veterans. They had drinking problems and lacked regular jobs, but they had good souls and good spirits. Perhaps tragedy and anguish and trouble attracted me right away as a little girl, more than the easier parts of life.

Also, the Laguna people lived in a matriarchy, and in a matriarchy one is more afraid of what women may say and think about oneself. Children feel less powerful than their mothers, and men seemed more interesting to them because they too had less power and were more like themselves.

Needless to say, women are a lot happier in a matriarchy than in patriarchal society. Also those elements that had given women their strength and continuity were not nearly as shaken by outside pressures as were those reserved for men. I think this was mainly because when outsiders came in they didn't realize the women's power, and so they left them alone. They stopped more of the things that men did traditionally than those that women did. So you see the men were more broken apart by the invasion. The government imprisoned men for practicing the Pueblo religion. Then of course war came, and the Second World War and the Korean War were devastating for men.

The Pueblo world is the reverse of Anglo-American and mainstream culture, where the final word is the man's word. In the Pueblo world, women have the final word in practical matters. This is a simplification, but women own all the property, children belong to their mother's clan, and all the mundane business—quarrels, problems—are handled by women. The female deity is the main deity, and in the Kiva ceremonies, men dress as women. But formerly the matriarchy was more evenly balanced, for the men were responsible for the hunting and religious ceremonies.

Boos: On the other hand, I've heard the theory that because the Euro-American legal system was so patriarchal, it destroyed certain aspects of Indian life that favored or protected women (by enforcing nineteenth-century laws, for example, which gave a married woman's property to her husband). If so, imposition of foreign laws sometimes diminished women's authority.

Silko: Well, we're only seeing that starting with my generation. It's taken that long for western European misogyny to arrive in the Pueblo. It's true that the conquerors negotiated only with Pueblo men, ignoring the clan mothers, but in the long run, when they destroyed what they thought was important, they left behind the authority of women.

Yet it's true that women are sometimes disadvantaged. A lot of tribal councils were established which didn't give women the right to vote, even though tribal organization was matriarchal. But that's a superficial level of damage, when you think that if the Conquistadors had really understood how important women were, they might have tried to [undermine their power]. Patriarchal attitudes have touched the Pueblo people only in a superficial way.

Boos: Does your identification with Tayo perhaps suggest that an author should try to identify with someone of the opposite sex as a way of moving towards a full presentation of reality?

Silko: Totally. When I was growing up, for a long time I felt that I was "just me." That was easy to be in a matriarchal culture, where women have access to the wide world. Women are everywhere and men are everywhere women are. There isn't this awful segregation that you find even now in the Anglo-American world . . .

Boos: In university life!

Silko: Yes, in university life. In the Pueblo, women crack dirty jokes to men who aren't their husbands or close relatives. There's a lot of banter, and a real feeling of equality and strength within the community. There weren't places where a little girl was told, "Oh, you can't go there!," or things of which a little boy was told, "Oh, you shouldn't do that!" I wasn't told that because I was a little girl, I had to dress or act a certain way. So for a long time, although I didn't think I was *really* a boy, I kind of . . .

Boos: . . . didn't learn *not* to identify with men.

Silko: Yes, I didn't learn not to identify with men. I had a horse and was kind of a tomboy, and I was glad of it. Although I was intensely attracted to men and males, I saw that as a part of being interested in them and watching their activities.

I finished writing *Ceremony* in 1977, when it was still not politically correct for a woman novelist to write from a man's point of view. Feminism in America was still so new that feminists wanted women to write of their own experiences, not those of men. Perhaps too, because my name is Leslie, which is kind of androgynous, they may not have realized that I was a woman author. For awhile I didn't hear anything from the feminists. I felt I was punished for using a male protagonist, but that was the only way I could write.

Boos: I'd like to ask you about some of your fellow contemporary women writers who have written novels about their own cultures—Michelle Cliff,

Toni Morrison, and Maxine Hong Kingston among them. Are there contemporary women writers whose works you've read a great deal, or whose works you believe resemble yours in any way?

Silko: Of course Toni Morrison's work has been important to me, and that of Maxine Hong Kingston. Both women have encouraged me to believe that I'm on the right track, and that we share something—that it's not so lonely, for there are other women and other people thinking and writing about the same sorts of things.

Boos: It seemed to me that you portrayed discrimination profoundly from within, not preaching about it, but analyzing its different layers and guises. Might I ask you to comment on contemporary Native American political issues and conflicts?

Silko: I'll tell you what's happening in terms of history. The largest city in the world is Mexico City, and officials don't really know its population. The uncounted ones are the *Indios,* the Indian people. A huge, huge change is on the horizon, indeed it's already underway—and there's nothing you can do.

A couple months ago at sundown, a freight train came up from Nogales through Tucson, covered, crawling with human beings. People were sitting on top, people were hanging on the side—and so the great return to Aztlan which the Chicano people talk about is coming to pass in a big way. The Zapatista uprising on January 1, 1994, was one of the most important signalings of what is to come. After that, small demonstrations were held all over Mexico and the United States and Canada, showing the solidarity of Native American people throughout the Americas. We sense that the rising on January first was a sign of this awakening.

The most important thing right now which people must watch out for is jingoism and hysteria about immigrants and immigration. [The U.S. government] is building an iron curtain, a steel wall—Rudolfo Ortiz calls it the Tortilla Curtain—but it's ugly. They're trying to seal off Mexico from the United States. But [those they are sealing off] are Indians, Native Americans, American Indians, original possessors of this continent, and [those who hate them] want to create a hysteria here so that it will justify U.S. troops opening fire and shooting and killing. The future could be a horrendous blood bath and upheaval not seen since the Civil War.

Right now the border patrol stops [Indian] people. I've been stopped three or four times and have had dogs put on me.

Boos: Oh!?

Silko: This happened to me on my way from Albuquerque to Tucson. Many peopole in the rest of the United States don't understand that the U.S. government is destroying the civil rights of *all* citizens living near the border. Something terrible is developing, and it's being sold to the American people, or shoved down their throats through this hysteria over immigrants and the fear that their jobs will be taken. But I see a frightening collision on the horizon! I'll tell you something—the powers that be, those greedy corrupt white men like Rostenkowski and all those criminals in the United States Congress—their time is running out very soon! The forces from the south have spiritual power and legitimacy that'll blast those thieves and murderers right out of Washington, D.C.

Boos: Are there particular Native American groups that you see working effectively against government wrongs?

Silko: Ah, ah, this change that's coming will not have leaders. People will wake up and know in their hearts that it's beginning. It's already happening across the United States. The change isn't just limited to Native Americans. It can come to Anglo-Americans, Chicanos, African-Americans as well. Every day people wake up to the inhumanity and violence this government perpetrates on its own citizens, and on citizens all over the world. That's why the change will not be stopped, for it will be a change of consciousness, a change of heart.

We don't need leaders. They can't stop [this revolution.] They can shoot some, they can kill some—like they have already—but this is a change that rises out of the earth's very being—a Hurricane Andrew, a Hurricane Hugo, an earthquake of consciousness. This earth itself is rebelling against what's been done to it in the name of greed and capitalism. No, there are no groups which bring change. They aren't needed. This change that's coming is much deeper and much larger. Think of it as a natural force—human beings massed into a natural force like a hurricane or a tidal wave. It will happen when the people come from the South, and when the people here [in the North and Midwest] understand.

One morning people will just wake up, and we'll all be different. That's why the greedy powerful white men will not be able to stop what happens, because there will be nothing to grab onto. There are no Martin Luther Kings to shoot, so the FBI can give up on that!

There's no one that can stop us, because [the return to Aztlan] will be a change inside of *you!* It will happen without your knowing it. And this won't happen because someone preached at you, threatened you with prison, put a gun to your head. No, you'll wake up [yourself]. It will come to you through dreams!

Boos: No Martin Luther King will have helped bring about change, but what about Leslie Marmon Silko? How do you see yourself contributing to this movement?

Silko: Just by telling people—"Look, this is happening!" As I tried to make clear in *Almanac of the Dead,* you don't have to do anything, for the great change is already happening. But you maybe might want to be aware of what was coming, and you might want to think about the future choices that you might have to make. Though as I said, in your heart, you will already know.

Boos: Amen, and thank you.

An Interview with Leslie Marmon Silko

Thomas Irmer and Matthias Schmidt / 1995

First appeared at the Alt-X Online Network at http://www.altx.com. Reprinted by permission.

Alt-X: Is this your first trip to Germany?

LMS: Yes, it is. And I am very excited to come to Leipzig because I am very interested in the transition that is going on here.

Alt-X: This interest is related to the themes of your most recent novel, *Almanac* . . .

LMS: Yes. You know when I began writing *Almanac* the wall had not come down yet. But this is very complex. First of all, back then, the people in the Philippines stopped the tanks when Marcos had to leave, and I have my character in *Almanac* who watches satellite television and thinks, "Oh, people all over the world will see this." This is the idea of Marshal McLuhan, the global village. And then, when all these other things occurred, it seemed to me that, perhaps, that's how my character could imagine all these events. And when the big change came here, I had been working and writing on that part. It was pretty amazing.

Alt-X: Most critics call you the first Native American woman novelist with your first novel *Ceremony.*

LMS: I guess that's true. The reason I hesitate in my answer is that we in the United States have so much ignorance about our own history. There might have been some Native American woman long ago that we don't know about. But I suppose no, I am the first. It seems hard to believe that it would take so long.*

Alt-X: No one else was in print before *Ceremony?* If this is true, it means that you established a new line in American literature.

LMS: I guess so. [Laughs.] You know I just do things and later on people tell me, "Oh, this and this!" but it was not what I had in mind.

---

*Editor's Note: In fact, two novels by Native American women are now known to have been published before Silko's: S. Alice Callahan's *Wynema, A Child of the Forest* (1891); and *Cogewea, The Half-Blood,* by Hum-ishu-ma, or Mourning Dove (1927).

Alt-X: But this is a great achievement for a writer. You started writing poetry, drawing from old Indian legends handed down by your ancestors.

LMS: Yes, when one grows up in the Pueblo community, in the Pueblo tribe the people are communal people, it is an egalitarian communal society. The education of the children is done within the community; this is in the old times before the coming of the Europeans. Each adult works—with every child, children belong to everybody, and the way of teaching is to tell stories. All information—scientific, technological, historical, religious—is put into narrative form. It is easier to remember that way. So when I began writing when I was at the University of New Mexico, the professor would say, now you write your poetry or write a story, write what you know, they always tell us. All I knew was my growing up at Laguna, recallings of some other stories that I had been told as a child.

Alt-X: So this type of education was exclusively based upon oral traditions and not on a written culture, as in McLuhan's terms.

LMS: Yes, it is a culture in which each person has a contribution to make. The older you are the more valued you are but each person is valued. The oral tradition stays in the human brain and then it is a collective effort in the recollection. So when he is telling a story and she is telling a story and you are telling a story and one of us is listening and there is a slightly different version or a detail, then it is participatory when somebody politely says, I remember it this way. It is a collective memory and depends upon the whole community. There is no single entity that controls information or dictates but this oral tradition is a constantly self-correcting process.

Alt-X: What is the significance of the content of these old stories and legends today? In *Ceremony* and *Storyteller,* old legends literally appear in your stories which are set in the modern world and which clearly show the impact of degeneration and even self-destruction—alcoholism, unemployment, disillusionment, uprootedness, and alienation. What is the power of these old stories today in the Laguna Pueblo reservation?

LMS: Something in writing *Ceremony* that I had to discover for myself was indeed that the old stories still have in their deepest level a content that can give the individual a possibility to understand. What frightens human beings is to not be able to understand or to see what is happening. So in *Ceremony* I worked with some of the old stories, for example the Ck'o'yo gambler, Pa'caya'nyi. He was a magician and in the old story he came, and he tricked the people into neglecting their care of the corn fields, of their devotion to the Corn Mother. This magician told them they didn't have to work hard, by magic he could do things. Listen to him, come to him. So, in the story, the people leave their corn fields and neglect the Corn Mother's altar and they are amazed by this magician. But that is all that it was, all magic. And while the people were enamored by this magician, the Corn Mother became angered and sad and then she left. And all the animals left and all the plants went away, a great drought came. The people found themselves in a terrible disaster; they had been lured away by this flashy, interesting, fast-talking conman. So in *Ceremony* we have in this old story the idea that we human beings are not dependable creatures. We are easily lured from one way or another. We get out of balance and out of harmony with our natural surroundings, and also we can get out of harmony with one another. And then it is quite difficult and painful, but necessary, to make a kind of ceremony to find our way back. I began to realize that hasn't changed. Human beings can have lessons of things that happened in the past, in history, and say, look, this is what happens. But somehow people sometimes won't pay attention, won't listen, and we have to suffer through and have to learn again, remember all over again why it is that we have to have a certain respect or care for hard work and for working with one another. There is no magic that is going to hand things over. When I wrote *Ceremony*, I realized that this old story is still very relevant, even now; even though these old stories take place in the past they have meaning now. Oral literatures of the indigenous populations worldwide contain these kinds of valuable insights. When Sigmund Freud wrote his *Interpretation of Dreams,* he began to respect folklore. You can look at the old stories that were told among the tribal people here in a north country and see that within them is the same kind of valuable lessons about human behavior and that we need them still.

Alt-X: Could one say this is a reinterpretation of the old legends?

LMS: Well, no, it's not reinterpretation. I think their spirit is unbroken because of the oral tradition. If you think, five hundred years, that is how long Europeans are in the Americas, is not a very long time. Because for 18,000 years there is evidence, and perhaps longer, of the Pueblo people being in that land. So for five hundred years of Christianity and the conflict with it, how many generations are this? Not that many. The interpretation of the old stories remains the same because of the oral tradition. It goes back through time so that the immediacy is now. It is very important how time is seen. The Pueblo people and the indigenous people of the Americas see time as round, not as a long linear string. If time is round, if time is an ocean, then something that happened five hundred years ago may be quite immediate and real, whereas something inconsequential that happened an hour ago could be far away. Think of time as an ocean always moving.

What is interesting to me about Einstein and post-Einsteinian physics and some of the discoveries in particle physics is what they have discovered about the nature of time. The curvature of time in space. So I grew up among people whose experience of time is a bit different. In their sense of time five hundred years is not a far distance and that's why there is no need for the reinterpretation. That passage of time doesn't mean the same thing to us as it might mean in a culture where the people stretch the string out and say, oh, this was a long time ago. That is not the way my people experience time.

Alt-X: So the wisdom of storytelling doesn't need reinterpretation, doesn't need the making up of new things?

LMS: No, not at all. I was waiting to come over here because I am very interested in the pre-Christian traditions in Germany and the British Isles, very interested in what the people were like before the Christians came up here. Because, in a sense, there are many similarities. I am not trying to say it is the same but, perhaps, there are some similarities of what happened with the tribal people that were once here, the people that were so close to the earth and the trees. And then Christianity comes in the same way it came to us. There is an old story from the British Isles about a white cow, the magic cow, and she would give enough milk to take care of the people. They must never take too much. So then when a witch comes with a bucket with holes in it and keeps milking the cow and takes too much, the cow goes away. This is an old folk story from England. What is it telling us? Not to be greedy, if the cow is symbolic of the natural forces.

There is a wisdom in these old stories, and it is no accident that filmmakers and novelists have used archetypes out of these old stories because that is the wisdom. So even now, in film and literature deep down underneath, these old stories stay with the people. Christianity has tried continuously to make fun of them, to devalue them, to laugh at them. Also, one of the reasons I was interested in coming to Germany is because so many Germans have been interested in Native American culture. I wonder why. Why? Because I think there is an old longing and not so much has been lost either. You cannot stop it, the land speaks to you. This is maybe the reason for the emergence of the Green Party from here; you must not be so quick to think that some of the old things are not here anymore.

Alt-X: But in your novel *Almanac* you have a character say that the German Green Party could also stand for reactionary politics that is driving at the process of natural selection, a king of ecological biologism against the people.

LMS: [Laughs.] Yes.

Alt-X: I have one more general question, please. Could you tell us about your career? It seems remarkable that your beginnings as a writer coincide with the revitalization of Native American culture in the U.S. in the 1970s, with the breakthrough of N. Scott Momaday in the late 1960s, with the politics of self-determination, when Indians got a lot more attention or, for example, Indian art, like on the book jackets of *Ceremony,* went into the museums. Could you please contextualize your own biography?

LMS: It was a kind of renaissance, I suppose. Actually, in the 1930s there was a novelist, a Flathead Indian named D'Arcy McNickle, who published some novels then. It was a brief moment of hopeful liberalism, but it quickly disappeared because of the war and everything. It is difficult to pinpoint why, but in the 1960s, around the time when Momaday's books got published, there was this new interest. Maybe it was not new, but people became more aware of indigenous cultures. It was an opening up worldwide, there was this interest in Asian religions and so forth. It wasn't just in the United States. That the Germans are interested in Native Americans is good for us in the U.S. Anyway, this came about and it is odd. It is just a coincidence that I would be starting to write in this moment and Momaday's *House Made of Dawn* would be published as a success. It is hard to account for the coincidence of time, and it becomes even more spooky and strange with the *Almanac* and its timing. I think it has to do with that shift worldwide, but this was for outsiders. The Pueblo people, for example, never forgot that we were an independent nation. The King of Spain gave land grants to us long before there was a United States, long before the Pilgrims ever settled on the east coast. We Pueblo people were dealing with the Spanish government and the King of Spain. We were conquered nations but we were still sovereign nations and they applied international law to us. We did not forget, even though the Anglo-Americans came from the east coast of the United States and stole that land from Mexico and took over. Our peoples, we still always have the feeling that we were sovereign nations, and even though these ignorant Anglo-Americans came and tried to treat us as some kind of lesser human beings, we knew the truth and we already had these relations in international law earlier. So we had our pride innocent of nationhood or community, and when this interest suddenly came up in the 1960s, it came from the outsiders, the ignorant Anglo-Americans that suddenly let us publish our books. But we had always had these other feelings. From generation to generation the people had been telling stories, and Scott Momaday could not have written that book if it had not been for the careful nurturing, for the care of the stories and his old grandmother he talks about. It is the same with me. We were just waiting for this and then the time was coming. And now the door is open, is open wide. But to open the door I have to thank the Germans, the Japanese, I have to thank all the rest of the world. Because if we just depended upon Anglo-Americans and their attitude towards us, who knows what would have happened to us. In other words, we feel that we get cultural, intellectual, spiritual support from all the people outside the United States. So this renaissance, in a sense, was helped, everyone participated including the Germans who have been so interested in things Native American. There are no isolated people, there is truly now a global village and it matters.

Alt-X: Almost every German child grows up with stories about Indians and novels about the frontier. Of course, there is always this double image of the American Indian, the noble savage and the mysterious evil. This phenomenon certainly needs some psychological interpretation, as you say yourself, why so many people feel attracted to indigenous cultures. Have you read Karl May?

LMS: No, I have not, but I heard a lot about him.

Alt-X: So many Germans are familiar, one way or another, with American Indians and some of their traditions, but not with the term you use for them. What is your definition of "indigenous people"?

LMS: When I say indigenous people I mean people that are connected to the land for, let's say, a thousand or two thousand years. But of course human populations were always moving, moving, moving, and if it is true what scientists say that the mother of all of us is from Africa, we all spread from Africa. I use that term because I like to think about people all over the world. If I just say American Indian or Native American that is precise and that pinpoints what I am talking about for the moment. But my interest is in people that were connected to the land, indigenous people all over the world including in Europe. The idea is if you were born sure you have a place in this world. So everybody is indigenous. More specifically, I mean it to apply to populations who have been connected to a land for at least some thousands of years. You can see similarities in some of the struggles of indigenous peoples in Africa, in the Americas, in Asia. But then, if you go back in time, think about ancient people here and how the outsiders came in and brought in this other religion and began to destroy the tribal organization that the people here had. That's why I think, maybe, the young Germans have this interest. Maybe it is not about us. Sometimes things appear to be about another culture, but maybe this phenomenon is really about *this* culture, that there is some need that human beings had. I believe that human beings are a force of nature. Huge mass migrations like what happened in Rwanda, the boatloads of people from Albania to Italy, then you think, Wow! people are like water, like waves. So we are natural, we are part of the natural world, we are not separate. There is some yearning, some longing; we know that we are part of the trees, and the earth, and the water. Although Christianity and other sorts of things have tried to come in and to separate us, that old, old longing is there. So, perhaps these young German boys and girls, if people want to pretend to be American Indians, maybe it is really about something long taken away from the people here.

Alt-X: It doesn't have to do, in the first place, with the nomadic tribal culture? Because there are also American Indians that built their own cities, the Maya built great cities, an urban culture we would say today. What is the character of indigenous people here; is city life in opposition to nature?

LMS: These cities were not considered to be in opposition to nature or the countryside. There were tribes who moved around, but there were also tribes who established their own place. But there is no contradiction in the cities. For example, the way these cities were made and laid out, not only the Maya but also in Peru, the Inca cities, the positioning of the buildings was in harmony with astronomy, so that the city itself worked as an observatory. It was all dictated by the positions of the stars. So that the cities had this organic connection to the natural world. And the worship centers in the old Mayan cities would always have a connection with the underwater springs. So the way that people perceived themselves in their cities was not in opposition to nature but it was a part of it. In the European world this opposition between the urban and the rural plays a great role, but those people didn't see it that way.

Alt-X: Our cities are organized by banking, insurance companies, and the stock market.

LMS: Exactly. I see all these cranes and equipments for the reconstruction of Leipzig's downtown from the window of my hotel. What's going on here is a kind of colonization. There is such a contrast between the old and the

new. Yes, it is all about bankers and investments and capital. I wonder how
long we can use these artificial constructs of currency exchange and investment theories. I wonder how long we can use those rules to dictate to flesh
and blood, to the earth, to water, to trees. Remember that human beings are
a natural force. It is very disturbing; I was just reading in the financial section
about the difficulties for agriculturists in the European common market. Because of currency exchanges, it makes it so difficult to move the produce. In
the old days in Mexico City they had a huge market—trading was very important—and exchange; it was so easy to trade some corn for some bananas.
But now because of these currencies and finances, a simple transaction—I
trade you this; you bring me that—they have made it into something really
not connected with any reality at all. It has actually been this way for a while.
In the U.S. they dump milk, they pour it out on the ground, and they burn
food because they want to brace the prices. This is some kind of madness
and no human beings in the whole wide world in other times had less respect
for food. But we are told they must do this. Why? Because of these strange
rules of international banking, investment, and currency exchange. This is
what all people worldwide have to face; this is what we have to think about.

Alt-X: Again, we are at the heart of your novel *Almanac of the Dead*. I
like to call it a novel about the collapse of the Christian-capitalist society in
the near future. . . .

LMS: Thank you. [Laughs.]

Alt-X: . . . and I have rarely come across a book as complex and immense
as your novel. Peopled with many characters, it is a novel full of action, but
actually a book about the idea that the order of things will change soon, that
the tribal people will take over the Americas as well as African tribal people
may take over Europe, a millennial book about five centuries of injustice.
Could you tell us how this novel emerged? Was there a center in the beginning before you went to work on it for more than ten years? How was the
actual process of creation?

LMS: In the beginning, it was supposed to be a short simple novel, my
second novel. Everyone tells you, if you are a novelist, that after your first
novel, if it is very successful as mine was, for the second one you better take
it easy. So I thought, okay. I had moved from New Mexico to Arizona, to
Tucson. It was all a very new landscape for me; there is a big difference
between the landscapes. I noticed in Tucson that there was a lot of drug
trafficking. In the early 1980s, there were all these activities and rumors in

Tucson. So I decided I would make a very short, simple, commercial novel. Something that anyone could read, not political, something that I would call a cops-and-robbers novel about cocaine smuggling.

Alt-X: A political thriller?

LMS: Not even a political thriller. Part of me said, you will be okay to sell out, make something commercial, something they will eat up. And then, I started looking into the police in Tucson, and they were so corrupt, and then, as I started writing I found out that the U.S. government was bringing the cocaine in because they wanted to finance the Contras to fight the Sandinistas. That is common knowledge and yet a big scandal, and the U.S. covered it up. The CIA glutted the cocaine market in the U.S. and brought the price down. They would bring it in with military aircraft. So this was common knowledge in Tucson, and when I started writing I began to realize this is not simple, what is going on. I began to lose control of the novel and to feel that all of the old stories came in, and I felt the presence of spirits. It was taken over. I meant for it to take only two years to write, and pretty soon after the years went by and it just went on and on. And I began to remember reading about Zora Neale Hurston, who has a wonderful book, *Tell My Horse,* and this title is a reference to voodoo religion, a new religion that was born in the Americas. African slaves ran away in the Caribbean and met the Caribbean Indians. Together they made a new, indigenous American religion. Zora Neale Hurston's book talks about when the spirits come they ride you, you become their horse. They use you. And so I began to realize that from the time I was a little girl and the old folks at home had told me little stories about the loss, and the hurt, and the anger of five hundred years that I had been always groomed—I had not realized it—but for generations they have been waiting for somebody. And now it seemed it came down upon me, but not just for me, or for the Native American people, but to think about all people. So the novel had to be bigger. That's why I had to bring in Germans and to talk about Japanese. A burden that had come down to me over hundreds of years, I believe. I was the one that had to serve these spirits. So the first part of the book was very, very difficult. I was horrified when I wrote about the killer of the little boys, this serial killer, I was horrified—where did this come from? In 1986, I stopped for a while because in Arizona we had an election and a terrible, racist man was elected governor. I was outraged and he had been elected with only thirty-five percent of the vote, one of the peculiarities of our political system. So I went down to my writing office, and I was having trouble with getting control of what was happening, so I went outside and sprayed graffiti on the side of this building against this terrible man who had been elected. Voters decided that we had to get rid of him, and the only way was with signatures, which was almost impossible. So I put the graffiti on the wall and I was very much involved with that and I left the book for a while. One morning I went there and thought, what is going to happen with my novel, and I looked at the wall and saw a giant snake. I would paint a giant snake on the side of the wall. So I went inside to get paints—I am a frustrated visual artist—and painted a giant snake on the wall. This wall is very prominent in downtown Tucson.

Would I make a fool of myself because everyone can see this crazy lady painting? I kept painting and painting, and I decided if I could make it work and look right I could finish the novel. I worked for about six months and the snake came and a message came and it was in Spanish: the people are cold, the people are hungry, the rich have stolen the land, the rich have stolen freedom. The people cry out for justice, otherwise revolution. I put it on the wall in Spanish because at that time in Arizona they outlawed Spanish; they made English the legal language. That's bullshit in the American Southwest where Spanish has been there longer than the English language. In rebellion to that, I put my language in Spanish. So there is a giant snake and he has skulls in his stomach and that's his message. In the part of town where I was working, the homeless, especially women and children on the streets, were an increasing number due to the U.S. policy of the 1980s. My painting was very close to the place where people were camping out and living in cars. When I finished that drawing I was told at home that the snake was a messenger—it is a messenger to the Pueblo people, you see—and that he came to help me finish the novel. And the other two thirds of the novel went just like that—because of the snake. That's how Mexico came in, the revolution, the uprising in Chiapas, that's how I knew.

Alt-X: Did you use historical materials for writing the novel? I was reminded of Eduardo Galeano's books, *Memories of Fire,* for example, or his first one that translates in German, *The Cut Veins of Latin America.*

LMS: Oh, yes! He was working on his recent books at the same time I was. He is an admirer of my work. He sent me copies, even in the galley, and I opened the package and thought, oh, somebody else is doing the same thing in the same breadth of vision. And then I looked and I realized he was doing it in a little different way. But of course, I work with the novel and he is a historian. Maybe both are complementary. Yes, I was aware of those books and I admire them. He also admires the *Almanac.*

Alt-X: A more technical thing: What about the chapter headings? I read that at first the whole *Almanac* was one block of text but the publisher didn't agree with that. And then you came up with the wonderful idea of a map, and one could also say that the novel maps the history of the Americas.

LMS: You know *Ceremony* is just one piece. When I delivered *Almanac,* yes, it was like a mountain and my editor couldn't bear it. He said, maybe we could have three or four chapter breaks. Then I remembered almanacs, not just the Native American Mayan almanacs but also Western European almanacs or medicine almanacs in the U.S. have many little, different sections. All of a sudden I became aware of, yes, what needed to be done was many, many chapters so that the chapter headings themselves could tell a story or express something.

Alt-X: But then, the chapter headings transcend the normal geography and history and lead us into the fourth and the fifth world. I only know the term fourth world from how the French philosopher Jean Baudrillard uses it for the disenfranchised. What is your understanding of the fourth world and the fifth world?

LMS: The fourth world now is the disenfranchised, and the fifth world is different. The world that the capitalists envision is the one-world economy; that is their fifth world. But the fifth world is a new consciousness in the hearts of all human beings, the idea that the earth is shared and finite, and that we are naturally connected to the earth and with one another. Arbitary political boundaries will fall away, so my reference to the fifth world is totally different from the one they are attempting to bring in now, this single capitalistic system.

Alt-X: Is it a transformation of the fourth world, does it grow out of there?

LMS: Yes, a gradual transformation. My sense of it is it's inexorable, unstoppable, it's emotion, despite what we see around us. For example, the earthquake in Kobe, Japan. Let's think about the earth, let's think about natural forces. Human beings have deluded themselves, fooled themselves to think that they can control nature, that they can control the human body which is a part of nature. They make war on the human body, telling you what you can eat and not eat. They cannot control nature. They put the ports at Kobe because it was believed to be the safest area; there was not supposed to be an earthquake like that. And yet that earthquake comes and it shakes the stockmarket in Japan. Or this little capitalist who has been with some English bank in Singapore, and boom! it went down. Over time, this is my

notion of things, this organic transformation is very slow and interior. It is
within human beings. It is not some outside political or governmental force.
This change happens from within, and it is a change that recognizes that
human beings cannot and do not control nature. I still feel confident that over
time I am able to feel hopeful. It was difficult writing this novel because so
much of it is to confront what is now the fourth world, and not to say it is
better to commit suicide. That was one of the deeper messages of the old
stories: the earth will humble us. It humbled us just recently and it will
humble us again and again, that we would have faith in the earth and that the
people will correct these aberrations.

Alt-X: One of your characters, Angelita, admires Karl Marx a lot, but only
as the great storyteller who vividly talks about exploitation while his theory
lacks the wisdom of human spirituality and the earth. Do we need theory and
analysis at all unless they come as stories and tales? There is a lot of political
theory in your novel, but always embedded in the stories.

LMS: That dichotomy that separates so much in Western European
thought leads to a kind of schizophrenia. As I was referring earlier to it, there
is plenty of food and people are starving. How can that be? It is a kind of
madness. Certainly we can have theory and abstract thinking. Let's go back
to the Mayans; they possessed the zero. Only the Chinese, the Arabic, and
the Mayans had the zero with which to perform higher mathematics. The
Arabic people introduced the zero to the Europeans so that they could begin
doing higher mathematics. For the Mayans all knowledge in history, technology, and religion was embedded in narrative. That does not prevent ambitious
thinking. They were great astronomers; they could calculate the passage of
Venus. I read this one book that today even with computers one cannot understand the precision of the Mayans. So it is not necessary to separate the two.
It is important not to let the story, the narrative, that connection wander too
far away, because then it becomes too separated and it is no longer any real
living benefit. If you leave this kind of speculation in the narrative, it always
grounds it with the people and with history. My character falls in love with
Marx. In the U.S. people are not familiar with his work, and I had a hard time
to get all the books for my research. I had been reading in *Das Kapital* the
stories about exploitation, and I found the beauty of his stories and their
power. It is all there. It was at the time when all the totalitarian capitalists in
the U.S. were celebrating. I was thinking: more than ever he is important. So
I decided that I would have my character express the power of those stories,

even though I understood that the most disillusioned people were the ones who had to live with Marxism. But I differentiate: I say his followers blew it, in the same way perhaps Jesus Christ's followers corrupted his ideas, or perhaps Mohammad's followers too. I realized that Marx and Engels had looked at egalitarian communal societies in Native American communities. Marx read one anthropologist describing those. So I decided to make this joke that Karl Marx was on the right track when he was studying Native American communities practicing their communism. Well, he got it wrong because he missed the spiritual part. But that did not invalidate his ideas about communal living. We should never stop thinking about that. Also, I am a rebellious person and at the time when everybody said, Capitalism won, Communism lost, I was going to say: Baloney!

Alt-X: Maybe we can put it this way: his stories about the exploitation in nineteenth century England were the groundwork, but then he came up with the wrong conclusions, which were another variety of the great rationalization process, another form of the rationalization of the economy. Morris Berman's *The Reenchantment of the World* comes to my mind here. This concept of rationalization within Marxism is not explicitly discussed by your character, yet she sees herself in conflict with the orthodox Communists from Cuba. Another interesting point in *Almanac* is that you always associate economic greed and its political forces with sexual perversity. Do you have a specific theory about this?

LMS: I did not realize that myself until the writing; then it emerged for me too. Before I wrote this novel I would not have connected them. I cannot rationally explain this but I do believe it comes from living in the United States. There was a famous cannibal who lived on Long Island, Mr. Fish, a descendant of one of the Mayflower families, these distinguished founding families. And here is the connection with Marx: he talks about "the devouring of children" in nineteenth century exploitation. There was something about Mr. Fish eating children on Long Island for nineteen years before they caught him. This is what you hear more and more these days: dismemberment of bodies . . .

Alt-X: The serial killer phenomenon of the 1980s . . .

LMS: Yes, it was weird. More and more appeared as I was writing my novel. After I had written this part of the novel, Jeffrey Dahmer was discovered. He was eating his victims and I was writing my novel. My God! I don't know whether it is true but again, I think it has something to do with that the body is nature, and they try to control rivers and now it is about the body. Is this the final thing when you have the selling of organs? Capitalism is about the bottom line. Right now we have a discussion about health care in the U.S. They are talking about cutting costs and somebody pointed out that it is cheaper if someone dies than if he lives. That's a fact. The irony is that the best thing for us is to all die. This is the quickest thing to do when we get sick: let us die. The purpose of the worker in the U.S. after they have been replaced with machines is to provide a new frontier. Now—they want people to be sick because they make money out of their sickness, and if it comes down to the bottom line, they better die. Also, we have about one million people in prisons; it is an industry now. Poor unemployed people take drugs and end up in prison. They make laws to enforce these on them, a new industry. Drugs and prisons—we pull apart the body and break it down—for profit. Then the organ transplants . . .

Alt-X: In nineteenth century machinery one arm was needed, now it may be a liver or a kidney. There is only a part that is needed, not the whole.

LMS: Not the whole. Isn't that interesting?

Alt-X: How was the reception of *Almanac* in the U.S.? I haven't read a contemporary anti-capitalist novel like that. The apparently white reviewer in *Time* magazine felt so threatened that he charged you of self-righteousness. How do you deal with this?

LMS: [Laughs.] There was even a worse review in *USA Today* by a political science professor at Yale. He starts out, oh she wrote *Ceremony,* that's a great novel. You know he wants to start out like he is rational. When he started to talk about *Almanac,* he completely lost control. The *Time* magazine and *Newsweek* reviewers kept their emotions under control but he just exploded and said: she needs psychiatric help because of her preoccupation with the male organ. It was outrageous. So the review was beautiful because it would make people read my book. Honestly, I was very nervous and expected worse in *Time* magazine, worse in *Newsweek.* I was afraid. For ten years I was locked in my room and not only was I sensing things like Jeffrey Dahmer but also the feelings of other Americans. So there is a whole stack of reviews which show that they understand; they got it. We Americans are very ignorant of Marxism, of our own history, and actually I was amazed and gratified that it was as well received. I expected the hysteria of all of these old Anglo-American males. In the Native American community people love this book; it gives them hope. When I started out in 1981 I had no idea it would be a statement against capitalism. You know, when I sold *Almanac* to Simon and Schuster, a very conservative publisher, I sold them the first 600 pages of the manuscript when it still was a dope novel. I tricked them. If they had seen the whole thing they never would have bought it; they got tricked. The publication in the U.S. is probably by accident; they didn't understand what it was.

Alt-X: A cultural terrorist act?

LMS: That's what it was. When I finished the novel the suitcase was already on the airplane. Simon and Schuster was embarrassed by it, and there were attempts to suppress the book. The enemies, in trying to attack it, created great powerful allies. It was too late. Sometimes the more you try to suppress something the more you help it.

Alt-X: Actually, it is a surprise that you are here with U.S.I.A., sponsored by the U.S. government.

LMS: It makes me happy. [Laughs.] You know the U.S. government to me is an illegitimate government; it is founded on stolen land, founded on the bones and blood of the African slaves and the Native American slaves. So it is my birthright to use the U.S. and it is important. Somebody has to tell the truth. I believe that all over the world the people are better than their leaders. Maybe in our evolution, we have evolved to the point where we don't need governments, these centralized, authoritarian, totalitarian institutions, masquerading oligarchies. The earthquake in Japan, the great bushfires in California—when disaster comes people organize themselves, which is fine.

Alt-X: What will the future be like? In *Almanac* you have your characters speculate about a whole bunch of scenarios with open endings: eco-warriors, a guerilla war in southern Mexico (which is happening right now), New Age philosophy, the end of history with rich people in outer space, or with total war, ecocatastrophies, etc. What do you personally see is going to come?

LMS: I don't know. The reason I leave many open endings is to let the magic of the *Almanac* work. Me, personally? I believe we will have these complex convergences. The earthquake in Japan brings down a bank in England. I see the synergy, the interrelation that all things could coalesce in a hopeful way. The people will take care of themselves locally. Decentralization, natural catastrophies, riots, more migrations . . .

Alt-X: How about the electronic revolution, as with the computer specialist Awa Gee in *Almanac*?

LMS: Hackers like him will be part of it. If all these forces could interconnect in a way that would bring down this world capitalism . . . See, a few
Mayan Indians in Chiapas shake North America; the Brazilian market, the
Argentinian market is shaky. I went down to Chiapas and saw how powerful
these 30,000 people in San Cristóbal de las Casas were. It wasn't just poor
Indians, it's Mexicans, white people. What is happening in Mexico is the
change of consciousness. Of course, it is the middle class that has the most
to lose, but people start thinking about things wider and bigger. There is
some spirit rising out of the land. To answer your question, I see something
positive. It doesn't matter if I live to see it. The people I come from, we don't
say everything has to happen in an individual lifetime; how egotistical.

Alt-X: What led to the German publication by Rogner and Bernhard with
Zweitausendeins, a publisher with some renown for courageous and risky
books? Were others not interested?

LMS: Possibly it was due to the length and also the subject matter that no
one else picked it up. Rogner and Bernhard had published *Ceremony,* and I
am just glad that they continued with the *Almanac.* Only the Germans have
been brave enough so far. A Spanish translation is being discussed. I sent a
copy to China and I wouldn't even mind if it violates international copyright.

Alt-X: How do you see your position as a writer between different cultures? Is one right to say you are a global writer, a global novelist of an open
world?

LMS: I see myself as a member of the global community. My old folks
who raised me saw themselves as citizens of the world. We see no borders.
When I write, I am writing to the world, not to the United States alone. I do
believe that the things I am talking about will finally, maybe not in my lifetime, will turn out.

Alt-X: Are you currently working on another novel?

LMS: Yes, I decided to write a novel about two women and their gardens
and flowers. Absolutely no politics. But then I started to study the history of
plants and where they came from. Oh my gosh! Right behind the conquistadors came the plant collectors. So my new novel will focus on gardens and
flowers, but it turns out gardens are very political.

Alt-X: Evolution has become political.

LMS: Yes, I think so. It is all one. That is one of the strengths of the
narrative tradition: it oversimplifies to break things apart, to fragment, but
the truth remains comprehensible, in beautiful patterns, in a beautiful way.

Listening to the Spirits: An Interview with Leslie Marmon Silko

Ellen L. Arnold / 1998

From *Studies in American Indian Literatures* 10.3 (1998): 1–33. Reprinted by permission.

The following is a portion of an interview conducted on August 3, 1998, at the kitchen table of Leslie Silko's ranch house outside Tucson, in the midst of her extended family of horses, dogs, cats, birds, and one big rattlesnake. On that table is a manuscript copy of *Garden in the Dunes,* the new novel Silko has just completed, which will be published early in 1999. At the time of the interview, I was about halfway through the manuscript.[1]

Garden in the Dunes is a richly detailed and intensively reserached historical novel set at the end of the nineteenth century. It focuses on the lives of Sister Salt and Indigo, two young Colorado River Indian sisters of the disappearing Sand Lizard tribe, who are separated when Indigo is taken away to boarding school in California. Too old for school, Sister Salt is sent to the reservation at Parker, but escapes to make her way among the construction camps of the closing Arizona frontier. Indigo runs away from boarding school and is taken in by Hattie Abbott Palmer, a scholar of early church history, and her botanist husband Edward, Easterners who have come West to look after the Palmer citrus groves in California. Thinking Indigo is an orphan, the Palmers take her with them on a summer tour of East Coast and European homes and gardens belonging to wealthy family members and friends.

Taught early by her Mama and Grandma Fleet the intricacies and pleasures of gardening in the sand dunes along the Colorado before her people were driven out, Indigo is an attentive and appreciative observer. Through her we experience elaborate mannerist gardens in Italy, English landscape gardens, and their American interpretations on the estates of the New England Robber Barons. Amidst this lush and loving description, Silko unfolds a gripping narrative of intrigue, betrayal and revenge, loss, reunion and renewal.

EA: In *Yellow Woman and a Beauty of the Spirit,* you described how *Almanac of the Dead* originated in a series of photographs you took that came together and made a story. How did *Gardens in the Dunes* begin?

LMS: *Garden in the Dunes* goes way back. Somewhere in my papers I had a sketch for a story about the gladiolus man. It was supposed to be a short story about a man who, when he was young, went to Sherman Institute in Riverside, and at the school they taught him how to cultivate gladiolus. He goes back home and on a piece of family land plants the gladiolus, and then the clanspeople get really angry because it's not a food crop; it's a flower. The idea being that this person is just so lost and in love with these flowers and their colors, even though they're ridiculous and useless. But of course, that comes head-on with the needs for food and economy. And so for years and years, I've intended to write this short story called "The Gladiolus Man."

Then I got interested in gardens and gardening. I've always tried to grow things. At Laguna, I could have a vegetable garden. Since I came to Tucson, it's a real challenge to try to get something to grow down here. I do have the datura growing around the house. Here in Tucson there's the Native Seeds Search group. They try to take care of heirloom seeds, and seeds of indigenous plants and indigenous crops. Since I've come to Tucson, I started to think more about the old time food and the way people grew it, not just in the Pueblo country, but in this area, in the Sonoran Desert.

So I'd been thinking about gardens, but I guess what cinched it is that everyone was complaining—not everyone, but some of the moaners and groaners about my work, who think that Chicano or Native American literature, or African American literature, shouldn't be political. You know, easy for those white guys to say. They've got everything, so their work doesn't have to be political. So, I was like, oh, okay, so you want something that's not political. Okay, I'm going to write a novel about gardens and flowers. And so that's what I thought, though I should have known that even my idea of the gladiolus man, my character who planted flowers instead of food, was very political. I'd always wondered too, why seed catalogues are so seductive, and plant catalogues. I was real interested in the language of description and the common names of flowers. So anyway, I just started reading about gardens.

I had this idea about these two sisters, and I knew right away that they weren't Pueblo people. I knew that they were from the Colorado River. There are some Uto-Aztecan groups mixed in with the Yuman groups over there. These were some of the people that lived in some of the side canyons on the Colorado River. So many of the cultures along the Colorado River were completely wiped out. There's no trace of them left. And it was done by gold miners and ranchers. They didn't even have to use the Army on them. Just the good upstanding Arizona territory, the good old boys, slaughtered all these tribes of people that are just gone forever. So I decided that my characters would be from one of these remnant, destroyed, extinct groups. They'd be some of the last of them.

So I started writing, but then it wasn't too long before I realized how very political gardens are. Though my conscious self had tried to come up with an idea for a non-political novel, I had actually stumbled into the most political thing of all—how you grow your food, whether you eat, the fact that the plant collectors followed the Conquistadors. You have the Conquistadors, the missionaries, and right with them were the plant collectors. When I started reading about the orchid trade, then suddenly I realized, but it was too late then! I realized that this was going to be a really political novel too.

In *Almanac of the Dead* you have the mention of the Ghost Dance. I didn't realize that this [indicating *Gardens* manuscript] would also be wanting to look at the Messiah, at Jesus Christ of the Americas. There are many different Jesuses. That was another thing I started reading about, the Gnostic Gospels—Elaine Pagel's wonderful book, *The Gnostic Gospels.* She was in the first group of MacArthur fellows with me, and they called us back to Chicago in 1982 for a reunion. Later she had her publisher send me a copy of her book, *The Gnostic Gospels.* Well, I was deep in the middle of writing *Almanac of the Dead,* and that book sat on my shelf for years. So recently I wrote her a letter and thanked her for it, and I said, oh, and by the way, I wrote a whole novel partly because of your book. I started to realize that there are lots of different Jesus Christs, and the Jesus or the Messiah of the Ghost Dance and some of the other sightings of the Holy Family in the Americas were just as valid and powerful as other sightings and versions of Jesus. And I didn't realize until just recently that there are all kinds of Celtic traditions of Saint Joseph and Mary being in England and Ireland. There's always been the Messiah and the Holy Family that belong to the people. And so that got mixed in too.

Lots of things came together then, and maybe that's what always happens when I write. You can see this idea from years ago, about the Gladiolus Man—my grandfather, Henry C. Marmon, went to school at Sherman Institute, and the early part where Indigo talks about the Alaska girls who came and got sick and died, Grandpa told me that. That really happened. So a lot of what this is, is a kind of accretion, a gathering slowly of all these things I've been interested in, I've heard about, I've read about, a book someone's given me.

And then, in 1994, I went to Germany to promote the German translation of *Almanac of the Dead,* which is more copyedited and more technically correct than the English version, because for my German translator, Bettina Munch, it was a labor of love.

EA: I can imagine *Almanac* in German. It seems like German would be a really good language for it.

LMS: Yes. And she's got it in there! Anyway, my German publisher, Rogner and Bernhard, arranged for Bettina to travel with me, and I flew off to Leipzig. That was our first stop, old East Germany. In that very church building where the Democracy movement, the movement that made the Wall finally fall down, began, I did my first reading. And then Bettina would read in German, and it was just beautiful—in English and in German. It was standing room only. So the energy there was. . . . I had no preconceived notions, but I have German ancestors. I could just feel that in that realm, those ancestors are not like human beings who differentiate, that my German ancestors were right there for me. I didn't expect it. I guess that's when you're most open to it, when you're not consciously thinking about something. Then those things can happen.

So not only were my German ancestor spirits really close, but the young East German women were just devastated at that point, by what the change, what unification meant. They lost daycare, they lost jobs, they lost the right to terminate pregnancies they didn't want, so their world was collapsing. They'd had all these dreams about what unification would mean, and now they were just being crushed. Leipzig was being colonized by huge construction cranes to build skyscrapers. Capitalism was trampling them and crunching them under its boot. I had so many German women come up to me and say they felt hopeless, they felt completely despondent over the betrayal of what they had hoped unification would be, and then they read *Almanac* and they found hope in *Almanac.* And I was like, Yes! I wrote that novel to the world, and I was thinking about the Germans, I was thinking about the Europeans. I believe that the Pueblo people, the indigenous people of the Americas, we're not only Indian nations and sovereign nations and people, but we are citizens of the world. So I had all these people come up to me and say, Yes! And the ancestor spirits were there, and it was almost like they were creating. . . . There was a medium, a field, of positive and real communication. And so Berlin, same thing—standing room only. It was wonderful. Munich, And then, Zurich.

Zurich. The book tour was in the spring, so it was around the time of
Fasching Festival, their spring rites. Right at sundown I was walking with the
publishing rep through the narrow downtown streets of Zurich, with all the
revelers and parades they do for Lent. It's like a European Mardi Gras, but
of course it's pagan. And so I'm loving it, and I think that's one of the
reasons that maybe I could feel the German ancestor spirits out, because even
though they consciously don't know why they're doing it, the Europeans
when they dress up in their masks and go around like that, that's an old rite.
And even though they consciously aren't aware of it, they're still doing what
they're supposed to be doing. All of a sudden, we were walking down the
street, and up ahead there were these giant blackbirds. And they moved
through the streets in this kind of silence. Someone who might want to ratio-
nalize it might say, oh you just saw another group of people masked, but the
whole feeling of it, the silence, and watching them move through the street,
was like a kind of apparition. So I saw this apparition of these raven or
blackbird beings move through, and when we got to where they had been, we
couldn't see them anywhere. We just found one little black feather.

So here I am on book tour, and what a time it was! There was some kind
of heightened energy, and it had to do with the old spirits, and that they
would come. That they didn't care about where you come from, that they
don't make those kinds of boundaries. I felt welcomed. I felt at home. And
then two years later, when I spent three weeks in Italy with my friend Laura
Coltelli, who's also my Italian translator, there were blackbirds that were
there with me. And I also have blackbirds who live here with me. So there's
something about blackbirds.

When I came back, my whole experience of Germany and Zurich was just
like, whoa. I also have ancestors from Scotland, and I've always been interested in their old stones, and of course I'm a stone worshipper. I've got stones
around, you know. You're a stone worshipper. Lots of stone worshippers!
And so, by golly, once I knew that Indigo was going to go to Europe, I knew
that she was going to see gardens in Europe, and I knew that something of
what's alive there, that there's a kind of continuity. . . . I mean Europe is not
completely Christianized. The missionaries were not completely successful.
There is a pagan heart there, and the old spirits are right there. When I went
to Rome, I saw the old cat cult. The old Mediterranean cat cult never died
out. It's there in Rome and all these old ladies and old men feed cats, and the
cats look at you, and you look at the cats, and the cats say, this is all ours. So
going into *Gardens in the Dunes,* I had a tremendous sense of the presence

of the oldest spirit beings right there in Europe, and that lots of Europeans, even the ones that don't know it, are still part of that. As hard as Christianity tried to wipe it out, and tried to break that connection between the Europeans and the earth, and the plants and the animals—even though they've been broken from it longer than the indigenous people of the Americas or Africa— that connection won't break completely. That experience was so strong that I wanted to acknowledge it a little.

EA: So in a way, you can see *Almanac* giving birth to *Gardens in the Dunes,* by taking you to those places.

LMS: By taking me to those places. Exactly. It was with the *Almanac* where I first realized that there are these spirit entities. Time means nothing to them. And that you can have a kind of relationship with them. They rode me pretty hard in *Almanac of the Dead.* But then I learned not to be afraid of them, to go ahead and trust them. Yeah, I was meant to go there. And the spirits were waiting there, probably called around by *Almanac.* But by then, I was also able to see fully the whole of it, that there was so much positive energy. And the old spirits that made me write *Almanac,* they meant well, even though two-thirds of the way through, they're about to . . .

EA: They're about to do us all in!

LMS: They're about to do everyone in, me included, believe me! You can really see how this grows out of that experience.

EA: What that gives me a sense of, too, is that we want to describe a lot of the things we do as "remnants" that don't have the same meaning any-more, without thinking about the fact that there are things that are living through us, even when we aren't consciously aware of it.

LMS: Exactly.

EA: That we're being used to keep these things alive.

LMS: Exactly. And then as usual, I start out with a conscious idea of what I think I'm doing, and then the Messiah came into the novel. The garden is so important in early Christianity, in the Bible, and gardens are so important to the Koran. In the three great monotheistic religions—Judaism, Moslem, and Christianity—garden imagery is real important. Once I had my Sand Lizard sisters down on the Colorado River, I remembered from my reading for *Almanac for the Dead* that in 1893 there was a Ghost Dance at Kingman (now in my novel, I fudge and move it over to Needles). Then as soon as the Ghost Dance comes into the novel, I know that Jesus and the Messiah are in there, and then I know the Gnostic Gospels have to be in there. And then my whole sense that in Europe, there's the corporate church, that kind of Christianity, and then there's this other Jesus. Jesus would have a fit, just like I wrote in *Almanac of the Dead,* if he could see what his followers did.

So there's very much a connection [between the novels], even though the effect on the reader is very different. *Gardens in the Dunes* is meant as a reward, something less rigorous for the reader. If you make it all the way through *Almanac,* it makes you strong. But it's like one of those stronger remedies. You do have to tell some people, hey, if it starts to bother you, put it down. Rest. Take it easy. Every now and then I'll run into someone who, by god, read *Almanac of the Dead* in three days, just read it. And I'm like, whoa, isn't it toxic to do that?

EA: One of the reasons I had so much trouble reading it is because the Los Angeles riots happened right in the middle of my reading it, and I could hardly pick the book up without feeling like it was coming to life all around me. It was very frightening.

LMS: The book seemed to know that. Even the urgency to go ahead and finish it. I look now and I see thats and whiches that shouldn't be there in *Almanac,* but it was like those little spirits who rode me, they said: your vanity? Your vanity about how your prose looks on the page, your vanity about wanting to satisfy the Ph.D. students and readers, your vanity? Your vanity! When I tried to get it finished and published within two or three years like the publishers wanted, the old spirits said, your vanity? You want to do something on a schedule like that? No, it's our book. You swallow all your hopes and pretensions. You swallow all your vanity. And then the urgency, when it kept saying, it's about time, it's about time, time coming, time, it has to go out, your vanity, no. And so I did that, and then Simon & Schuster chose November 2, 1991, as the pub date. November 2 is the Day of the Dead. November 2 was the day in 1977 that the doctors told me that I would probably die in surgery. And so the thing about time, and the urgency, and the spirits saying no, this thing goes out now, and then how when you were reading it—everything about the *Almanac* has been really eerie. When I got done with it, Simon & Schuster couldn't have known or timed it, they just arbitrarily brought it out on November 2. They don't know what day that is.

EA: So that is actually the day that they brought it out?

LMS: It's called the pub date; it's a literal date that's connected with all books; it's like a birth date. And that was its day. The other thing that was interesting about *Almanac of the Dead* is that it's ISBN number has 666 in it. I love that! [Laughter] I didn't ask for that! I didn't ask for November 2! And of course the ultimate thing that it did—January 1, 1994, I pick up a Sunday paper, and it says that the Zapatistas in the mountains outside of Tuxtla Gutierrez. . . . Then the hair on my neck stood up.

EA: Mine too! And everybody else who'd read it.

LMS: It went out over the internet. It blew people away. Well that's why, it had a sense of time. The spirits had a sense of time and things about dates and time. It's like *Almanac of the Dead* did everything that it wanted, that's how it's been. And it didn't care about editing or copyediting, and it did not care about my vanity. It did not care about being shaped into a more traditional novel. Some people have said, oh *Almanac of the Dead,* you could break it into four or five of that kind of fiction that's so popular, the quick read or the page turner. But that's not it at all. I was not allowed to. I completely was taken over, and everything about it was meant to be. The spirits just wanted it out there. And so I let go of it, and then that's what happened in terms of getting that particular ISBN number, that pub date, for you to be reading it when the riots happened, for the Zapatistas. . . . They knew, and I knew somehow, now that I can look back.

What's interesting is Commander Marcos [spokesman for the Zapatistas] went to the mountains in 1980, and that's when I started to have transmissions. I started to have to spontaneously write down things from the *Almanac.* So there's a real parallel there, which works on that plane that extends across the universe, where stuff travels faster than the speed of light.[2] So the *Almanac,* everything about the way *Almanac* has gone out into the world and since then, is so spooky.

EA: In *Almanac,* the Reign of the Death's Eye Dog is a male reign. It seems that what you see in *Almanac* is the ultimate of a patriarchal system. *Gardens* seems so very female. Were you consciously balancing that?

LMS: No not consciously, though very soon I became conscious of it. And then I thought, well, yeah. Of course there are males in this female world, like Big Candy, that I was interested in.

EA: But they're very different men from the ones who were in *Almanac!*

LMS: The *Almanac* men, everything in *Almanac,* isn't quite realism. This [*Gardens*] is more going back to a kind of literary realism. No, almost all of those characters are so intense or extreme as to be almost mythical. This

[*Gardens*] was to try to explore and see if I could make a book so that, if you had a scale and you put *Almanac* on this side, they could balance out. And I think *Gardens* explores dimensions of history and has a span almost like the span in *Almanac,* but it's just a different way of looking at it again.

While I was writing *Almanac,* I got an invitation to go to Gettysburg College. I thought maybe I shouldn't go, because I was working on *Almanac,* and I was trying to get it done. And then I thought, oh well, I'll go. I took *Almanac* with me. I took the manuscript I was working on with me. And do you know, I'll never try to go to bed and sleep at Gettysburg. Those dead souls and spirits, they were just overwhelming. And that's where the part of *Almanac of the Dead* came from, where some character says that the Civil War was the blood payment for slavery in the U.S. Actually the war was only a partial payment. That part comes from spending that night there, and do you know, I lost part of the manuscript of *Almanac of the Dead* there. It stayed in Gettysburg. It was a section about Zeta, Lecha's sister in *Almanac of the Dead.* It was so precious, and somehow I managed to lose it. It disappeared there. Oh boy, I won't go back to Gettysburg. Those big battlefields like that, and those burial grounds, and those things that aren't supposed to be there. . . . Gettysburg was very powerful, and I doubly won't go back to Gettysburg now. There are so many souls and spirits howling and crying in the Americas, not just indigenous ones.

EA: I haven't finished the manuscript yet, but one of the things that I feel really strongly in *Gardens in the Dunes* is the artificiality of the lines we draw between people, between peoples and nations. The battles and the Messiahs, these are the kinds of things individual people share in common. If you set them apart from the politics behind them, people in Europe and the indigenous peoples in the Americas have a lot more in common than they have that divides them.

LMS: Exactly! And those who would make the boundary lines and try to separate them, those are the manipulators. Those are the Gunadeeyah, the destroyers, the exploiters. I'm glad that comes through, because that's what I was trying to do, to get rid of this idea of nationality, borderlines, and drawing lines in terms of time and saying, oh well, that was back then. And because I felt that in Germany. I felt that when I was talking with those women. It's because I've experienced it. And the more you really feel it and believe in it, the more angry you get at these manipulators who would divide people. Our human nature, our human spirit, wants no boundaries, and we are better beings, and we are less destructive and happier. We can be our best selves as a species, as beings with all the other living beings on this earth, we behave best and get along best, without those divisions.

EA: Something that disturbs me is that much of the literary criticism that's written about Native American literature perpetuates those divisions. It's always Native Americans versus Euro-Americans, and it falls out that way even in literary interpretations. People have to make those political distinctions and draw those lines even when they're writing about novels.

LMS: Right. I really wanted to dismantle that in this novel.

EA: And you'll get criticism for that, don't you think?

LMS: Oh, I'm sure I'll get all kinds of criticism.

EA: Elizabeth Cook-Lynn, for example, criticized *Almanac* for not working towards tribal sovereignty.[3] And I can imagine that some people would object to this book for bringing Indians and Europeans together in a way that I don't think has happened in a Native American novel.

LMS: No, I don't think it's happened before. I can foresee the possibility of the greatest of changes, but they can only happen if the people from the South work at it, and all the people here, including the non-Indian. Everyone would have to take part. It would be working toward what the continents and the old tribal spirits and people believe. Even for the old folks I grew up with, the Indian way is to learn how a person is inside their heart, not by skin color or affiliation. That criticism grows out of more of a non-Indian way of looking at things. That's why the indigenous people welcomed the newcomers. They didn't draw lines like that.

EA: They were bringing new things in.

LMS: Yes. The old folks who showed me and taught me that way of seeing the world, they're not here now to defend that way of seeing. But it really was an inclusive one. In the old way, the old folks would say, just like in *Almanac,* all of those who love the earth and want to do this are welcome. That's the old, old way. That attitude about nationalism comes in much later, that's much more a European way of looking at things. The truth of the matter is, if you really want to think about the retaking of the Americas, it has to be done with the help of everybody. It has to be done with the help of the people from the South. Everyone has to agree. And the retaking of the Americas is not literal, but it's in a spiritual way of doing things, getting along with each other, with the earth and the animals. It would be for all of us.

It's true that the way the old folks looked at things got them into trouble, because they welcomed these newcomers. But that was how they saw the world, and it was the right way. Just because everyone wants to fall in and draw lines and exclude, well, that's the behavior of Europeans. A lot of that's been internalized. A lot of the times when my work is attacked, it's attacked by people who aren't aware of how much they've internalized these European attitudes. The old time people were way less racist and talked way less about lines and excluding than now. So that that way of being in the world and in the Americas is not forgotten, we've got to be reminded of how the people used to see things. And if being yourself gets you into trouble, which it did, if being so inclusive and welcoming of strangers didn't turn out well, the old prophecies tell us that it still doesn't matter, and it's all going to be okay. That's the only way that it can be, including everybody. That's the only way that the kind of peace and harmony that this earth of the Americas wants is going to happen.

So yeah, I can see making everyone mad. I can see all the tribal people could be mad, and all different kinds of Christians will be mad. Actually this novel could be more dangerous for me and more trouble than *Almanac of the Dead* was, for just those reasons. And I'm aware of it, but I refuse to forget how generous, how expansive, how inclusive the way of the old people was, of seeing the world and of seeing human beings. You can see it being eroded. Even the racism that came into the reservations, brought in by the Bureau of Indian Affairs, and then the next thing you know, somebody thinks that's Indian tradition.

EA: When you read from the novel in Montgomery,[4] you said that you had invented the Sand Lizard people. Why did you choose to do that rather than to draw on a real people?

LMS: Because I didn't really feel like I knew any of the Colorado River people that are left. I know a little bit, and I've met people from the different Colorado River tribes, but I hadn't lived that experience of being a Yuma or a Mojave. I also wanted them to be gone. Lots of people were wiped out and gone forever, and lots of people had to be the last ones. That's where a lot of the bitterness and negative attitudes against white people come from, from the terrible crimes that were committed. I didn't want to mitigate or lessen. I wanted them to be from a group that was completely obliterated. But also I wanted the artistic and ethical freedom to imagine them any way I wanted.

EA: So you wouldn't have people jumping on you about ethnographic accuracy?

LMS: I didn't want anyone to think that what I said about the Sand Lizard people was factual. I wanted that freedom. I did do lots and lots of reading about the Colorado River area and the tribes and the people, and then I tried to imagine a people who had characteristics that made others remark that they were different—characteristics that, in being who they were, it set them up to be destroyed. Maybe that's what happens here to me as a writer. You just have to go ahead and be a human being, be who you are. So I was interested in imagining a group that, when they were fighting, instead of obliterating their opponents if they were winning, they would stop. I love that.

EA: Is the canyon of the Sand Lizards a real place, or did you create it?

LMS: I just created it. I can just see it. I just know it. It's based on a spring on family property south of Laguna.

EA: So this is the same Dripping Spring that's in *Ceremony*?

LMS: Yeah, that's the same spring. It's the same spring in *Gardens of the Dunes,* but I've added some big dunes. And of course I moved it, but there is that sandstone geological formation that makes springs come out of cracks that does occur all the way across north central Arizona and New Mexico. There are places like that all along the Colorado River in the side canyons. The shallow cave and the snake that's there. You're right. That's what I did. I took that spring. That spring's not in *Almanac* though. But guess what? *Almanac* ends with the snake—I didn't mean to, I didn't plan this, I shouldn't tell you about the ending—but there's a snake at the end [of *Gardens*]!

EA: I'm not surprised!

LMS: I was! I wrote it, I finished it, and then I stepped back, and I was like, wow! I did it again. I didn't mean to, I didn't plan it, but that's how it is.

EA: Speaking of snakes, I walked down and looked at the wall [of the building on Stone Avenue where Silko painted her snake mural while she was writing *Almanac of the Dead.* Since then the building has been sold, and the new owner has painted over the mural.][5] The paint is very thick, but it's beginning to peel off right in the middle. What's underneath it is the white-wash, and you can see a little faint color under the whitewash. So it's beginning to peek out.

LMS: What happened is that after [the mural was painted over], there was a group of people stalking the guy who destroyed it. They really tried, you know. The TV station did a piece on it. The whole neighborhood tried. It's so sad. It isn't like it was hated, and everyone wanted to get rid of it. So I don't feel bitter, like I didn't have any help or anything. It's just that the destroyers—it's a guy with money.

EA: It's the private property thing.

LMS: It's private property. They even took it to City Council, and that's what they [the Council] said.

I was working along on *Almanac of the Dead,* and I'd reached a point where I wasn't sure. I was right at a midpoint, and Mecham got elected [Governor of Arizona], and I got really angry because he called black people pickaninnies, and he was elected with twenty-seven percent of the vote. I wrote *Almanac* inside that building. So when Mecham first got elected, I did this to the side of the building [indicates photograph]. I made it look like graffiti, so that my landlord wouldn't get into trouble. I was just so outraged. It started out: Arizona Democrats are you dead?

EA: So your landlord at that time was sympathetic.

LMS: Right. He let me do that. We left it up until the sonofabitch Mecham was recalled. As soon as people rallied around, as soon as we got rid of Mecham, then he painted over the graffiti. So one morning I drove up, and I didn't know what I was going to do [about *Almanac*]. I've always been a frustrated visual artist, and I always have paint, and I had paint down there inside my writing office. That morning I drove up and I could see a snake, and then I knew that the snake had the skulls in it.

Like everything that I write or create, it just kept growing, and I left off the novel. I came to the middle of the novel, Mecham got elected, I freaked out, and I didn't know what I was going to do. I didn't know what happened in *Almanac*. But of course, the spirits are writing *Almanac*, not me. I decided if I could successfully complete the mural, I could by god finish the novel too. So I stopped writing *Almanac* for awhile, until I got the mural along. I worked and worked, and when I got it to the point where it was pretty much finished, I went back inside and finished *Almanac of the Dead.* The whole Mexico section, it all came. It all came.

This was it's first incarnation [points out another photo]. The early incarnation, the blue snake, doesn't have the hummingbird and spider. It was chosen one of the best new pieces of outdoor art in 1988. It was up for about six years, and it was so gratifying. You know there are those graffiti guys, taggers and gangs, and they respected it so much, they never laid a hand on it. They would put their tags nearby it, and people would write me notes in Spanish and thank me for it. It lived out there for years and nobody ever harmed it. The sunlight and pollution worked on it, but you know, when you make a piece of art and you put it out in public, it's completely defenseless. It's just there. And yet it was so loved. The taggers didn't tag it, and the graffiti guys left it alone, and there are other outdoor murals in Tucson where right away— you know, the public art, real bland, don't offend anyone—those guys come. That's not art, that stuff they call public art. So anyway, all these years it stays up, and then in the fall of '93, I decided it needed to be freshened. At Laguna they keep the same outline, but they sometimes will use different paint [shows another photo].

EA: Oh, it's red!

LMS: So by god, this time the snake was red. In November I paint it red, finish in December, and in January the Zapatistas rise up! And then I freshened up more. It took me years to get the whole thing done.

EA: [Reading from newspaper account] "Leslie Silko, an award-winning writer, began small with painted graffiti."

LMS: "This was a good year for public art. . . . But other artists took funding and commissioning into their own hands." Yeah, I did it all with my own money. These public artists that have to have approval and money, the work has to be so bland. I did it all on my own, because of course, no one would ever okay it for public art, no one would ever fund it.

EA: So the new owner painted over it and then put something else on there, and then painted over that too?

LMS: Yeah, he painted over it [first with whitewash], and it would always start peeking out. People would drive by and put the words on it. He just recently did that heavy paint, so it'll take a while. It'll come back.

But because of its destruction and the way it was done, it really made a big impression on people. It was a lesson about greed, and how little art matters in America. Now there's an international convention that protects art, but the U.S. didn't sign in time to save the mural. It's just a little recapitulation of everything that makes it so hard to live in the United States.

I got this law firm, and they looked into it. Since that time, that lawyer's learned a whole lot about that Bern Convention. But he couldn't help save the mural. So that happened in '97, the whitewashing, and then that thick, thick stuff, he just did that in the past three months. If it's already peeling after three months, it won't be long.

EA: It's just really hard to imagine.

LMS: It was sad. But then, when they came after it, if I hadn't been embroiled in personal troubles, and trying to finish *Gardens in the Dunes,* and having Simon & Schuster after me, I might have been able to make a better stand. But some part of me wants to paint it again. Of course, it probably will never be exactly like that, because I would get bored, but as long as I know I can do it again, I don't really mourn that much. I just need a wall. My fantasy is that something will happen to that Mr. Dickhead that destroyed it, eventually that wall will. . . .

EA: . . . will become available again.

LMS: It will become available again. You bet. Either that or it'll fall down.

So all that time, no one harmed it. Not the taggers, not the homeless, not the crackheads, not this or that. It's this wretched dickhead of a rich man. And he does it against all the wishes of the people. And he said he did it because he hated what it stood for. He didn't do it for any other reason, but for the worst kind of reasons. So it was a little education for all these Tucson liberals who think it's such a nice community.

But the importance of this mural is that when I got it done, I walked inside and finished *Almanac of the Dead.* The whole Mexico section came in, and it all came together. I honestly didn't know why I kept having so many snakes in the early part of *Almanac of the Dead.* And then after I painted the mural, I started reflecting on them, and I went inside and wrote the end. The mural was terribly important ultimately to the novel.

The other happy thing, too, in its destruction it became more known. Just this summer, here in Tucson, there was a summer program for kids. They hired local artists to work with the children and the junior high and high school kids to make art projects to keep the kids out of trouble. One of the groups made this great big giant snake! It's three dimensional, a sculpture in concrete, and then they covered it and painted it. You know it's an offspring of that snake. So the big snake is still around. It's out and about in town. That big snake's never going to leave town.

EA: What about the stone snake in Laguna?

LMS: Well, it's really interesting. The tribe moved a state highway to keep people from going too close to it. It came back into this world so close to that highway. So the way I describe it when I first approached it and saw it, now that description doesn't function anymore. The road is moved.

EA: Nice.

LMS: Nice. But radical, too, to move the whole road, because you know it costs millions of dollars to move a highway.

EA: So is that a place people in the community still go?

LMS: Oh, I imagine so. Absolutely.

EA: You referred in an earlier conversation we had to the woman who wrote the invented story about your being banished by the Tribal Council. There's also speculation that it happened because of the stone snake, that the story about Sterling in *Almanac of the Dead* is about you and the filming of your movie. Do you want to lay those stories to rest?

LMS: It's fiction, okay? And yes, authors do combine imagination with things that they find out in their lives, and things that happen to them. Novelists are always having to explain this, the difference between what happens to them in their lives and where they create a character that has characteristics like theirs. The Laguna people, as I've said before, are way more tolerant and broad-minded than outsiders want them to be.

I just decided I would have that be the reason for Sterling being banished. The real reason I left Laguna and moved down here was that I was going through a divorce and I had to leave. And I came down here. I was called down here, actually, because of the *Almanac* and the spirits. Besides being Laguna, I have Mexican Indian in me too. I have Cherokee, I have lots of tribes. I have lots of callings, and lots of spirits. But the proximate reason for moving to Tucson and moving away from Laguna was the divorce. It was nothing about the tribe, nothing about the people.

EA: So you have NOT been banished by the Tribal Council? Will you say that definitively?

LMS: [Laughter] No, I have not been banished by the Tribal Council! The Tribal Council has more important things to do. Laguna is not like that. At first I thought it was a misunderstanding, because there were a couple of people that had done some things. At first I thought maybe that woman who wrote that about me being banished was confused. But she willfully wanted to rewrite my life and rewrite my relationship with the Laguna Tribal Council and the community. She wanted to make me resemble Dante, and because

Dante got in trouble for what he did with municipal authorities, she had to have my life parallel Dante's life.

EA: I guess a lot of that speculation started with that essay by Paula Gunn Allen saying you should not have revealed the clan stories.[6] It seems like it has persisted since then, the desire to understand that you did something outrageous, for which you could not be forgiven.

LMS: [Laughter] Could not be forgiven! The stories that I have and work with are the stories that were told to me by Aunt Alice, who was my grand-aunt, my grandpa, people within my family and clan, and people that I knew. That was given to me. My sense of that, the hearing and the giving, especially with *Almanac,* was that there was a real purpose for that. I had to take seriously what I was told. There was some kind of responsibility to make sure it wasn't just put away or put aside. It was supposed to be active in my life. We'll never get past the openness and expansiveness that once was, and how the Conquistadors, the invaders, came, and the dampening of that openness and wanting to share and give. So you start to get into secrecy, closing things off. That's not the original Pueblo way. That's reactionary, protective, and that's a kind of a shrinking away or a diminishment of the spirit of what the people had been able to do. And I just won't bow to it.

But I feel confident that I've never divulged anything that was kept secret. So much of that ownership stuff and talking like that is so—again, who talks about ownership all the time? That's such a Western European kind of thing. And even the anthropologists that Paula is relying on, so much of that material that they work off of was gathered by ethnologists. Even the terminology in English, the way of talking about it, is a secondhand kind of thing. You just can't worry about it. You'd end up just being silent. They want to silence you. Even the *kats'ina* dances at Laguna that are closed and guarded. The way the Hopi people did it for so long was the way all the Pueblo people must have done it. It was open to the world. It was for world renewal, and all this closing down, that's a reaction to the incoming. That's not the Pueblo way. But of course, people have been hiding and closing down things and closing up for so long, now they're forgetting the older, more open and expansive way.

EA: I really understand the need to do that though, in terms of the lack of respect.

LMS: Oh, yes! I understand that, at the rituals. But as far as for writing, or expressing yourself, it's like when people used to go back to Oxford,

Mississippi, and ask about Faulkner. Wherever a novelist or an artist or a writer works, the local people always have some kind of gripes about, oh they shouldn't have written about this, or they shouldn't have talked about that.

EA: Let's go back and talk some more about *Gardens in the Dunes*. You said earlier that Hattie was influenced by Margaret Fuller.

LMS: Yes!

EA: How did you work her into all these other things?

LMS: I've loved Margaret Fuller for years and years. She's a great hero of mine, ever since I was an undergraduate. In my junior year at the University of New Mexico, Hamlin Hill, the great Mark Twain expert, was giving a class on American Transcendentalism. We studied all the Transcendentalists. And of course, I just loved Margaret Fuller. What a woman! What a hero! Free love, so brave, goes to Italy, has a baby out of wedlock, hangs out with all of the Freedom Fighters in Italy. And then, just such a mythical death, within sight of home, with her baby and her husband. The boat sinks off of Fire Island, and she's gone . . . oooh.

I knew of her, and I've always thought of her. Then when I was on book tour, I went to Black Oak Books in Oakland. Often when you're promoting a book, sometimes if you bring in a lot of people, or just as a courtesy to the author, they give you a gift. And so I walked around in that bookstore, and by golly, there was a used copy of a biography of Margaret Fuller's early years. So I have her Italian years and then I have a biography leading up to that, so I started reading them. And then Alice James, that biography. So Hattie's part Alice James too. Alice James was really thwarted, and sort of an invalid. In a sense, Alice James is what Hattie avoids, through her affection and involvement with Indigo, and the firming of her resistance to the way she was railroaded by the culture and the people. Hattie is more like Margaret Fuller than she is Alice James, but Alice James is a good example of the kind of destruction that was set up to happen to a character like Hattie. And it was an example of the fight that Margaret Fuller would have had to carry on if her boat hadn't sunk. So that's how Hattie relates to those two characters.

EA: What about Transcendentalism itself?

LMS: It had a big influence. That course was very important to me. We studied some of the minor Transcendentalists, and one of them was from a rich St. Louis family. He went out into Oklahoma Territory, and he lived for years and years with the Indians. So he was a Transcendentalist who saw

something transcendental about Native American views of the world and relationships. Even to this day, I point to American Transcendentalism as a sign
of what the old prophecies say about the strangers who come to this continent. The longer they live here, the more they are being changed. Every
minute the Europeans, and any other immigrants from any other place, come
on to the Americas and start walking on this land. You get this dirt on you,
and you drink this water, it starts to change you. Then your kids will be
different, and then the spirits start to work on you.

I point to American Transcendentalism and say, if you don't think the
change isn't already underway, well, you're a fool. Because the American
Transcendentalists are a sign. It's true a lot of their influence comes from the
East, but still, it's called American Transcendentalism. And the links with
Whitman, and with Thoreau, with earth and land and animals—it's my evidence to the world of the change that's already happening. The Europeans
come to this land, and the old prophecies say, not that the Europeans will
disappear, but the purely European way of looking at this place and relationships. So the American Transcendentalists, they're the first important sign
that this is already underway. The influence of American Transcendentalism
is still very strong, whether people recognize it or not.

EA: Where do you see that change continuing now?

LMS: It's a change in consciousness, and it's ongoing. It has to do with
the changes in the way people see, with the whole environmental movement—and a lot of the environmental movement and environmentalism has
been co-opted and turned into a capitalist tool. But I would point to, not just
the Greens and environmentalism, but the subtle turning of the people toward
simplifying. It's just in small ways. We look back in retrospect and say, oh,
here's American Transcendentalism. Right now we're in the middle of what
it is. But if I have to point at one thing I would say, look at the awareness of
more of a oneness—not that it helps in the face of the greedy capitalists—but
there is an awareness of plants, animals and earth being much more of a
holistic unit.

EA: *Almanac* and *Gardens in the Dunes* both are about capitalism and the
effects of capitalism.

LMS: If you would tell me to sit down and write about capitalism, I would
just go a-i-i-i-i! [Laughter] I think that sounds so boring. So it's accidental.
Of course *Almanac* is a post-Marxist novel, and so is *Gardens in the Dunes.*
But if it turns out that they're about capitalism, it's totally unconscious or

subconscious. That isn't how I start out writing. But it turns out that way, and I think the reason is because capitalism is so much in the forefront of the destruction of community and people and the fabric of being, and always was—I mean, slavery in the Americas, the destruction of the tribal people, of the world and the animals. And who did captalism start destroying first? White people in Europe. The poor factory workers that got ground up in the spinning machines that Marx wrote about. Both of the books end up being about that, but that isn't how they started out. If they're like that, if they're about capitalism, it's only because everything around us right now is so permeated with capitalism that I can't help it. You know, just like I said that I wanted to write a novel about gardens, and I thought it wouldn't be political. [Laughter] No, you just can't write an apolitical novel about gardens! Or I couldn't.

EA: The gardens that you're writing about, at least some of them, are very dependent on a capitalist economy to make them possible. So I have really mixed feelings when I'm reading about the gardens. I'm not sure how I'm supposed to feel about those gardens, especially when sixty-foot trees are being transplanted to make the gardens perfect.

LMS: That's why Indigo had to be the one to see the Robber Baron gardens on Long Island. Because she could love them, and see them differently from the reader. There's nothing evil about the poor trees, or about the gardens themselves. It's the conspicuous consumption. You're supposed to be grossed out.

EA: So you're asking us to do something that is very difficult for some of us to do, which is to love the gardens and at the same time question how they came to be.

LMS: Yes. That's why you have to try to stay with Indigo. Indigo just sees it and it's all wonder. Indigo wanders through and she sees the blossoms, and she doesn't make any kind of judgment. But of course Hattie's put off by it, Edward doesn't like it, because it takes so much money to keep them going.

I'm interested, you have to be interested, in the plants. They come from all over the world, and they're also another way of looking at colonialism, because everywhere the colonials went, the plants came back from there. But it's spectacle, so I would imagine the reader's feelings would range somewhere in between the feelings of Hattie and Edward, and Indigo. If the reader's completely put off and hates all these gardens, that's fine, because you could.

To me, *Gardens in the Dunes* is mostly funny. And the reader is supposed to be more amused [chuckles] than angry and outraged. I mean, they built these gardens and these ladies really did have Welsh gardeners, if you read about what really went on. It's conspicuous consumption to the max. While Susan Palmer James is making her landscape gardens, they are already going out of style. That is supposed to be ridiculous. You're supposed to kind of feel contempt and amusement. You can like those gardens or not, depending on how much you know or care about the history of them.

But I try to have Indigo see the gardens without all the baggage that comes along with them. I want her to think, oh, Grandma Fleet would love it! I gotta take these seeds back! Because that would be a kind of pure, innocent reaction. And that's one of the reoccurring things in it—gardens, innocence, safety. But also gardens can mean betrayal, plotting. The wicked old Popes used to go into the garden to plot the deaths of Bishops and Cardinals they didn't like. Jesus got betrayed in the Garden of Gethsemane. That's intentional, to have that range of possible ways of looking at the gardens. Yeah, I would expect that the reader would probably be put off by those. . . .

EA: By the excess.

LMS: Yeah, by the excess of the Long Island gardens! The ice to ice down [the greenhouse]! But hey, they're still doing that! Up in Phoenix people are getting truckloads of ice now to put in their swimming pools, spending hundreds of dollars. Or like the year in Palm Springs some people spent thousands of dollars to truck in snow for their Christmas party! When I got done writing, I thought, a hundred years later, this is the same place. William Gates builds that huge house out on that little island, it's the same thing. These robber baron computer guys are building huge conspicuous consumption homes and gardens. In a hundred years, nothing has changed. That's the weird thing. So this novel is really about right now. It just so happens that, for other reasons, [chuckle] I chose to set it back in 1900.

EA: It's a feeling that I get a lot of the time just in ordinary life, that there are many things that are very beautiful to look at and experience, and yet you can't get away from that sense of what made them, where they came from, what was required to produce and maintain them.

LMS: Exactly. Exactly.

EA: *Almanac* has a lot to say about the effects of capitalism on the lives of people, the way people get consumed. Is there something in *Gardens* that you see as kind of an antidote to that? Are there hints in this book about how to get away from that? How do we move out of that?

LMS: *Almanac* told you how to move out of that. That's where *Gardens in the Dunes,* I think, is different. *Gardens in the Dunes* is related to *Almanac,* but I don't think *Gardens in the Dunes* lays out how it will all be dismantled. So in that sense, *Gardens in the Dunes* is under the umbrella of the *Almanac.* *Almanac* talks about how capitalism destroys a people, a continent. This [*Gardens*] is very personal. This is about what capitalism makes people do to one another—what those guys with Edward did to him, what Edward does with Hattie. There's all the anxiety for Edward and Hattie over the debts he owes.

As far as saying how do we get free, or what do we do, *Almanac* is the one that says, this will come and this will happen. *Almanac* just says, now this is going to happen and this is going to happen, and you mother fuckers, you better watch out, and then this is coming! And I stand by it, because you can still see it coming.

Gardens in the Dunes really is about now. It all connects together and it gives you a psychic and spiritual way to try to live within this. I think that's what I'm trying to say about spirituality and the different Jesuses and the Messiahs. It gives you a way, but it gives you a quieter, more personal, more interpersonal way, whereas the *Almanac* lays it out in a more community, worldwide kind of way. This [*Gardens*] still has the world in its structure, there's something within this that will help you see a way, but it's much less political in the overt sense that *Almanac* has it. I guess it's offering people another way to see things and possible ways to connect up, in a spiritual way, to withstand. In the end I think there's a kind of spiritual and interpersonal accommodation. By trying to go into this personal, spiritual solution, it can't have the kind of bigness of solution that you see in *Almanac of the Dead.*

EA: I think one of the reasons that so many people are attracted to writing by Native Americans is because they're looking for a different way to live, searching for some way to exist in all of this that doesn't feel so contributory. It seems like you have really addressed that.

LMS: Yes, that's what I've tried to do.

EA: Did you consciously set out to do that?

LMS: I just do it instinctively, or intuitively. And then after I've done it for a while I can begin to see, and sometimes I go, oh, all right! And as I said earlier, that impulse to look at things and shift it around, that's how we survive as a species, the instinct for people to seek different ways. That the seekers seek, and that I try to help in what they are seeking, that's something that's in our DNA as human beings. They have a sense that I'm there, and I have a sense that they're there, and that it must be done. That we have to take what we are given, that's so oppressive and destructive, and ask what can we do? It's all in how you look at it. And I feel very proud of it [*Gardens*]. It is going to cause a lot of trouble, because people aren't used to looking at things this way. They're just not. I mean I wasn't; I'm different now after writing *Gardens.*

So that time in Germany was terribly important, and that's where the *Almanac* is still involved. I have a real sense of those people; it's something that comes to me. It's almost like even with this book, I was writing for the seekers without knowing it. Sometimes I wonder why I write what I write, why I do what I do. And then it's later on, after it's written and out in the world, I meet people like yourself, Greg,[7] other people, like the women in Germany, and then I say, okay, now it's complete. Because it's a dialogue.

EA: For me, *Almanac* told me that I needed to be more angry about a lot of things, to speak out, to not let so many things go by. And it seems like this [*Gardens*] is more about how you sustain yourself while you do that, how you keep your insides alive, while you do what you can to fight.

LMS: Right. That's exactly it. That's why I have my women characters. They're basically like my Sand Lizard sisters, the most powerless, at the mercy of everything. These characters are all terribly vulnerable. That's why the characters are powerless, helpless, the last of their people, peaceable people. Look at how vulnerable Edward was. He was way out of his league, and his whole family—you get the feeling that it's falling apart, they're decaying aristocrats, the money had run out. So in this capitalist world, there's a pecking order among the people with money.

EA: And you get a sense of Edward as somebody who started out a fairly decent person, but just sort of got taken in, swept away by all that.

LMS: He deteriorates, over time.

EA: Trying to do what's expected of him.

LMS: Yes. And he's more and more vulnerable too in his own way. I purposely made no terrible, terrible villains. Even the Australian doctor is really funny. I think the whole *Gardens in the Dunes* is pretty funny. I think *Almanac of the Dead* is pretty funny too.

EA: I do too. The second time I read it!

LMS: Yeah, the second time. [Laughter] That's right. When I was writing it, I didn't think it was so funny, but after I went back over it, I thought, this is pretty funny. So yeah, this is about being a little powerless person. It's not about great movements of armies and people, like *Almanac of the Dead*. This is about, what do you do if you're not only a woman, but also most all of your people are killed off, what do you do? You're right, it's about how you hold yourself together, and how, in that situation, seemingly powerless people can get things done. How people can mean things to one another, how humans, on the most simple interhuman level, can help to sustain each other. How the embattled animals and plants and the embattled people can help one another and keep one another going. So I'm really careful. There are no guns. Well, actually there are some guns [laughter], but they're being delivered South to the revolution, and there are no shoot-em-ups. There's some violence, but it's off-screen.

EA: So you feel like capitalism is unredeemable. No matter how you start out, it's going to do you in?

LMS: Capitalism, yeah.

EA: What are the alternatives?

LMS: The logical thing is that there's finite water, there's finite land, there's finite food. Wherever the water and the land and the food are taken away, hungry people just come after them. So the capitalists and the monsters, they have to kill and kill and kill more, and they don't sleep better at night. There's no way around the fact that you have to share, that in the long run to have peace, for the well-being of everybody, for the health of the planet, for the health of the species, you have to share and take care of one another. And if you don't, then you get what's coming, what the *Almanac of the Dead* says is coming if you don't. Capitalism is absolutely irredeemable.

Now I'm not talking about the free market or private property. I'm talking about laissez faire, trample-people-into-the-dirt, destroy-the-earth capitalism. The indigenous people of the Americas had markets. A lot of people want to apply [the term] capitalism to: you make something and you come to the market, and I make something and I come to the market, and we trade. That's not capitalism. You made it, I grew it, we traded with one another, there's no money, there's no bankers, and there's no in-between guys. There's no false baloney. That's not capitalism, that's trade, that's human economy, that's personal enterprise. Capitalism is the middle men, the banks, the government, that kind of economic system that favors the giant and crushes the little person. And we've had giant Communism. Big Communism is no good. Big Socialism is no good. And by big, I mean that some kind of huge apparatus that bosses and tells what the little people do.

Regionalism is the hope. Regionalism—what human beings did with plants and animals and rivers and one another before you had the nation-states tramping in—that's where the hope is. Getting rid of all national boundaries. Getting rid of all borders. With regionalism, you do that. You have a region that's organized around Sonoran Desert or Chihuahuan Desert.

EA: Bioregionalism.

LMS: Yes, bioregions. We get rid of all kinds of national boundaries. Of course, we're going in the opposite direction, with the European union. But that experiment will probably break down.

So yeah, big anything is doomed. Big capitalism is evil. It's flat out evil.

EA: So it's more the size of the system. It seems like that's the same thing that's happened with the religions you were talking about. They get to the point where the system takes over, and everything else is lost.

LMS: Exactly. You exactly have it. That's how I see it about religion. There's even a little episode [in *Gardens*] in a Corsican village. There's an abbey that was built years before to house a portrait of the Blessed Mother that's in gold and silver, and that picture does miracles. So pilgrims would come, and there are monks there; they're there because of that picture. But in the meantime, a few years before Edward and Hattie and Indigo get to this little Corsican village, there's been an apparition on the wall of the school. That actually happened down in Yaqui country, and it might even be in *Almanac of the Dead* in a different form. That would be interesting. But there's an apparition on the wall, so the people start going to the wall, and they stop going up to the abbey. And that angers the monks. There's a scene where they come down angrily, carrying their crucifixes, to scold the villagers for taking visitors to this schoolhouse wall. So you have this fight against the corporate church that tries to tell people what is holy. And yet there's the persistence of the Virgin to appear on schoolhouse walls and not stay with the silver.

EA: And that's the appeal of the whole Gnostic tradition, that it's unmediated.

LMS: Yeah. And that's why ultimately I hope this is a gnostic novel.

EA: It makes me think about how hungry people are for more direct experience, for something that is more personal, that they have more control over. And that's where the church stays alive, not in the system.

LMS: Exactly. That's another reason why what I'm doing with this novel tries to be more on a personal level. It's a whole different dimension from *Almanac,* on purpose, and I try to keep it like that too, for the reader.

In the Americas, that's where I got inspired. Early on, the Spaniards hadn't been there giving religious instruction for more than five years before all the people got in tune with the Christian spirits, the Christian saints, and took them right in. That's what the Voudun religion is about. That's what happens in the Americas, because it's all inclusive, it excludes nothing. You come here, you'll never be the same again. You'll be taken in and churned around, and what comes out is American. I don't care if it came in European, or it came in Chinese, it comes out American. It's changed by being on this very soil, on this continent.

In Peru and in Mexico, right away the folks started doing that. That's what the Nuestra Senora de Guadalupe is about too. It just freaks out the Europeans, because the Europeans, and a lot of cultures, are so exclusive and want to keep things pure. But here in the Americas, yeah. It was so funny. They weren't here long, and they had to see their Jesus, their Mary, their Joseph, their saints, go native, just like that. And they couldn't stop it.

EA: I think your writing itself really models the kinds of things you are talking about. Part of what draws me to it is the fact that you take so many different ideas, you take what you like and what's useable out of it all, and don't reject things outright. I'm thinking about the kinds of arguments people get into, over capitalism versus socialism for example, as if those are the only two ways and there isn't anything else. And neither of those work, so what are you going to do except stay in the one you've got?

But you take Marx and you use Marx for what he has to say to you. You don't throw him out because he screwed up somewhere along the line, or didn't do it all, which I think is a trap that we fall into. We're trained to think that way. If they messed up on this point, throw them out and go look for somebody else who does it all, who gets it all right.

LMS: The whole impulse of the Americas is to do just that, to say, well, let's look at it and see if there's anything we can use. But of course, you only include what you want. That's an outgrowth of that old, old way, which I fear so much we're losing. That's what so special about the Americas and about the tribal people of the Americas—that impulse to say, no, wait, we'll keep what we can. The people who do that [argue for exclusion] become like the destroyers. Then you've become like them, starting to see things just like them. And there are Native Americans out there who see things that way too. And there are Anglo-Americans. That's why it's not valid to use race or skin color, and never has been. What matters about human beings, and that's what the old folks knew, what matters is how you feel and how you are and how you see things, and not how you are on the outside. That's what's so tragic about the ugly lessons of racism that have seeped into Native American communities, because the really old folks didn't see things that way at all. That's why in *Almanac* the only hope for the retaking of the Americas is that it's done by people of like hearts and like minds.

EA: You expect *Gardens in the Dunes* to come out early in 1999?

LMS: They're saying April of '99. That's if everything goes all right with Simon & Schuster.

EA: So you're feeling like they aren't going to push for a lot of substantial revision? [In an earlier conversation Silko told me her editor wanted her to shorten or remove the first book of the novel, which describes Sister Salt and Indigo's early life in the canyon of the Sand Lizards.]

LMS: I won't do it. I won't. If they won't publish it like it is, I'll buy it back from them. They can't make you do anything, but they can not give you any money to promote it.

EA: What happens to you if they don't invest much in selling it?

LMS: There's nothing I can do, but I'm not too worried. If the worst happens, and they do it the way I want it, and don't give it any kind of budget, it will have to get out into the world through persons like yourself and Greg and other people.

What I'm hoping is that out of their own greed, they won't do that. *Ceremony* made it onto the *Utne Reader*'s list of 150—I don't know what kind of books they are[8]—and *Ceremony* has 500,000 copies in print. But *Ceremony* took off slowly. As time goes by, the books don't change, but the culture changes. When *Ceremony* first came out, it was considered to be really challenging, for the most sophisticated reader. And then gradually, graduate students could read it, then juniors and seniors in college were considered to be able to read *Ceremony.* Now, precocious juniors in high school suddenly can read *Ceremony. Ceremony* didn't change. Something changes within the culture. And the same way with *Almanac*. It'll fit in better and better. If the worst happens, *Gardens* will just come out more slowly. It'll hurt me personally, economically, but the book itself and what it means to the world won't be changed.

EA: Will they send you on a book tour this time?

LMS: I hope so.

EA: Do you enjoy that? Some important things have happened for you on tour.

LMS: Oh yes, I think I do. It's dialogue.

EA: But it's got to be exhausting.

LMS: It's exhausting, you bet it's exhausting. They schedule you way too heavily. That's the part I don't like. But meeting the people who have read the work, that's important. I wouldn't trade meeting the people in Germany for anything. The worst part is that it's systematized. They set it up, and the pace of it is really grueling. And the way the media people treat you, because you're a part of the same complex that sells movies and albums.

EA: The entertainment industry.

LMS: Yeah. That part I dislike, and that part seems to try to feed off that cult of making the maker of the work the point, and not the work itself.

My readers waited ten years for *Almanac of the Dead* to come, and then when I went on book tour, I didn't think anyone would come. Why should they wait for ten years after *Ceremony*? But there they were! They were there. So I like to take a lot of time. Each person comes up for me to sign the book, and they'll say something like, I've been waiting, and I'll say, you waited! I didn't know whether you would! And we talk.

And then you can see the handlers and the bookstore people. They're looking at the clock, they're looking at the length of the line, and they want it to go like a fucking machine. That's one thing that I really, really will not do. These people waited ten years for this book! These assholes, they don't care about my relationship with the readers. So I have to fight them.

It's incredible, you know. I have a sense that they're there, and that sense sustains me. How can I not? And then there they come! For me it tells me that what I sensed was true. I can't not talk with them. But it certainly flies in the face of the machine.

EA: What's next?

LMS: I've got all kinds of ideas. But I don't know what it might be. The conscious one who sits here and talks to you doesn't know. The one that knows the most is the one that doesn't speak in this form, and that one is working on all kinds of things.

EA: What about Flood Plain Press?[9] Do you intend to keep doing things like that?

LMS: Oh, Flood Plain. I'm still making the books. My son [Robert, a bookseller in Tucson] and his friend mail them out, and I still sell some. Yes, I have that entity there, and I think about making and doing other things, but in the spirit of these handmade books, just like I've done before. I'm still doing my photographs and puttering around with things like that. I don't have anything offhand that I'm doing right now, because I'm at a fallow time.

EA: Do you have a sort of post partum depression after you finish a novel?

LMS: April 27 I put down what I know is the last sentence, and then . . . yeah, there's a form of post partum depression. I didn't want to do anything else, even though there was cleaning, all kinds of other things. There was nothing in the world that I loved more, or I wanted to do more, than to make this book, even though towards the end, I knew I had to get it done, and there were all these pressures. The metaphor, or the comparison I would make is, I once had a mother goat, and she had a premature kid and it died. And the goat just was lost, and she kept looking for it, and she would go to the same place where it was. And so I would keep going, I would go just like the old mother goat, to where it was, to the work table, and then get up and wander, and not be able to do anything else. There's a real bereavement and separation. And you'll think of anything, and I did. I did try to think about starting up another book, even though I don't think I'm going to yet. You try to do anything. But there's nothing like the one, nothing can replace it.

Except then I did something I had forbidden myself to do. I was so bereaved, I did something I hadn't allowed myself to do since 1991. I started to think about those characters in *Almanac of the Dead,* the ones who are still alive. And the scariest thing that happened during this post partum time was to hear that siren call. [Laughter] Oh my god . . . I let myself listen. I was so bereft, that all of a sudden something in my mind went click, click: remember? You meant to kill off a lot more of them than you did. Wonder where they are? Wonder what they're doing?

EA: That's so wonderful for readers to hear, especially students who've been taught to think there's a right way to read a book, to know that even for the person who made the book, it's got a life of its own.

LMS: It has a life of its own! Someone said to me after they read *Almanac of the Dead,* that they didn't know I knew so much. And I said, well, I didn't know I knew that much! There's something magical that's going on, and it does have a separate life, and it is an exhibit or an artifact or a part of something greater than just the author's life. It's a part of a culture, and a time, and it reflects that. And it does know more and it does say more than any individual human being. That's why art, whether it's a novel or a play or a symphony or a song, that's why the arts are so mighty and powerful. Some alchemy happens with the individual human being, so that through that human being some kind of connection is made through space-time, through all eternity, that's way bigger than the individual.

That's why I always caution students when they ask me, well what was this about or that about? I try to remind them that this is my take on what I did. And then I tell them it's not mine anymore, it belongs to them. And that it doesn't matter what I say I think that section is about, that I cannot limit that work. The work is separate, and part of the process is that it is to go to the reader, and that the reader makes these connections, and that's how it flows on.

EA: I was thinking about that when you were talking about *Ceremony* and how at first it was just for advanced readers, and then it moved its way down into the high schools. It's not just the times that have changed around it, though. It's changed the times. The book itself has made some of those changes.

LMS: You're right. What happened was, a few teachers of teachers taught it, and then teachers of teachers of teachers taught it. The book appealed to the teachers, the teachers and the book interact. The book helped make that change. It's so beautiful.

EA: You said something the last time I talked to you that I really loved. You talked about the magic of how words are so tiny, yet giant worlds spring up from them. And it ties into some of the things you say about physics too. Something's going on there that we don't know about. Something's happening there on that plane that you were describing before.

LMS: Yes, exactly. I first had the sense of it the day the hardcover of *Ceremony* arrived. It was a few weeks before they shipped it out to the bookstores. I worked two years on it, and I was so nervous about it, and I had no help, no one looked at it. And it was a troubled time in my life, I had such a hard time. It was such a struggle. So then the book came, and I opened it up, and I burst into tears, because a book is so small. It just seemed so insignificant and small. That was the conscious, the one who talks to you now, those are the kinds of reactions I have. But then, luckily the other level within myself, my little hands, I opened it up and I looked—I don't know what part I opened—and I started to read. And then it was like WOW!

It just turned around, and it was like within this little object are worlds! Inside of here, the mesas and the sun! Animals and the water and the people! Open it up and remember the magic of language. And so that was the first time. Without that sense of what language does, you're just reduced to weighing things and measuring them.

Even with this [*Gardens*], once I got it far along and I would think about the characters, they're alive. All my characters are always alive. I was getting really close to the end of *Gardens in the Dunes,* where Hattie is reunited with the girls, and I knew that this certain thing was going to happen. I thought Hattie's folks would come for her and take her back. I thought that was what was supposed to happen. I was really close to the end, and I'd been rolling along so well. But then I started to feel the novel not want to go. I had to stop and say, well now, what's wrong? What is it that I'm not doing right? It's with Hattie's character. Hattie, what is it? There's something you don't like.

Hattie didn't want to just leave. Hattie wanted to get even, so wait till you see what happens. She wasn't going to go softly or quietly away. So I did it, and it was like whoosh, and it was okay. That was really shocking, when I wasn't doing what that character wanted me to do. Not what I wanted—the one who sits here and talks to you. I thought I had this idea about how it would go, what Hattie would do and how she would go out of the novel. And it really was as if that character was saying no. No, this isn't quite right. This isn't what I did, or I want to do. There's something else. I had sense of the Hattie character saying, you know there's something else. Okay, I do know, oh, that's what you want to do! Wow! All right, now I see why you were unhappy with me. I was just going to have you leave like that? Oh, okay.

EA: This novel seems to be very much about the subconscious. You feel it at work in there all the time. The characters are operating on one level, but all these other things are working underneath on them. And in them and through them.

LMS: Good. That's good.

EA: I know you've read all of Freud's work. You've talked about that many times. Were you thinking of that while you were writing?

LMS: No.

EA: This is his time, the turn of the century.

LMS: No, I think I forgot it until you mentioned it. But of course, it must be very important. Again, the one who sits here doesn't know anything about that. [Laughter] You're exactly right. But yes, I hope that it's seen as a tribute to him, because *Almanac of the Dead* is my tribute to Marx. I might have mentioned Freud in *Almanac*. He has some part in there, because when I was blocked during writing *Almanac,* I read Freud. Whoosh, right through.

EA: Volume one through eighteen!

LMS: But yeah, this is exactly what I wanted to happen. That wasn't what I was thinking when I was doing it. When I was doing it I was just struggling. But now that you tell me that this is what's going on, then I can say, oh, good. That would be just what I would like to do, especially for Freud. You have all his dimwit followers and misinterpreters. Feminists and all kinds of people have their complaints about Freud. He was only one man and one lifetime, and he wrote like an angel. What he uncovered about that connection with language, it's right there, and I lived it. It all happened seamlessly or effortlessly. I guess my subconscious is really wanting to acknowledge him and I'm glad I could do it like that.

EA: I'll have to think about that in Indigo, though, because she seems whole in a way that the other characters aren't. Her conscious and her unconscious are not separated in the same way.

LMS: You're right; she's a little bit different.

EA: She's just very much present in her experience all the time.
LMS: Yeah.

EA: And part of that is that she's a child.
LMS: She's a child.

EA: But there's something else too.
LMS: Something else too, yeah. Oh yeah.

Epilogue: A Prophecy

LMS: You're in this situation, no one's ever seen it before. All of the old ways don't work. There's nothing to be done. There's an old Pueblo story about that. That's why Kochininako goes off with Buffalo Man, that's why she has a propensity for adultery. Adultery symbolizes breaking with everything that's known or supposed to be. The people are hungry, and she goes off with the Buffalo people and makes that liaison, and the people survive. One can imagine long, long ago when the Ice Age started to come, or there were terrible cosmic or volcanic and tidal waves and things like that. When everything that's been thought or known no longer holds, then that's when a person like myself, who doesn't fit in, who is a little bit frightening, a little bit strange to the others, that's where that vision comes in and is necessary.

EA: Like the Year 2000 problem [the potential computer crash]!
LMS: Exactly.

EA: It's very likely that we'll see just how important that vision is.

LMS: There'll be reports in the aftermath, and there'll be all these people saying, the people at Laguna, or the Navajos, gee, they didn't have much trouble during that time. Well yeah, because they had managed to barely cling. Or some of the folks up in the mountains everyone is always making fun of, they'll hardly notice. I learned that truth years ago, when some of my students at Navajo Community College wrote about the Great Depression. Hey! There was plenty of rain that year. They remembered the depression years as good years, years of plenty. Why? Because they didn't have anything to do with that paper charade on Wall Street.

The fear is that the instability in Asia, the overpriced stock market, and then the Year 2000 bug—those things together [will cause a disaster]. And in the aftermath, how ever many years later, you watch. We'll laugh because we already knew it was developing. They'll be writing about, oh, it was so interesting, who was affected and what was affected. And of course they'll find out that the people with the more diverse ways—whether they were forced by political, economic, geographical, whatever exigencies, to do things differently, to not be hooked into the web. Then hopefully out of those summations and conclusions will be, we must never again all be hooked! We must remember! But no, right now, we'll have to all go through it and suffer.

Some of us have been trying to say it all along. But no, it seems like they have to have something like that. In a way, I'm glad it will be something as apolitical, so universally loved as computers. That it won't be the usual things over some kind of religious issue or something like that. It's perfect. It's just beautiful. And oh, the old Mayans will laugh, because they understood how to use the zero, in mathematics. And what was the undoing of the modern world? Was it a war or a bizarre machine? Was it a virus or an asteroid hitting the earth? Oh no. Only two zeros. And what does a zero mean? What does a zero stand for? Nothing. What did them in? Nothing. [Laughter] They're always talking about the Western European fear of nothingness. Here it is. Oh, it's nothing.

EA: Nothing brought it all down.

LMS: Nothing brought it all down. Nothing. Zero zero!

Notes

1. This portion of the interview was selected to focus on *Almanac of the Dead* and *Gardens in the Dunes.* It has been edited for clarity and continuity.

2. In previous conversations, Silko conveyed her excitement to me about recent experiments in particle physics demonstrating that twinned electron or photon pairs, when split apart in a particle accelerator, still seem to communicate with each other instantaneously over long distances. She called my attention to an article by George Johnson in the July 31, 1997 *New York Times,* "The Unspeakable Things That Particles Do."

3. Elizabeth Cook-Lynn, "Cosmopolitanism, Nationalism, the Third World, and Tribal Sovereignty," *Wicazo Sa Review* 9 (1993): 26–36.

4. Southern Humanities Council Conference on Justice, Huntingdon College, Montgomery, Alabama, March 20–22, 1998.

5. A black and white photograph of the mural is reproduced in *Yellow Woman and a Beauty of the Spirit,* pages 150-51.

6. Paula Gunn Allen, "Special Problems in Teaching Leslie Marmon Silko's *Ceremony,*" *American Indian Quarterly* 14.4 (1990): 379–86.

7. Gregory Salyer, who did the first book length study of Silko's work, *Leslie Marmon Silko* (New York: Twayne, 1997).

8. "The Loose Canon: 150 Great Works to Set Your Imagination on Fire," *Utne Reader* 87 (1998): 52–59.

9. Silko's own press, which published *Sacred Water,* among other things (Flood Plain Press c/o Fine Print, 2828 N. Stone Avenue, Tucson, Arizona 85705).

Index

104–05; "Escape Story" (short story), 6;
Gardens in the Dunes, vii, ix, x, xi, 161, 162–73, 179–89, 192–93; "Humaweepi" (short story), 73; *Laguna Woman*, vii, 52, 97, 113, 140; "Lullaby" (short story), 8, 41, 63; "The Man to Send Rain Clouds" (short story), 5, 29; "An Old-Time Indian Attack" (essay), 73; "Private Property" (short story), 136, 138; *Sacred Water*, vii, x, 122, 136; "A Story from Bear Country" (short story), 136; *Storyteller*, vii, ix, x, 41, 70, 72, 77–78, 97, 113, 136, 137, 147; "Storyteller" (short story), 27, 41, 42, 58, 137–38; *"Toe'osh*: A Laguna Coyote Story" (poem), 10, 14–16; "Tony's Story" (short story), xi, 6, 37; *Yellow Woman and a Beauty of the Spirit*, vii, 162; "Yellow Woman" (short story), 12
Simon and Schuster, xii, 94, 105, 119–20, 133, 160, 168, 176, 188
Snyder, Gary, 8, 74
South Africa, 63
Stein, Gertrude, x
Steinbeck, John, 5–6, 42, 91
Stone Avenue mural, 98–99, 155, 173–76

Tapahonso, Lucy, 94
Third Woman, The, 49
Thoreau, Henry David, 180
Thought Woman, 54
Time magazine, 107, 108, 132, 133, 159
Tohono O'odham, 122

Transcendentalism (American), 179–80
Treaty of Guadalupe Hidalgo, 102
Trinity Site, Alamagordo, N.Mex., 44, 52
Ts'its'tsi'nako. *See* Thought Woman
Tucson, Ariz., 97–102, 113, 114, 119, 122–23, 129, 143, 153, 154, 162, 163, 175, 176, 177

USA Today, 108, 132, 133, 159
Utne Reader, 189

Vietnam War, 34, 44
Village Voice, 132

Washington, George, 8
Waters, Frank, 30
Welch, James, 40, 43, 46, 51; *The Death of Jim Loney*, 40, 51; *Winter in the Blood*, 51
Whitman, Walt, 180
Wittgenstein, Ludwig, 81
Women's Review of Books, 132
World War II. *See* Second World War
Wounded Knee (1890), 64
Wright, Annie, 104
Wright, James, 104, 105

Yale University, 140
Yaquis, xii, 102, 123
Yellow Woman, 12, 58, 76–77, 194

Zapatista uprising. *See* Chiapas
Zeilik, Mike, 109
Zen Buddhism, 106